‘**7
Lan
Villag

CW00348984

THE VILLAGES OF BRITAIN SERIES

Other counties in this series include:

Avon*

Bedfordshire*

Berkshire*

Buckinghamshire*

Cambridgeshire*

Cheshire*

Devon*

Dorset

Essex*

Gloucestershire*

Hampshire

Herefordshire*

Hertfordshire*

Kent

Leicestershire*
  & Rutland*

Lincolnshire*

Middlesex*

Northamptonshire*

Nottinghamshire*

Oxfordshire

Powys Montgomery*

Shropshire*

Somerset*

Staffordshire*

Suffolk

Surrey

East Sussex

West Sussex

Warwickshire*

West Midlands*

Wiltshire

Worcestershire*

*Published in conjunction with County Federation of
Women's Institutes

The Lancashire Village Book

Compiled by the Lancashire
Federation of Women's Institutes from notes
and illustrations sent by Institutes in the County

Published jointly by
Countryside Books, Newbury
and the L.F.W.I., Preston

First Published 1990
© Lancashire Federation of Women's Institutes 1990

All rights reserved. No reproduction
permitted without the prior permission
of the publishers:

Countryside Books
3 Catherine Road
Newbury, Berkshire

ISBN 1 85306 076 3

Cover Photograph of Turton
taken by Joan Horsfield

Produced through MRM Associates Ltd., Reading
Typeset by Acorn Bookwork, Salisbury, Wilts
Printed in England by J.W. Arrowsmith Ltd., Bristol

Foreword

To many people, Lancashire conjures up a picture of factories, grime and the architectural monotony of Coronation Street. This book on Lancashire's villages should go a long way towards setting the record straight. It tells of the splendid variety of rural Lancashire, from the seafaring settlements around Morecambe Bay to the hill farms on the slopes of the Pennines, from the villages to the east of the county, sturdily built of stone, clustering around a central mill, once busily working, but with the green moorland on the doorstep, to the fertile Fylde plain, once known as the granary of Lancashire, and to the market gardens of the drained marshland to the southwest. It links the present to the past as it introduces the reader to the interesting buildings, the colourful characters, the local customs and the thriving communities of the Lancashire villages. It tells of change, but change which has led to growth, not stagnation. I hope all who read it, whether Lancastrians or not, will enjoy their excursion through this stalwart and beautiful county and will go on to savour for themselves the riches it contains.

Joan Fenlon
County Chairman

Acknowledgements

The production of this book has only been possible by the enthusiastic research of the contributors and the untiring efforts of Mrs Vera Proctor and Dr Joan Wilkinson who co-ordinated the whole. To all these and to others who helped in any way the Lancashire Federation Executive offer their grateful thanks.

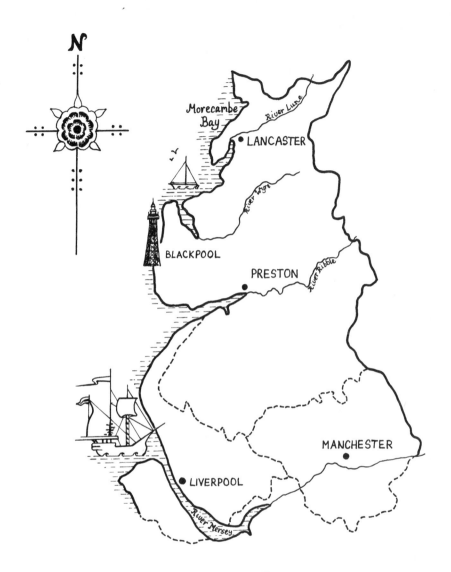

N

Morecambe
Bay

River Lune

● LANCASTER

River Wyre

BLACKPOOL

PRESTON
●

River Ribble

MANCHESTER
●

● LIVERPOOL

River Mersey

County of
LANCASHIRE

The boulder over the witch's grave at Woodplumpton

8

Abbeystead ⁂

Abbeystead is in the parish of Over Wyresdale, ten miles south-east of Lancaster. The name suggests that there may have been an abbey at some time but there aren't any ruins or documents to show where it was. The village is in the centre of the parish and consists of Abbeystead House, known locally as 'the Mansion', the school and eleven houses.

Wyresdale church is about a mile from Abbeystead and is of an early foundation. In 1894 it underwent a thorough restoration including stained glass windows, each depicting a scene from the Bible on the theme of sheep and shepherds. Consequently it is often called the Shepherds' Church, but its real name is Christ Church. The organ was also installed in 1894, but the delicately carved pulpit is dated 1684.

The Quakers of the district built a meeting house and school in 1670, which continued to be used until both were closed about 25 years ago. The school has been made into a house. A Wesleyan chapel was built at Emmetts in 1891, replacing an older one which had been built in 1824.

The most notable character of the past was Mr William Cawthorne, who had Abbeystead school built in 1674. A local man, he held the position of clerk to the governors of St Bartholomew's Hospital, London, from 1661 to 1675. He left land and property to endow the school and he also built a residence for the schoolmaster.

The school is also the social centre, where monthly WI meetings, the Horticulture Show, the parish party and Christmas whist drives are held. There is a Field Day in June with sports and fancy dress. Sheepdog trials are held once a year too, and activities are run by committees drawn from every part of the parish. There is a sports club hut behind the school which is very popular with the men of the district, while the teenagers have a youth club and use the Church Sunday school building for their activities.

In the 1880s the Earl of Sefton bought the area and built Abbeystead House. Though small compared to other houses built by the great landowners of that period, the rooms are spacious as it was intended to be used as a shooting lodge after the style of shooting lodges in Scotland. During the building of the 'Mansion', lodges, Home Farm and coach houses, the stone was quarried on the estate and dressed on the site, an undertaking quite outstanding when every load had to be moved by horse and cart from a quarry on Tarnbrook Fell.

When King George V came for the shoot in 1926 and stayed for a week, he attended the church service on the Sunday morning. After the last Lady Sefton's death in 1980, the Duke of Westminster bought the estate and members of the Royal Family, including the Queen, have been to stay on several occasions, on private visits.

On 23rd May 1984 there was a terrible disaster at Abbeystead when visitors from St Michael's-on-Wyre came to see the massive water scheme called Lancaster Conjunctive Use Scheme. While they were in the pump house an explosion occurred which killed 16, while many others suffered severe burns. Methane gas had collected in the tunnel and caused the awful tragedy.

There are some unusual buildings in the parish, the most prominent being the Jubilee Tower on High Cross Moor. It is a square tower with stone steps leading to the top. It is not very high but gives a panoramic view of the surrounding area and the sea coast, and was built to commemorate Queen Victoria's Jubilee.

There is a small square-built house in the Trough of Bowland called the Tower Lodge, but known locally as 'The Canister'. At Ortner and Lower Lee there are two square summer houses, and near the Lee there is a long open-fronted building called the Gad House, for the cows to hide in when being chased by gadflies. Across the road from the school at

Emmetts Methodist chapel, Abbeystead

Abbeystead is a round pinfold where stray sheep would be left for their owners to collect in days gone by.

Wyresdale is a place of contented people, which is really something in this age of unrest. For generations the young folks have lived on at home, the sons taking the farms on after their fathers, or working on the estate, but now with travelling made easier the young folks can pursue other work or attend college or university.

Abbey Village 🐚

Abbey Village, we are led to believe, was given its name because of its connections with Whalley Abbey. According to tradition there was a route to the abbey from a secret passage at Brinscall Hall, through the Roddlesworth area (where a cross may still be seen on one of the farm buildings) and from there towards Whalley. Roddlesworth is just outside the village.

After the Industrial Revolution Abbey Village, as we know it today, was built to serve the large cotton mill which then provided employment. Unfortunately the mill closed in about 1970 and the houses built for its employees were sold. Recently the mill has been divided into small industrial units, but the village has become another dormitory area.

Situated as it is on the A675 Bolton to Preston road, Abbey Village is an opening onto the West Pennine Moors, a beautiful area with walks and an abundance of trees, plants and birdlife.

Ainsdale 🐚

The first settlers in Ainsdale were Vikings, who gave the village its name. Ainsdale is mentioned in the Domesday Book under its Viking name, Einulvesdel. Later it became Aynesdale and then finally Ainsdale. It was a relatively poor settlement.

After the Conquest the land was transferred to a series of Norman landowners. Years later, after a legal dispute, the land came to the Halsall family. In 1630 they sold Ainsdale to Robert Blundell of Ince whose family continued to hold lands in Ainsdale until the 1950s. The last of the Blundell line, Charles Robert, bequeathed the estates to Joseph Weld Blundell of Lulworth in Dorset. The additional surname was assumed in accordance with the terms of Charles Robert Blundell's will.

The Blundell and Weld families had been friends for years.

In the 17th century the village comprised just a few cottages and farms, and a corn mill which was a local landmark. The village started to grow with the arrival of the railways in 1848, and by 1891 the population was 811. The first church, St John's, was built in 1886 and the primary occupations at that time were farming, fishing and managing the large rabbit warrens in the sand dunes.

At the outbreak of the First World War in 1914 the population had grown to 2,000. Better houses were being built and gas and electricity were being installed. The Wesleyan school was offering free education to children of all denominations.

It was during the 1960's that major changes took place with the disappearance of familiar landmarks including the corn mill, black-smith's shop and bowling green. Thatched cottages and farms were removed to make way for new housing estates for the ever-growing population. In 1967 Pontins built the holiday camp near the shoreline. The level crossing gates were replaced with 'continental style' barriers. These changes, although necessary for 'progress', caused much concern amongst local people but, by this time, the population was rising towards 12,000 and a new style community had developed, earning its living in a whole variety of ways.

Ainsdale's main claim to fame is its magnificent beach and vast area of sand dunes, rich in flora and fauna and home of the rare Natterjack Toad. For many years now the dunes have been maintained as a nature reserve and, along with the beach, are responsible for attracting thousands of visitors in the summer months.

Appley Bridge

On the banks of the river Douglas, in the Douglas valley, lies Appley Bridge, approximately six miles from Wigan and 15 miles from South-port. Through the village the Leeds and Liverpool Canal (the longest single canal in Britain) runs parallel with the river Douglas in many places. The village is overlooked by Ashurst Beacon, built during the Napoleonic Wars to warn of the threatened French invasion. The beacon was never lit and is now a local beauty spot.

The Dicconson Arms pub, named after a local family, is better known as Dangerous Corner. The story is told that a local farmer's wife died, and as her coffin (on a cart) was being carried round the corner, it fell off

The canal at Appley Bridge

and the corpse 'awoke'. Years later when she finally did die, as the cortege approached the corner, the farmer shouted 'Now take care lads, this is a very dangerous corner'. Hence the name.

Skull House is a strange house, with mysterious cupboards, massive beams and a priest's hole. A human skull is kept at Skull House and legend says that ill fortune will befall anyone who removes the skull. There are various theories – that the skull belonged to a priest at the time of Cromwell, or that it was the skull of a knight who lived in the days of King Arthur, but medical evidence says that the skull is female. Historians now think it unlikely that the past will ever reveal its secret.

Primitive Methodism in Appley Bridge began in 1830 when Matthew Guill got permission to preach in a room of a house in 'the slacks' (a local beauty spot). Later Old Mill House was used. There were 24 members when the present church was opened in 1859.

In 1894, the foundation stone of the old mission church was laid. In 1897 the mission became a dual building and a day school was started. A new Church school was built in 1968, the final phase being completed in 1971. As Appley Bridge was growing in population, the Blackburn

13

Diocese decided in 1972 that it could become a separate parish and sever the connection with Parbold. Since then a new church has been built and it was opened in March 1982.

A bill for the Leeds and Liverpool Canal, which runs through the village, was passed on 19th May 1770. This was to prove the most difficult engineering problem of that time, involving a cut of over 120 miles and nearly 100 locks. It took 46 years to build and cost £1,200,000. At first it was used by horse-drawn boats, and later by steam and diesel, to transport stone, brick, flour, coal etc. Basin Cottage (unusual in that it had no back door) was set at the side of the basin. Stables attached to the cottage provided rest and refreshment for the boatmen's horses. Tubs containing stone from the quarries ran along the narrow railway lines to the canal sidings, to be loaded on the boats. Douglas Valley Sailing Club now use the basin for mooring and hold an annual Easter Boat Rally.

With the coming of the railways and increasing road traffic the canal became overgrown. British Waterways have cleared the canal, repaired tow paths and positioned seats, so it is now extensively used by pleasure craft, fishermen and walkers. The villagers enjoy the local beauty spots of Fairy Glen and the Douglas Valley, where there is a wealth of wild life.

Appley Bridge changed over the years from a farming community to a thriving industrial village in the 1930s. Now there are not as many industries but there are two churches, two schools, a village hall, railway station (Southport/Manchester line), several inns, a village hall, garden centre and a telephone exchange. One village postmaster served for 48 years and once most of the inhabitants worked in the village, but now villagers commute to the cities. Appley Bridge has grown in population over the years, but the villagers hope to preserve the history and character of this Lancashire village.

Aspull & Haigh 🦢

The earliest reference to Aspull is in 1212 when it was described as 'ploughland' – the inference being that it had been cleared of trees and its tenants were living by farming.

Centuries later the presence of the coal pits, together with the farming of the district, resulted in a growing population for which an ale house was established, but records show that unfortunately 'it was not kept in a manner satisfactory to the magistrates'. Several of the substantial farm-

14

houses of this period still remain; Kirkless Hall, Gidlow Hall and Highfield House.

The Industrial Revolution increased the demand for coal and greatly increased the importance of Aspull, where the world's largest limited company was established – the Wigan Coal and Iron Company. The miners and cotton spinners of the period supported the building of eight churches between 1833 and the turn of the century.

Adjoining Aspull district is the rural parish of Haigh where Haigh Hall is an important feature. This was the residence of the Earl of Crawford and Balcarres until after the Second World War when the Earl moved to his Scottish seat at Balcarres, allowing the township of Wigan to purchase the Hall for the use of the public. In recent years it has become widely known as Haigh Country Park with many popular amenities, and the Hall itself is available for public and private functions.

In the village of Haigh there is much to remind people of the Crawford family, who built the school and the two inns, the Balcarres Arms and the Crawford Arms. An important landmark, in a field on the road down to the Hall, is Haigh windmill. Its use in the past was said to be for pumping water, but now it is restored and preserved, presenting a most pleasant pastoral scene.

The parish church of St David stands at the entrance lane to the Hall, opposite the Balcarres Arms. Here the Crawford family worshipped – the church entrance is still known as the Crawford Porch. It is a 'Waterloo Church' – built from funds allocated after the battle of Waterloo. An interesting and beautiful feature is the baptistry donated by Vicar James and his wife as a memorial to their four sons killed in action in the First World War.

At the centre of the village a five storey brewery stood, and here many locals were employed. Though the brewery itself has been demolished, many of the cellars still exist. One of these remains under the Haigh school building. During the working days of the brewery, employees working in the cellar used to complain about the clatter of the children's clogs above, whilst in turn there were embarrassing moments when the quiet of the school was disturbed by some choice words not intended for tender ears.

The Leeds and Liverpool Canal runs through the New Springs part of Aspull and on past Haigh Hall Park. Its use as a busy thoroughfare for transport of commodities – sugar, wheat, coal – is past, its present use being confined to pleasure craft, as it wends its way towards the Haigh boundary.

In a field almost opposite to the Crawford Arms is the remains of a colliery known locally as the Button Pit – a place avoided by the local people. Here in 1863 a heinous murder took place when a workman, whose duty was to keep the fires going and attend to the pumping engine, was foully murdered and his body disposed of in the boiler fire. Investigation resulted only in the discovery of a few buttons and two buckles. In 1866 the murderer paid the penalty for the crime. Hence the title 'Button Pit'.

Astley

Astley has been in existence since Anglo-Saxon times. The name means East Fields, relating to a small settlement about two miles to the east of Leigh, sheltered by rolling hills to the north and bounded by mossland to the south.

In 1606 when Adam Mort took up residence as lord of the manor he found a small hamlet, the tenants scratching a meagre living from the land, but without a church, market place or school. He soon set about building a chapel and a small free grammar school, but because Astley was part of Leigh parish the church was known as a chapel of ease until 1867 when Astley was created a separate parish.

Another great man who had an influence on the village was Ambrose Barlow, born in Didsbury, Manchester in 1586 and canonised in 1970. He was ordained as a Catholic priest in 1617 and as a Benedictine monk made his headquarters at Morleys Hall, Astley. It was there on Easter Sunday in 1641 as he celebrated Mass (forbidden by law in those troublesome times) that he was arrested, committed for trial at Lancaster and after four months was found guilty and sentenced to be hanged. A large Catholic secondary school was erected in the early 1970s and land was acquired for a new Roman Catholic church and primary school to be built at Lark Hill.

Alfred Hewlett was the third influential person to leave his impact on Astley. He arrived in 1832 to take up the position of curate. He found the chapel in a dreadful neglected state, dirty and damp. He worked hard, cleaned up the chapel, opened the school in the vicarage barn and being a great preacher slowly gathered the villagers under his wing. In Victorian times the art of oratory made him widely known and he was invited to preach in many parts of the country but he never neglected his village.

Alfred Hewlett was vicar here for 50 years. During that time he saw many changes. The village had already been divided in two when the Bridgewater Canal had been dug in 1790, then in 1830 the Manchester to Liverpool Railway was laid across Chat Moss (part of which is in Astley) on a foundation of bales of cotton. 1833 saw the opening of a cotton mill built by James and Robert Arrowsmith on the banks of the canal. This employed about 200 people. The fact that it was engaged in both spinning and weaving was most unusual.

For centuries the villagers had burnt wood and dug peat from the moss to burn on their fires. Coal was discovered in 1840 and early attempts were made to mine it from sloping shafts. But after the Gin Pits were sunk about the middle of the century, Cross Hillock Pit was opened. It was worked until 1886 when it had to close due to flooding. Astley Green Pit was sunk in 1905/6 and gradually, where agriculture had been the main source of employment, mining and mill-work took over. The mill traded until 1951 when mining subsidence damaged the old foundations and brought the company to extinction, so ending an industry almost as old as the village itself.

When the pits and the mill were working, the Manchester Colliery horses and the barge-horses were stabled at Peel Hall Farm. May Day was a day to remember – to see the horses dressed was a sight never to be forgotten. Walking Day was also much enjoyed by the villagers. The village was a busy happy place, so hard to imagine the number of shops – butchers, several grocers, a shoe-shop and cloggers, a hairdresser, a barber, a post office and even a bank. Now, sadly, all are gone but for the post office.

The village was once again cut in half by the opening of the new East Lancashire road from Manchester to Liverpool (A580) in 1934. There are now only a few shops in Blackmoor. Agriculture still thrives and there are some very good arable farms on the Moss, even a maggot farm for the anglers! Peat is still cut and a modern plant has been built for the gardening industry. A small industrial estate has also been built at Cross Hillock for light industry.

Older residents remember with horror the evening of 18th June 1961. After the procession of witness had taken place a youth set the old church alight and, due to the inadequate supply of water, St Stephen's church was damaged beyond repair. Many old and valuable documents and books were lost in the blaze. The corner of Church Road will never look the same. It was 1968 before the new church was consecrated. It was built alongside the new infant and junior school on land known as The Ley, starting another phase in the history of the village.

17

Mining came to an end in 1970 when Astley Green Pit closed. The engine house has been made into a mining museum and the pit head still stands against the skyline.

Banks

Banks village has a population of about 3,500 people. The historical name of the village was North Meols, which in Viking days meant 'northern sand dunes'.

Over the years Banks has been known as a fishing village, mainly for cockles and shrimps, but since the 1960s fishing has declined. The river is silting up and there are only a few fishermen left. The women of Banks used to go out to the cockle beds and the men went out shrimping in boats and horse-drawn carts. When the shrimps had been boiled, the womenfolk sat and shelled them by hand. Women in the village today still carry on this traditional work.

The names given to many of the roads in the village have historic roots. Ralph's Wife's Lane for instance, has a lovely legend as to how the name came about. It is said that many years ago there were only a few fishermen's cottages in that area. One night a fisherman called Ralph set out in a winter storm to go fishing. When he had not returned after the expected hour, his wife went searching for him across the marsh, which lay behind their cottage. She is said to have been heard calling 'Ralph, Ralph', over the misty windswept marshes. He did not return and the legend goes on that her ghost wanders along the lane on windswept winter nights – still calling for her lost husband.

Many of the older Banks people have nicknames. Some families acquired these names over a hundred years ago, when a pirate ship went aground. The old fishermen climbed aboard thinking the ship was deserted. When they realised that it wasn't, to prevent themselves being identified, they called each other by peculiar names. The names stuck and have been handed down from father to son. Some nicknames are still in use, such as Silver, Mustard, Snig, Shuffle, Voughton and Fudge.

Banks is a thriving market gardening area. The best salads are grown here and distributed to markets and shops all over England. Over the years, the women have taken their own fresh shrimps and the well known Southport potted shrimps to the markets. In the early days they used horses and carts for transport and later the railway, especially useful

18

when travelling to the mill towns of Blackburn, Preston, Bolton and Bury. Today this work is still carried on, but on a much smaller scale and using car, van or lorry for transportation.

There are two churches in Banks, both having celebrated their centenary year some time ago. Both churches have a day school as well as Sunday schools, youth groups and groups for adults. Each year they hold a Sunday School Anniversary and a Procession of Witness through the village, led by the Banks Brass Band, which was formed about 100 years ago. It was originally called the 'Banks Temperance Band'.

Up to the 1960s, Banks was known as 'The Dry Village', because there was no public house. Then a farmhouse situated in the centre of the village was converted and licensed. It is now named the Fleetwood House Hotel.

Lord and Lady Scarisbrick lived for many years in the mansion house, called Greaves Hall. During the Second World War, the Hall opened as a hospital for patients who were evacuated from Liverpool. Later, the local Health Authority took it over and Greaves Hall became one of the largest hospitals in the area for the mentally ill. Greaves Hall Hospital provided a great deal of work for many of the local people and still does, though not quite on the same scale.

There are many societies in Banks village, catering for almost everyone; Parish Council, youth organisations, women's clubs, men's clubs, football, cricket, bowls, pigeon flying, the Band, and not too far away are some very good golf courses.

Barley

Barley is a small village of around 200 residents, nestling at the foot of Pendle Hill. In 1324 it was known as Barelegh, meaning infertile lea or meadow.

Pendle Hill, 1,835 ft high, dominates Barley and the surrounding area of lush farmland. It is believed that the site of the beacon of Pendle was originally a Bronze Age burial mound, possibly 7,000 years old. The beacon was used in past centuries to warn of Scottish raiders. Pendle is also associated with the Pendle Witches who were sent for trial at Lancaster Castle, found guilty, and hanged on 20th August 1612. George Fox had a vision on Pendle Hill in 1640 during a thunderstorm, after which he began the Society of Friends or Quakers.

During the Lancashire cotton boom, Barley had two mills, one spinning and one weaving cotton, but both are now closed.

Barley is a close-knit community with a village hall which houses various activities. The Methodist chapel has a Sunday school and services every Sunday.

There are five large sheep farms in Barley. The local post office serves the three villages of Barley, Newchurch and Roughlee. There is one pub, a restaurant, a guest house, a builder's yard, a joiner's shop, a company that sells textiles by mail order and a soft furnishings company, so Barley still has textile connections. There is also an Outdoor Education Centre, but mostly people commute to work.

Barley is a friendly village, very picturesque and historic. For the many visitors to the village there is a car park and information centre, and a picnic area where people can relax and admire the scenery.

Barton 🐑

Barton is a small township five and a half miles north-west of Preston in the Ancient Hundred of Amounderness. The population in 1851 was 370 and at the 1981 census 1,214. The acreage is 2,708, mostly open fields and woodland.

About a mile north-east from the southern boundary stands Barton Hall, on a slight rise. In 1834, Mr George Jacson purchased almost the whole of the property in the township of Barton from James Shuttleworth, lord of the manor, and lived at the Hall, previously Barton Lodge. During the Second World War, the Ministry of Aviation used the Hall as its North West HQ and many underground complexes were built. It is only in recent years that underground cables were removed from some private gardens. Today, Barton Hall is a Government Animal Health Centre.

A few yards from the Hall drive, Cardwell Bridge crosses Barton Brook, which rises eastwards above Inglewhite. There used to be a steep brow from here, and there were many accidents involving horse drawn traffic. In 1863 a man and three horses were killed, so in 1869 Stone Brig Brow was lowered, the cost of £800 being defrayed by the Misses Cross of Myerscough. On the east side of the brow is a polished granite tablet recording this.

There are four 'highways' covering Barton, running parallel. To the west is the Preston – Lancaster canal, which used to bring coal and wood to cottages and farms. Not far from the main road is the London – Glasgow railway, though Barton station has been closed for many years. Then there is the A6 – a great arterial road, and to the east the M6.

Just off the main road to the west, not far over the railway bridge, is the Roman Catholic church of St Mary Newhouse. Newhouse is mentioned in the Domesday Book. The first chapel, dedicated to St Lawrence, was built in 1742 by Father Roger Brockholes of Claughton. There was much Catholic activity in this area during the Jacobite rebellion of 1745. A second church, dedicated to St Mary was built in 1806, but this was replaced by the present church in 1905 at the expense of William Smith of Newsham House.

The word 'Bar' originally meant a corn farm or a grange. It is recorded that there used to be wild boars in Barton and legend has it that one particular boar in the days of the Bartons 'did much mischief'. So the head of the Barton family promised to give his daughter in marriage to the man who would kill the boar. A great hunt took place on St Lawrence's Day and one of the Shuttleworths killed the boar where the public house The Boar's Head now stands near the church of St Lawrence.

The parish church of St Lawrence cost £5,721 to build in 1895. Previously there had been Barton chapel on the main road for the use of the lord of the manor. St Lawrence's school started as a simple dame school with seven scholars in a cottage. A school house was built in 1848 at a cost of £300 with money given to Catherine Jacson as a wedding present. This small building is still used for some parochial purposes. A large new school on adjoining land was built in 1958.

Next to the church is Barton Grange, now a well known garden centre, hotel and conference centre, but originally the home of a cotton magnate.

The long straight stretch of highway gives open views of the country-side, with the Fylde plain (not forgetting Blackpool Tower!) to the west and the lovely Longridge and Bleasdale fells to the east, all of which are easily accessible.

At the end of June the village holds a Rose Queen Festival and sports day for all – particularly anticipated by the children as their teas are free!

There are many old houses and farms, too numerous to mention, some being Duchy of Lancaster property. There has been considerable residential development since the 1960s, mainly on the eastern side, due primarily to easy access from the M6.

There is still a considerable farming community. There are still fields to wander, bluebell woods to explore, kingfishers and tiddlers at the brook and enduring peace along the canal bank, accompanied by coot and mallard.

Bashall Eaves 🐚

A small hamlet in the parish of Mitton, from Saxon times Bashall Eaves has been variously known as Basclelf, Bakesalf and Beckhalgh. It is situated on the banks of the river Hodder to the west and Bashall Brook to the east, a tributary of the river Ribble.

Bashall Hall has great historical interest. In the 15th century it belonged to the Talbots, who were a power in the land at the time. In 1465, during the Wars of the Roses, they betrayed King Henry VI to his enemies, leading to his capture at nearby Brungerly. For this treachery Sir Thomas Talbot received £100 and a pension of £40 a year from King Edward IV. The Talbots also kept a private army. The 'barracks', a lovely half-timbered building, still stands behind the Hall on the banks of Bashall Brook, in an excellent state of preservation.

There is an old coaching inn, The Red Pump, dated 1756. It was also a small farm, where it is said, a teenage boy who was staying with his grandparents, was hidden under the hay in the barn to escape the press gang.

Two farms are known to have been ale houses, namely Horse Hey and Mason Green.

A field on the banks of Bashall Brook, called Mill Mains, was the site of a corn mill. In 1822 it was being run by John Halstead. On the Hodder was a paper mill, recorded on maps and old deeds, but now gone. Only older residents remember the ruins. Basket making once flourished, using local willows.

In 1786 Moor End was a schoolhouse for 'Protestant Dissenters', as well as a Quaker meeting house.

There is no church in the village and the Methodist chapel was closed in the 1960s. Church services were then held in the school, until that also closed. Part of the old school has been retained for a village hall, and the rest converted into three dwellings.

Losing the school meant losing old customs such as maypole dancing by the children. 'Pancaking' took place on Shrove Tuesday, always a half day holiday. At 11 o'clock, children dashed out of school and went 'hell for leather' round the village, knocking on doors and being given an orange or a penny, the spoils from this escapade being made into marmalade. Of course, those who ran fastest and farthest got the biggest haul.

When our grandparents were young, another custom took place on the Monday preceding Shrove Tuesday, known as 'Collop Monday'. This was a time of year for pig killing, so those less fortunate were sent to knock at the farmers' doors, saying 'Please we've come a'colloping'. If lucky, they were given a piece of bacon.

Until the 1920s the usual rural tradesmen such as blacksmith, wheelwright, joiner, stonemason and grocer, all supplied the everyday needs of the community. Various pedlars toured the countryside with essential small items for the housewife, including buttons, sewing thread, needles, pins etc. One such pedlar was known as 'Mary Ann Tin Box'. Two men kept up this trade on different rounds until the Second World War.

Only the grocer remains in business, in the post office and village shop, much appreciated by all the neighbourhood.

The appearance of the village has changed little over the years. Built of local sandstone round a village green, any conversions of redundant buildings have been carefully done and fit in well with the original.

This is entirely a farming area, mainly milk production, supplemented by beef cattle and sheep. Although now fully mechanised and with fewer people working on the farms, there is no unemployment. A small number work in nearby towns.

The village is situated on the road to Lancaster, through the Trough of Bowland. The Lancashire Witches passed this way to their doom. Now this route is much used by tourists and holidaymakers heading north to Morecambe, the Lake District and Scotland.

Belmont

Would you come to live and work in a district called Hordern, pronounced in the local dialect 'Hard-earn'. Not on your life! In 1804 Squire Laurence Wright and calico printer Thomas Rycroft thought you wouldn't also. So they changed the name and the village of Belmont was born. Belmont means 'Beautiful Hill', a far more alluring implication.

Belmont is an industrial village. Although it has an attractive setting 900 ft above sea level in the West Pennine moors, its character and dignity come from its foursquare artisans' cottages. It grew steadily until in 1851 it had a population of over 1,600. Unfortunately the village was

St Peter's church, Belmont

affected greatly by the textiles depression of the 1860s. Belmont became a ghost village with the population falling to under 300 and many streets in ruins. A slow recovery began in the 1870s with the establishment of the Deakin Bleaching and Dyeing enterprise and by the end of the century the population had reached 1,000 again.

A visitor to Belmont in 1900 could not fail to be impressed by three landmarks: Hilltop House on a bluff overlooking the village and home of the squire, the factory chimney of the so-called 'Top Works' and the tower of the new Congregational chapel. They symbolised the powerful social, economic and cultural influences on village life. Today few of Belmont's 525 inhabitants are employed at the dye works. Hilltop House was destroyed by fire 80 years ago. Sixty years later the chimney was felled and in the 1970s the chapel demolished. Only one village family can trace 200 years of continuous residence dating back to those 18th century days when the community was known as Hordern. Most contemporary Belmonters are recent arrivals, drawn by the beauty of the moorland landscape but working elsewhere.

The most famous inhabitant was Edward Deakin, successful owner and manager of the bleach and dyeworks. He became High Sheriff of Lancashire and was a friend of the first Lord Leverhulme. William Wall was the second vicar of St Peter's, the parish church. He was much loved because of his efforts to help villagers during the depression of the 1860s. A small man with shoulder length white hair, he presented an incongruous if homely figure as he strode through the village in his clerical gaiters and clogs. The first resident Congregational minister was Joseph Hornby. Before entering the ministry he was a railwayman and lay preacher and used to walk every Sunday from Bolton to Belmont, rain or shine. He led his congregation for 36 years and when he died aged 92 he was buried where the pulpit had stood in his first chapel. Sarah Read was not so much a village worthy as a village character. She was the village carrier and visited Bolton daily with her donkey cart. The donkey was called *Victoria* and Sarah wrote to the Queen to tell her that she had the same name as her donkey.

When you visit Belmont, don't overlook the dye works. It may seem prosaic but remember without it there would not have been a Belmont. Trudge like the earliest workers up Print Shop Brow to Maria Square, the first terrace to be built. Admire the prospect from the aptly named South View. Walk along the Potato Pie Path, named after the supper celebrating a successful defence of the right of way, cross the recreation ground and relax on the banks of Ward's Lodge, a local beauty spot. Before you leave, visit St Peter's church. It, together with the dye works and the terraces of cottages, is that part of Belmont's present which reminds us of its past.

Billinge 🐟

Billinge is dominated by Billinge Hill or Beacon, which is one of a chain of beacons in Lancashire. In 1988 the bonfire on the beacon was lit to celebrate the anniversary of the defeat of the Spanish Armada.

The very old villagers speak in the real Lancashire dialect. For example: Divvilsnose (currant cake), jiggert (tired out), powfagged (exhausted), baggin (lunch in the fields – mainly farm workers), peggies (teeth), shives of bread (slices), clem (starve), yon mon (for he or him), bo-bo's (sleep). One can understand why strangers staying in Billinge have great difficulty understanding the local people!

Before the advent of motorised vehicles, Billingers worked on local farms or in small coal mines, of which there were probably three or four within walking distance of Billinge. Walking three or four miles to a place of work years ago was considered quite normal. Today most people have cars or use local transport to get to Pilkington's of St Helens, or further afield to Liverpool and surrounding industrial estates.

Before the Second World War it was quite a small village, consisting of just one main street, with several small lanes or roads leading off. It has since grown quite considerably with new housing estates springing up on each side of Main Street. The rows of stone cottages that used to line Main Street have long since gone, replaced by red brick houses, plus a row of shops at the very bottom tip of Main Street, where it joins Rainford Road.

Just a few stone buildings remain, other than farms. Two very old cottages, lovingly restored, and Ye Olde House at Home (formerly a pub) are situated opposite St Aidan's church. A couple of hundred yards lower down stands Malt House and across the road Claremont House, which has been in the Mather family of local doctors for years. Villagers used to sit in the waiting room on settles whilst old Doctor Oswald Mather made up his prescriptions.

Claremont House is now a retirement home for the infirm, housing about a dozen people. There is also a larger retirement home – a Sue Ryder home – formerly Birchley Hall, situated opposite St Mary's church, Birchley.

Billingers in days gone by had to make their own entertainment, as was usual in village life. During very cold winters the nearby lake of Carr Mill was frozen for weeks on end and skating competitions were held. One famous skater hailed from Billinge – 'Our Nell's Jack'.

Billinge Hill was very popular for Sunday afternoon picnics, and Shaley Brow which runs from the hill down to King's Moss and Crank is a beautiful tree-lined road, where you could call in at a small hut for egg sandwiches, scones and tea.

A very popular pastime in the 1930s and 1940s was Billinge Picture House, corrugated tin outside but on a scale of grandeur inside, with red plush seats and twin seats on the back rows. Films changed Monday, Wednesday and Friday. All this for 2d.

The churches in Billinge and the schools were all constructed from local stone brought to the village from the quarry at the hill. There are four churches, St Aidan's at the top of the hill, the Methodist church halfway down, and St Mary's Birchley at the bottom end. A new Methodist church has just been completed and consecrated on the site of what was once the Old Square, next to the Labour in Vain pub which was reduced to rubble several years ago.

Bilsborrow

This rural village is on the A6 about 14 miles south of Lancaster and seven miles north of Preston. At its centre is a war memorial in memory of servicemen from the three parishes of Bilsborrow, Myerscough and Barton. Their boundaries divide the modern village, even cutting through the bowling green of the Roebuck Inn, and this makes tracing Bilsborrow's history a confusing task.

Discovering Bilsborrow's history through its architecture can be equally puzzling. The 17th century look of Bilsborrow Hall is deceptive; it was built just before the First World War by the Eccles family and is now a judge's lodging. The original manor was built in 1654 on the site of Bilsborrow Hall Farm, which is the home of the prizewinning Bilsborrow herd of Friesian cattle.

Real thatching and an A-frame construction give Guy's Eating Establishment an attractive medieval air, but it was built by John Toolan in the early 1970s on ground adjacent to School House Farm. This old house was the home of John Cross, who endowed the village school in 1718. In 1797 the Lancaster canal was built within yards of it. In the 1980s,

School House Farm was transformed into Owd Nell's pub and customers come to laze by the canal on summer evenings.

Notable 17th century buildings include Matshead Farm, built in 1618 by the river Brock. The Green Man Inn was a toll house on the turnpike from London to Scotland (now the A6) and the White Bull Inn has a real fire in its winter hearth.

The original Myerscough Hall disappeared to make way for the Lancashire College of Agriculture. Nothing original survives of Myerscough Lodge, the home of Thomas Tyldesley, the Roman Catholic recusant whose diary of 1712 to 1714 throws a fascinating light on the life of the lesser gentry of the times. However, Brook House, visited by John Wesley in 1775, still remains. The Methodist chapel in Bilsborrow Lane was opened in 1811 on the site of an old pothouse.

Built in the Early English style, St Hilda's church came into being because Jane Salisbury of Myerscough Hall met an untimely death crossing the railway at Brock station in 1922. She left her estate to build the church, which was consecrated in 1927. The peal of eight bells was added later and draws keen bell-ringers from near and far.

The oldest surviving building in Bilsborrow village, is what remains of a wattle and daub cottage in the yard of Raby's Farm, now adjacent to the M6 motorway. But there again ... is it really in Bilsborrow? The parish boundary snips its way across the cobbles of the farmyard leaving the cottage apparently in Barton!

Bilsborrow has some 30 businesses, including dairy farms, nurseries, haulage contractors, a well-established caravan park, a transport cafe, post office and working bakery. About half the population leaves the village each day to commute to work.

In this spacious village of trees and fields, gardens, hedgerows, underground springs and passing traffic, the surface soil is heavy, but beneath are rich reserves of sand and gravel. Fields in the north-west of the village have been restored since the last extraction of gravel which was shipped out on canal barges. It is rumoured that two of these barges sank in Bilsborrow basin.

Another mystery was the disappearance of a very large pipe left overnight in a ditch. Locals will tell you it sank in the quicksands which mark where an ancient coastline used to be.

The village calendar begins in January on Plough Sunday when a plough is still taken into the church for blessing. June is busy with the Children's Festival, a Strawberry Fair and a vicarage garden party. The produce show is in August and a Harvest Ball is held in September.

People come from far and wide to whist drives, dances, football matches and antiques fairs and new activities keep appearing, such as a microlight club on a local farm.

At present, Bilsborrow is alive and well, though changing. In 1989 Duncombe House became an attractive hotel offering annexe accommodation in canal barges and Brock Farm became a development of prestige houses. Plans are already in hand to extend tourist accommodation and to transform Head Nook Farm into a sand and gravel quarry. It is hoped that Bilsborrow can continue to be a living community, popular with country-loving visitors, where people say 'hello' and everyone knows almost everyone else.

Blacko 🐾

Blacko village, nestling under Tower Hill, has not altered in structure or shape during the last 50 years, though a small estate of new houses has been built on the outskirts, off the Beverley Road.

The village has its place in the history of the Pendle Witches. Malkin Tower Farm was a hide-out for old Mother Demdike and her 'coven of witches'. Stories of witches, boggarts and bogies were often used as threats to naughty children. Many of the old superstitions are still talked over and still partly believed, such as the belief that beads or a silver chain placed around a baby's neck or wrist will ward off evil spirits or the influence of witches.

Blacko Tower is a focal point; built by Jonathan Stansfield in about 1891 as a look-out, from where he hoped to catch a glimpse of his girl friend who lived in Gisburn. But the Weets Hill was higher than the old boy reckoned, and so the tower remained half finished, until a troop of Scouts from Colne built another round of stone, and cemented the tower to look as it is today.

There was a ghost in Blacko once, but the east wind was so strong that the ghost was blown away. A bed sheet at Stone Edge Farm had been left out overnight to bleach on top of the garden hedge. The Blacko women on their way home in the dark, suddenly saw a greyish white figure slowly rise – as did the hair and fear of the women as they fled home to tell the story of the Blacko ghost.

It is about 100 years since the post office came to Blacko. It was started by Billie Thompson and the posting box was red and white. The General Store, started by Norman Brown was the next nine day wonder, when

Norman displayed a bacon slicing machine! ''Ave yer sin yon contraption for cutting a bit of bacon?' Blacko was progressing into the 20th century.

Spout Houses – the nearby spout which never runs dry – was at one time the only source of water supply for the village. A focal point for gossip, and where many a village romance was begun as buckets of water were carried home for cooking and washing. In those days each house would have a rain butt to catch rain water. It was soft, good for washing hair and clothes.

At the neighbouring village of Roughlee John Wesley preached at the tiny village chapel. He had rested on his way to Colne, and paid for the refreshment provided at Roughlee by preaching. Alas, the little chapel has been demolished.

Blacko County primary school is under no threat of closure, as the local population seems to be growing. The village celebrated the centenary of the school in June 1989 with a very successful village festival.

Bolton-by-Bowland 🦡

Bolton-by-Bowland, so called because it is situated on a bow in the river Ribble, is a small village of about 400 inhabitants, which prior to the 1974 reorganisation was in Yorkshire.

It is a village which has physically changed little over the past century, no new houses having been built in the village itself. Barns have been converted, and in the neighbouring hamlet of Holden there are seven new houses. Farms have been amalgamated and the redundant farmhouses converted into country residences.

There is no industry apart from agriculture which is not now as labour intensive as it once was. Much of the village is owned by Bolton Hall estate, who over the years have endeavoured to maintain the rural aspect of the village, which could be described as typically English.

The cottages are grouped around the ancient church which stands on a small eminence in the centre of the village. There are two greens, one in the middle which has the remains of the old market cross and the stocks, whilst the school green is bordered by the former court house and the school. The school was built by public subscription in 1874, replacing an earlier school which had stood on the green since 1620. It is built of local limestone and was designed by Paley and Austen, the well known architects.

In the early 1980s the school was threatened with closure because of falling numbers, but after a vigorous campaign for its retention, was granted a reprieve, and is now flourishing with an ever increasing school roll.

The history of Bolton-by-Bowland revolves around the Pudsey family who lived at Bolton Hall for over 500 years. The Hall was demolished in the 1950s, but King Henry's Well, a circular stone building, reputed to have been built when Sir Ralph Pudsey sheltered King Henry VI during the Wars of the Roses, still stands in the grounds of the Hall. A later descendant, William Pudsey, created the legend of 'Pudsey's Leap'. He is said to have illegally coined silver shillings from a mine at Rimington and, while escaping from the Queen's officers sent to arrest him, jumped on his horse and leapt from Rainsber Scar, a sheer cliff over the Ribble. He rode to London and begged a pardon from his godmother, Queen Elizabeth I, who was on the royal barge on the Thames.

In 1865 the estate was bought by W.C.B.E. Wright of Doncaster whose family still own it today. Mr Wright lived in lavish style at Bolton Hall, employing practically the whole village as gardeners, grooms, maids and estate workers. He is reputed to have owned so many horses that the stables were built on two floors! He was a great benefactor to the village, building a reading and billiard room and giving generous donations towards the building of the school and restoration of the church.

In 1823 the village appeared to be very self contained. The population of 1,800 inhabitants included joiners, wheelwrights, stonemasons, tailors, hatters, shoemakers, corn millers, butchers, cordwainers, blacksmiths, shopkeepers, publicans and farmers. Today there is a combined shop and post office, and an antiques shop, a joiner's shop, two hotels and two nursery gardens.

Although the population is comparatively small, there is a wide range of activities, well supported and enjoyed by residents. A village hall was built in 1970 and extended in 1988.

Bolton-le-Sands ✍

The village of Bolton-le-Sands lies four miles north of Lancaster and Morecambe. The suffix 'le-Sands', not commonly used until the 19th century, distinguishes the village from the half dozen other Boltons in the north of England.

Its history is briefly summed up in the motto under its official coat of arms, 'Per Arenas, per Agros' (By Sands, by Fields). Generations of farmers, fishermen and cockle pickers made their living from the sea and the land. Now the cockle and shrimp pickers are gone. Farmers remain, though some of the shore-side fields have become popular caravan sites.

But the splendid view over Morecambe Bay is unchanged – the Furness coastline and Cumbrian fells (including, on a clear day, the highest point in England, Scafell Pike). Bird watchers too have a special interest in this area of the bay. The over-sands crossing to the Furness peninsula was in the past the quickest way north for pedestrians, horsemen and coaches. Drownings and deaths in the quicksands were not uncommon. The route is definitely not recommended today, the varying channels of the rivers Keer and Kent having made the crossing even more dangerous.

The population of the village, centred half a mile from the shore, increased from less than 400 in the 17th century to 639 in 1801 and at present is near 5,000 after extensive developments since 1945. Much of the old village has fortunately been preserved, unseen by the busy motorists on the A6 bypass. Dated buildings include 14 from the 1600s, the oldest date-stone being 1637 on the former grammar school, now used as a meeting place by village groups and societies.

Here William Stout (1669–1752) received his early education, when not helping out on his father's shore-side farm. William's autobiography, described by Lord Macaulay as 'highly valuable' historically, was first published in book form in 1851. He became a Lancashire shopkeeper and a dedicated Quaker and his detailed life story, which could be regarded as a North Lancashire Pepys, has even been published in the USA.

A less literate local farmer's use of the English language early this century is not so widely known, but has passed into village folk-lore. Rebuking a working lad for bad time-keeping, old Neddy Perkins is quoted as saying: 'I've telt you two times yance afore and if I've to tell you again I'll not tell you twice and you'll stop coming late soon!'

Bolton-le-Sands parish church, Holy Trinity (formerly St Michael's), is one of the oldest in the area, certainly existing in the 11th century. Altered and partly rebuilt in the 19th century, the church contains fragments of pre-Norman stone crosses and the 15th century tower still stands. The architecturally impressive Roman Catholic church, St Mary's, celebrated its centenary in 1984 and the third place of worship, the United Reformed church, formerly Congregational, was opened in 1935. All the churches are well attended and joint services are sometimes held.

The name of one of the three local pubs, the Packet Boat, recalls the

32

days when the section of the Lancaster Canal which passes through Bolton-le-Sands was opened in 1797. The railway to Carlisle followed in 1846, completing the parallel north-south communications by road, water and rail, which at the northern boundary of the village run within a few yards of each other. The canal, once an important carrier of passengers and Lancashire coal, continues to be used by pleasure boats, mallards and swans and its towpath by fishermen, dog-walkers and joggers.

A few natives of the village still remember Sunday school outings on the canal in the 1920s. The journey was made in a coal barge specially cleaned out for the occasion and drawn by horses to a field where games and races were enjoyed. Other highlights of the children's year were the Shrove Tuesday paper-chase, Easter Monday 'pace-egg' rolling and Ascension Day, appropriately the time for groups of children to be escorted up the church tower to hear the clock chime and to see the view across the bay through a telescope.

Many visitors appear in summer, but Bolton-le-Sands is not noticeably geared to the tourist industry. Though hedged about with its own residential suburbs, the old village green site at Crosshill is still surrounded by churches, the school, the Blue Anchor hotel, the library and old stone houses. A few minutes from open countryside, if you know which road to take, the heart of Bolton-le-Sands is still a village.

Borwick & Priest Hutton 🐚

The villages of Borwick and Priest Hutton, both mentioned in the Domesday Book, are three quarters of a mile apart and today, as in the past, rely on the support of each other.

Borwick contains Borwick Hall, dating back to at least the 14th century. The present building owes much to the Bindloss family, cloth merchants from Kendal, who were so good at time-serving that they managed to keep in with both the Royalists and the Roundheads during the Civil War.

At the beginning of the 20th century the distinguished music critic of *The Times*, J. A. Fuller-Maitland, still remembered by a few older villagers, restored the Hall to its former glory and brought much music to the area. It is now run by Lancashire Youth Clubs as a hostel.

Priest Hutton contains a school, sadly closed in 1978. Children are now bussed to neighbouring schools. The original school opened in what was the village tithe barn where church services were also held. A log book records much illness among the children in the early years of the century and time taken off for farm work.

The church, just in Borwick, joins the villages as does the Memorial Hall, just in Priest Hutton. The church was built in 1896 in memory of a loving wife, by a member of the Sharp family, whose descendants still live in Borwick. The original Memorial Hall, pulled down in 1988 to make way for a new one on the same site, was erected in memory of the men who gave their lives in the First World War. Full to capacity for all village entertainments, it was the venue for the Saturday night dances, when, after midnight, the cap would be passed round so that the musicians would play for another hour. Today's societies still meet there.

The canal, built in 1796, brought much work to the area and Methodism was introduced about the same time. Tewitfield chapel was within easy walking distance of both villages. The chapel is thought to have been originally an ale house, used by the canal navvies. One can imagine their reaction to a temperance meeting going on in their old inn. In later years a motorway was to cut off the Tewitfield locks.

In 1936 a Ministry enquiry showed that the water supply from wells, springs and streams, in some cases carried by bucket 600 yards, was unsafe. There was no drinking water in the school and the farmers relied on the rain for their stock and for cooling milk. Piped water was laid on shortly afterwards. It cost a special shilling rate to the parish after contributions from the Ministry of Health, Lancashire County Council and Lancaster RDC.

Until the 1940s, there were a few grand houses and many modest rented dwellings, inhabited by farm workers, chauffeurs, gardeners, shoemakers, blacksmiths, quarry and canal workers. There was a village shop, post office, slaughterhouse, joiner's shop, basket maker's and a smithy. Now, regardless of the absence of street lighting, pavements and village shop, and with lanes inadequate for 20th century traffic, every cottage has been extended into its outbuildings and every barn and shop, together with the smithy and the school, converted into stone residences.

Bradshaw 🌿

Bradshaw's church has an unusual dedication to the French saint, Maxentius. Records tell of a Norman knight from Poitou, living in this area and it is more than likely he built the Norman church and named it after the patron saint of his home town.

The present church, built in 1872, is one of a select number of Church of England churches built without a tower. The old bell tower stands in splendid isolation at the crossroads – the church to the south, the old village school to the north.

As the traveller from Bolton sits at the traffic lights near the elegant stone Royal Oak pub, the ever changing veil of trees hides the shopping precinct, health centre and the large housing estates, stretching up to Christ Church, Harwood, topped by the hills of Affetside, always pleasing to the eye of the native, whatever the season.

Not so many years ago, this land was farmed by small dairy farmers, with the names of Scowcroft, Haslam and Hamer.

One farm left in the area is the 17th century stone farmhouse on Lea Gate. On a summer morning the cows, ambling down the road, cause a hazard, not only for the impatient motorist, but for the unwary pedestrian as they slither on the many cow claps left on the footpaths. They wander down past the bleachworks workers' houses, the old Co-op and the pub set in the middle of a row of small cottages. When the first publican went to apply for his licence he was asked 'What is the name of the house?' 'It has no name' was the reply and so it has been The House Without A Name or the No Name as the locals call it, for more than a hundred years.

Bradshaw boasts an unusual Conservative Club. The old smithy with its smell of burning horses' hooves is just a memory, but the old beams and stone walls have been tastefully left in the bar. Standing proud at the junction of Bradshaw Road and Rigby Lane stands the old school house of 1807. In 1923 this lovely house became a post office. If three customers came in, it was overcrowded!

Walking through the tunnel of trees down Rigby Lane is a delight. The majestic house at the bottom was once a calico warehouse for the bleach works and after that for 75 years a mission church belonging to Manchester City Missions.

Across the bridge, Bradshaw cricket field is one of the most beautiful in Lancashire, if not in England, flanked by its tennis courts and bowling green. Its three-tiered, seated banking is surmounted by a lonely plain white cross, commemorating the young men who went away to the Second World War and never again put willow to leather.

Meandering past Andrew Hamer's wood yard and under the wide road bridge, the brook borders Longsight park and on through Timber-bottom. Long ago, on the farm there, a maid and her man were cruelly murdered. Their skulls stand together on a Bible at Turton Tower. If they were ever separated it is said that the occupants of the farm would not be able to sleep for their wailings and walkings.

Today many wild water flowers float in the clear water of the brook, and anglers enjoy the fishing. But in times past, when the workers at the bleach works were cleaning the dye vats, the polluted water ran red, purple, blue, green or yellow, killing all the fish and vegetation.

Small firms now use the buildings of the works but the lovely Bradshaw Hall is no more – cruelly demolished in the late 1940s. The Hardcastles owned the Hall, and the bleachworks which was the life blood of the village for generations.

Colonel Hardcastle, the last Squire of Bradshaw, was known to go big game hunting in Africa. On the school Sports Day he would stand in a field alongside Bradshaw Brook and throw gingernuts to the scrambling children, while his chauffeur, complete with black livery jackboots and peak cap, held the tins.

Brindle 🦜

Brindle has a pub, a church, village school and hall, and is set in the middle of rolling fields and lanes. It is thought that the name derives from 'Bryn' meaning spring. Today there are still numerous springs in the village.

Brindle is one of the oldest parishes in Lancashire and celebrates its 800th anniversary in 1990. A board containing the list of rectors over these 800 years hangs in the parish church of St James, situated in the centre of the village. Originally the church was dedicated to St Helen. The tower and Cavendish Chapel date back to the 15th century. Five fonts can be found in the church plus some beautiful stained glass windows.

The Catholic church, St Joseph's, stands at the far edge of the parish hidden down a leafy lane, a reminder of the time when Catholics were persecuted for their faith. The faithful had their own way of communicating where the Mass was to be celebrated – washing was hung out on certain trees, the location of which is still pointed out today. However, this did not prevent Father Edmund Arrowsmith from being captured on Brindle Moss and taken to Lancaster Castle where he was executed. At Arrowsmith House, the room in which he is reputed to have said his last Mass has been preserved intact.

The legend of the Brindle cuckoo developed in the Middle Ages. The story goes that the villagers of Brindle thought they would like to keep the cuckoo in the village all the year round, to have perpetual summer.

They all plotted together and when they found the field where the cuckoo was, they rushed out to build a wall around it. If only they had built the wall two bricks higher, it is said, they would have succeeded! Still today, babies born in the village are known as 'Brindle cuckoos'!

The main industry of the village has always been farming and its associated trades. With the prevalence of sheep, spinning and weaving have been an important part of the local economy. Weavers' cottages remain but are now desirable residences for the business people who enjoy the quiet of the village.

Other industries included the development of the Leeds–Liverpool canal in the late 18th and 19th century and the quarrying of stone from the hills surrounding Brindle.

Throughout the 19th century, Brindle was famous for its races. Every year in April, thousands of people thronged the narrow lanes to watch the horses over the circuit of approximately three miles between the rectory and the canal at Wheelton. Bookmakers were much in evidence and the marquees for refreshment, both liquid and solid, were busy all day. The event continued to the early part of this century with crowds of 20,000 being reported in 1905.

Christmas Day 1944 brought a nasty surprise for the villagers of Brindle. A bomb landed on some outbuildings in Gregson Lane, Brindle, wrecking two nearby cottages and blowing off the roof of a farm across the lane. Fortunately there were no casualties except some 30 hens – all that was left of their cabin was some feathers and straw in a 40 foot crater. Propaganda leaflets dropped from the plane were found around the area. News of the attack was kept 'top secret' for 3 weeks but eventually the leaflet story broke with the hope that if Hitler needed to resort to this kind of 'invasion' then there was hope.

About 20 years ago, a small cul-de-sac of 50 houses was built in the centre of the village. This has ensured that life within the village continues to develop. But the lanes and fields of Brindle remain a haven for wild life as well as those people who need a refuge from the encroaching developments of the town.

Brinscall

Brinscall was a small farming community owned by the de Hoghton family, who were lords of the manor in the 16th century. When the cotton industry came to Lancashire in the 19th century, a thriving community of handloom weavers was built up in the valley area. William Christopher Wood built the present Brinscall Hall in 1876, and a calico printworks which employed a number of people but which closed in 1928. The ruins of many of these buildings are now surrounded by woodland known as Wheelton Plantation.

In 1847 Liverpool Corporation bought the water rights of Withnell Moor from William Bashall Parke, a local landowner, and built Roddlesworth reservoir. The area is now owned by North West Water Authority and is part of the Anglezarke link of reservoirs and also a nature conservation area.

Halfway up School Lane, the main street of Brinscall, is Hillside Methodist chapel, where the famous singer Kathleen Ferrier was married.

The village school, St John's, was the first combined Church of England/Methodist primary school in Lancashire.

The swimming baths in Brinscall were built to celebrate the coronation of King George V, with generous donations from papermill owner and benefactor Herbert J. Parke. The cottage hospital was built to celebrate the coronation of King Edward VII by the same benefactor in 1902. The village cricket field, which accommodates three thriving teams, is held in trust by the villagers, also by courtesy of the Parke family.

Bromley Cross

The original 'cross' was shown as Kershaw's Cross on very old maps, situated somewhere between Bradshaw Road and what is now the Jumbles Country Park. Kershaw farmed land thereabouts, tenant to the Bromleys (or Bromileys), landowners in Harwood and Bradshaw. Kershaw's Cross eventually became known as Bromley Cross.

The growth area which is now the recognised Bromley Cross developed away from the original site in the 19th century, together with factories, mills and bleachworks, using water from the Eagley and Bradshaw Brooks. By 1938, Bromley Cross was part of a straggling 'district' administered by Turton Urban District Council. Today the old council offices are occupied by a commercial firm and administration is by Bolton Metropolitan District.

The area owed a great deal to such as the Ashworth family, millowners and thoughtful benefactors. Forward looking, they encouraged the formation of the Bolton–Blackburn Railway Company; they were among its directors and had their own little station, 'The Oaks', which was adjacent to the family seat near Canon Slade school. The family seat has gone, the mills have gone, and the little station's platforms are all but hidden in the lineside greenery. Only the former stationmaster's house remains, occupied, beside the level crossing at the head of Oaks Avenue.

Present day commuters to Blackburn, Bolton and Manchester keep Bromley Cross station, with its commuter car park supplanting the former goods sidings area, very much alive. Abutting the station booking office and waiting rooms is one of Britain's fast disappearing lineside signal boxes. Bromley Cross is the railway 'boundary' of BR's Manchester Division, therefore the signal box is manned around the clock, the next nearest box being Preston Power Signal Box. Commuters would hate to lose their friendly signalmen.

The village itself has many convenient assets, among which are good schools (one with swimming pool for public use also), health centre, supermarket, post office, bus service, attractive small unit shops, a well stocked library, churches to suit several denominations, and the local hostelries.

The star attraction, however, appears to be the one all the visitors have heard of, and which is situated on the northerly edge of Bromley Cross. This is Orrell Farm, by Goose Cote Hill. This was dramatically transformed in 1964 into the now almost nationally, if not internationally, known tourist feature, The Last Drop. This is a village within a village, if you like. It has cobbled streets, tea shop, craft shops, antique market, pub, village stocks, and a substantial Hotel/Conference/Banquet Centre. The name, somewhat ghoulishly, refers to the site of one of the last public hangings in England.

In olden days fairs were held in the village. There were people who played flutes, violins and concertinas. There were card sharps, brandy snap stalls, walking sticks for sale, and a peruke maker who bought hair from local girls for his wig-making business.

Another millowner benefactor, Stephen Blair, built a hospital in 1887 on high ground adjacent to what is now the Last Drop complex. This hospital, known today as 'Blair's', was principally a convalescent home for his own employees, but served the sick and needy of Bolton, too. It became a military hospital during the First World War, and in the 1920s Bolton Royal Infirmary was allocated some of its beds. In 1948 it came within the NHS and is invaluable even today.

Caring is also a way of life at Birtenshaw Hall, a very old manor at the southern end of the village, where children with all sorts of handicaps are looked after, many on a residential basis, who often take part in the life of the village.

Broughton (near Preston)

The origins of Broughton are peaceful and ancient, a far cry from the present day incessant traffic, which roars through the village at the crossroads.

The name 'Broctun', which is the early spelling of Broughton, means a farm enclosure, or an estate by a brook, and traces of the first settlement can be found by the Blundel brook, which flows just to the south of the church.

By 1260 the Singletons were the lords of the manor, settled in this sheltered spot where the meadows were rich and water was plentiful. A simple wooden church was established, and from that time Christian worship has continued over the centuries on the same site, but not always in the same building. In 1533 the stone tower of the present church, dedicated to St John the Baptist, was erected.

During the early years of the 19th century, churchwardens, bell-ringers and worshippers were able to meet and refresh themselves at the Church Inn, which rested under the shadow of the church; the inn was in existence when James Tuson the schoolmaster bought it in 1806, and he then ran it for the next 33 years. It is reported that on Guy Fawkes Day in 1823 thirsty bell-ringers went there to drink 20 pints of home brewed beer. All this conviviality came to an end in 1870, when the inn became a home for the sexton Mr Applebury, who, according to Fishwick's contemporary account, 'can ring in the steeple, dig graves, read responses in the church, make clothes, feed throstles, fatten ducks and look after Sunday school scholars'.

In a building next to the Church Inn was Broughton grammar school, endowed in the 16th century and free to the children of Broughton, Barton and Haighton. A school return for December 1833 records somewhat primly that there were 70 scholars; boys in one school, girls in the other. Discipline must have been strict. Fishwick reports that, 'Mr Alexander Jackson appointed in 1820 does not believe in sparing the rod and spoiling the child'. In 1843 a new stone building was erected on land opposite the church, and this can be seen today with additions to suit modern educational requirements.

For centuries the children attending the school were sons and daughters of farmers, craftsmen or labourers, but after 1928 the population of the parish increased and changed radically, as large suburbs were built to the south. The country children shared desks and learned their catechism with the new urban children who walked down the hill to school.

The commercial centre of the village never developed on this early site, but was to be found about half a mile further north, at the crossroads on the A6. Today this is just a bottleneck, as the incessant traffic grinds to a halt at the traffic lights. The roads that created the village long ago now threaten to strangle it, and there is talk of a bypass.

The old Toll Bar Cottage, jutting out onto the pavement, is a reminder of a time in the 18th century when people had to pay to use the roads, and tolls were collected for animals and vehicles; in 1760 the fee for a horse, landau, hearse or sledge was 6d.

Pinfold Cottage, just south of Toll Bar Cottage, is a pointer to the agricultural past, taking its name from the nearby enclosure in which stray animals were penned until claimed by their owner.

The cottages on each side of the road, now mainly private residences, served a very different purpose before the First World War. Here were all the essentials of a village. The new garage on the east side of the road has superseded the smithy, worked by successive generations of the Mercer family. Its presence was advertised by a large iron horse on the roof of the forge, and outside the nearby clogger's shop hung a large iron sign fashioned like a clog. On the north side of the smithy was a saddler, and just round the corner in Whittingham Lane stood the workshop of Richard Hardman, the village joiner, chorister, and churchwarden at Broughton church. Villagers and passers-by alike could meet and quench their thirst in the two public houses which still stand at the crossroads, and the women would find all they needed in the village shop, long since gone.

Until the early 19th century Broughton was populated by farmers, labourers, tradespeople, gardeners, dressmakers, washerwomen and quite a number of handloom weavers, but from the middle of the century a number of professional or manufacturing gentlemen began to see Broughton as a pleasant place in which to build a new residence. In 1833 J. W. R. Wilson, a Preston solicitor built Broughton House, with bowling green and pleasure gardens. In these changed times this fine house serves as an ambulance depot, and Broughton Park built in 1890 for James Clarke, another Preston solicitor, is now a country club and hotel.

Cabus 🦡

Cabus is an unusual parish with no church, no school and no real village centre. There is some new housing, clustered at the southern edge of the parish, on the fringe of the market town of Garstang. All the older houses and farms of Cabus are scattered along the network of roads.

Roads are the essential characteristic of Cabus, especially the A6 running north through the centre of the parish. Since Roman times the narrow strip of level land, between the mosses and marshes to the west and the Pennine fells to the east, has been part of the major west coast route to Scotland. Edward I may have led his army this way in the 13th century to subdue the Scots. Scots supporters of the Young Pretender, Prince Charles Edward certainly passed through nearby Garstang on their ill-fated march south some 500 years later.

Meanwhile, ancient paths from the ecclesiastical lands of Cockersand Abbey crossed the region, passing through the Trough of Bowland, to Clitheroe Castle. The stump of an early cross was found at a junction of lanes, now little used, near the western boundary.

The county archives have references to people who lived in Cabus long ago. '1516 – Margaret, wife of Nicholas Rigmayden, died.' There is still property called Rigmaidens, though the present home is a modern building. '1661 – James Davis and his wife Elizabeth, blind.' There is still a farm belonging to a Davis family. '1669 – John, son of George Weaver.' A large old farm is still called Weaver's Farm. There are also reports of repair to the highway and to Gubberford Bridge (also spelled Goversall and Goverton) over the river Wyre at the boundary with Scorton. There is a legend of a grey figure seen at this bridge. It is said to be the ghost of a servant girl, from Woodacre Hall, killed by her jealous soldier sweetheart.

Most of the land is good, fertile farmland and once belonged to the Dukes of Hamilton. The well drained, constructed and cultivated fields had good thorn hedges planted by men brought from Scotland by the Duke. Several of the farms and the woodland at Fowler Hill are now owned by the Duchy of Lancaster.

In 1751 the Preston to Lancaster road became a maintained turnpike and the toll bar remains as a private house at the junction between the old road from Garstang with the A6 bypass. One of two very strong, round gateposts which formerly belonged to the toll bar was unearthed during road widening and re-erected by the cottage. When the Royal Oak and other Garstang inns were staging posts the exhausted horses were led out to buildings in Green Lane to rest and graze before replacing the next stage-coach team.

Between the two world wars the A6 became a trunk road and several garages and transport cafés were opened, adding alternative employment. Best known was probably Dunn's Cafe where discerning businessmen also stopped to enjoy huge portions of ham and eggs, or 'taty' pies. After the opening of the motorway in 1965 there was a startling fall in traffic flow but the garages are still in business and one former transport cafe, May's, has become 'The Crofters', a palatial restaurant and hotel. Dunn's has been demolished but the oldest inn, the Old Holly, rebuilt in the Georgian era as the Hamilton Arms, is being refurbished. The Little Chef restaurant, opposite, serves fast food for travellers in a greater hurry.

Several of these establishments added small caravan parks before 1939 and these now provide important additional income in Cabus. There are over 200 caravans, almost half being residential. The others bring holidaymakers from industrial towns, who find Cabus an excellent recreational centre.

Apart from jobs and income generated by the roads, the main land-use is farming. Influenced by nearby Morecambe Bay and the prevailing westerly winds, the climate is ideal for stock rearing. The traditional dairy breeds are Friesian and Ayrshire. Some of the milk is bottled but there are several small ice cream and cheese makers in the area. Many farms keep flocks of crossbred sheep as well and one specialises in breeding and schooling horses.

There have recently been some light industrial units developed near the Garstang boundary, mainly agricultural. The smithy has expanded into farm machinery repairs. Horse boxes are being built and veterinary supplies sold.

Many residents have to travel to Preston or Lancaster to work and to Garstang for services like doctor or dentist. Permission has been given for a post office service in one of the shops. Younger children go to primary schools in Garstang, Winmarleigh and Scorton while teenagers go to high schools in Garstang or Lancaster. The only meeting place is the village hall in the centre of Cabus, but very good use is made of this asset.

Calder Vale 🦢

Calder Vale is an unusual village in many ways. Set in a steep valley, it is a small pocket of industry tucked away in a picturesque setting. The river Calder provided not just a name but also the source of power for two cotton weaving mills. The terraced stone houses were built by the mill owners for their workers, every house fronted by a garden.

When the industry was in its heyday the women were all skilled weavers and the men who were not employed as tacklers probably worked at the paper mill at Oakenclough, within walking distance further up the river. The village was a self-contained unit; families without a mill worker were rare although a few men would work on the surrounding farms.

The materials produced were beautifully embroidered cottons, linens, voiles and later nylons, many exported for Indian saris. Home dressmakers always had a wealth of samples to choose from and some exquisite bridal gowns have been made from 'mill weave'. Low Mill was at the very bottom of the valley and many workers took a short cut down 'the 40 steps' from the top road. The 40 steps are still there but sadly Low Mill was demolished over 20 years ago. Lappet Mill however goes from strength to strength, working shifts 24 hours a day. 'That's music to my ears' said one retired weaver, referring to the clatter of the looms disturbing a still summer evening.

At one time there were three shops and a 'chippie'. Senior citizens can remember Old Joe's toffee shop and the clogger's and a cafe. There are also memories which can stretch back to the days of shared toilets – 'petties', communal water taps, installation of electricity at £1 per light and the terrace known as 'Nosey-Row' – one wonders why?

Gradually the houses have been sold to their occupants, and the only shop today is the post office, which is also the newsagent's and store.

There is a village hall, a mission room shared by the Anglicans and the Roman Catholics, who hold their weekly services there, and a well supported Methodist chapel. There is no pub although there used to be a Temperance Hotel – no strong drink because the mill owners were Quakers. The social centre for many is 'the club', founded by the British Legion.

There is no road through the village, which helps to keep it unspoilt and definitely off the beaten track. There is a bus to Garstang on Thursdays and Saturdays, not used by many but vital to those who need it. By car the road ends at the mill square but there is a footpath past the mill lodge (the small lake formed from the river to provide water power). The ducks are tame and will look for any crusts you bring. The path is steep and takes you through woods to the church and school. In bluebell time this woodland path is a beautiful sight.

The church and school were so sited to serve the needs of both Calder Vale and Oakenclough. A worthy intention; but everyone has a long walk, or a longer drive by road. A delightful lingering walk for a child to school posed a problem for funerals in days gone by – there was a resting place for coffin bearers half way through the wood.

As with all high level villages the weather does not always show a smiling face. The rain clouds sometimes come down to sit on the surrounding fells and snow can soon shut us off from the outside world. The milkman has carried crates of milk down the blocked road and the coalman has humped bags of coal on his back down to the lowest houses.

But this is not a village living in the past. Far from it! An active WI helps provide for a Children's Festival in June when tradition is very much alive. The children are also given a bumper Christmas party and the over 60s are treated to their day out too. There is a playgroup for the tinies and the school has a very supportive PTA. The churches of necessity have fund raising events as well as social occasions. In a caring community like this most people support all causes.

Carleton

Carleton village, three and a half miles from Blackpool, was recorded in the Domesday Book as Carlentun and has been a more or less thriving community ever since.

A free school was founded in the late 17th century, finance being provided by the will of Elizabeth Wilson of Whiteholme. There were Wilsons still at Whiteholme this century. During the First World War two of the sons walked to Kirkham – some nine miles – to volunteer for the army, were rejected because they had flat feet, and walked back home to continue farming until after the Second World War. Their farm is now the site of the Blackpool and Fylde Technical College. The Carleton Church of England school, albeit in newer buildings, continues on the original site, and in addition there is now a very new school on Carleton Green.

The public house, which has been called The Castle Gardens since about 1890, was formerly The Weld's Arms, and this would date it at about 1750.

Dick's Mill, the date of construction unknown, was demolished in 1886 by 'a great Fylde gale which caught the sails' although the mill-stones were then being driven by steam engine. A row of houses built with the bricks from the mill now stands on the site, and one of these carries a stone carved with a windmill, and the words 'Dick's Mill Terrace 1886'.

Opposite the windmill was a smithy, the cottage of which was extended by 1861 to become Thornton Villas.

During the first half of the 20th century the village grew steadily, mainly by the establishment of new smallholdings and market gardens. As in most country villages of this time there was a busy social scene. Bowls was popular, men's on the Castle Gardens green from 1910 and ladies' on their own green on Blackpool Road. The present site was donated in 1917, with the men and ladies eventually uniting to form a single club. Football and cricket teams were fielded in due season, there was the annual gala in summer, and the Shrove Tuesday tea and concert is still remembered vividly by those who were there.

The Castle Gardens attracted excursions by holidaymakers from Blackpool to its 'theme park' of swing boats, aviary and afternoon teas. If the visitors wanted to go shopping, they would almost certainly buy from one or other of the three generations of Parkinsons who ran the village store for decades until Nellie retired.

There was a village baker and confectioner who supplied a large area of the Fylde. One of his bakers, Jonty Greenwood, was occupied all day and every day in winter, but only two days a week in summer, making crumpets, muffins and oatcakes whilst others kneaded, shaped by hand, and baked the bread and cakes. One of the girls working there was Alice Parkinson, and the only machine she remembers was for kneading the dough for white bread. This took batches of up to 120 lbs of flour and was operated by hand.

Collecting for parcels of 'comforts for the troops' in the Second World War led to the establishment of the first community centre, a shed behind the Castle Gardens. In 1946 the site, and a former RAF barrack hut, were bought to establish the Memorial Hall which, with some later extension, is still being used today.

In the 1970s a large area of land was made available for building to create the Carleton Green estate and this has been well executed with variety and spacious planning.

The village is now wholly residential, no industry, no heavy traffic, but with easy access to towns and motorway if these are needed. Around the Four Lane Ends are shops to supply any and every daily need for those who are too busy, or do not wish, to travel further.

Catforth 🪶

Catforth is partly in the parish of Woodplumpton, partly in that of Inskip and lies between these villages, some five miles from Preston.

The ground was once marshy so that drainage and infilling was necessary. The inn called The Running Pump and the house known as Spring Cottage bear witness to the presence of natural springs. Spring Cottage is thought to have been the brewhouse of the inn.

The agricultural past and present of the village is marked by the old smithy and the tithe barn (now a private house) and the number of working farms. Cottages once inhabited by handloom weavers and the name of Tan Pit Farm refer to former occupations in addition to farming; so does the malt house shown on the 1840s Ordnance Survey map as being on the canal bank.

The canal goes from Preston to Kendal and was cut in 1798. Two humped bridges, important features of the village, were built over it. There were wharves on the banks, where coal and other merchandise was unloaded. The canal was the main thoroughfare to Garstang, Lancaster, Tewitfield and Kendal. Wharf House still stands. Horses were changed at Swillbrook. Swillbrook House is said to be haunted by the ghost of a child who died in a trap set by her father for her unfaithful mother. It was a private school in the 19th century, before Catforth school was built.

Catforth National school, as it was first known, was opened in 1873. A Roman Catholic school was opened two years later, but it closed some years ago and is now a private house. In 1877 St Robert's Roman Catholic church was opened, next to the school.

There is no Church of England in Catforth, but the Methodists have had three chapels since the Primitive Methodists built the first in 1829. Prior to this they had met in private houses and in the open air, addressed by preachers of such fervour that they were known as 'ranters'. The custom of open air gatherings was long perpetuated by the annual Camp Meeting and Love Feast held on Whit Sunday, when a crowd would assemble on Carr's Green, an open space to the west of the village, to listen to sermons by well known preachers.

The Memorial Village Hall commemorates the dead of the First World

War. The architect was Walter Standen, son of a former headmaster of the school. It was opened in the 1920s. All that remains of a sports club erected at about the same time is the football field, but a bowling club, complete with floodlighting, flourishes today.

In living memory, the post master walked to Broughton for the mail and the only telephone in the district was in the post office. Now the motor car connects the village with a web of other villages, and a bus plies hourly to Preston and Poulton le Fylde. Pleasure boats gather on the canal and a marina supplants the working barges of the past. Canal cruises now pass the Swillbrook staging post.

Building in Catforth is severely restricted as Catforth is in the Green Belt. This means that it remains unspoilt, but it also means that no new generation is growing up ready to take over from the old.

Caton-with-Littledale 🌿

Caton and Brookhouse (one and a half miles east on the A683 from M6 junction 34) combine into a 3,000 population community of small-town size, but newcomers and visitors quickly discover a singularly friendly village atmosphere.

A monthly newsletter *The Link*, written and delivered by volunteers, tells every household about the busy life of the village, for there are more than 20 clubs and societies, two primary schools, two community homes for the elderly, five churches, health centre, twice-weekly library, three pubs and a range of tradesmen and shops including a chemist and cobbler.

Caton-with-Littledale, as the parish is named, climbs from the leafy glades of the Crook o'Lune, the magnificent scene painted by Turner where the river meanders like the shepherd's hooked staff, up to windswept heather and bracken-covered moorland fells commanding a panorama of Morecambe Bay.

In a green and pleasant situation in the lush Lune valley Caton and Brookhouse make a popular country village home for commuters. The village burgeoned with new housing in the 1950s and 1960s as a 'dormitory' for Lancaster. But Caton was more a workplace itself through the Industrial Revolution 200 years ago, with at one time about eight cotton and wood-turning bobbin mills. Mill owners built fine homes alongside farmer neighbours. A rural industry renaissance now awaits Willow Mill, thanks to a £¾ million Government grant to create craft workshops and offices. Former textiles factory Low Mill is soon to be converted into new housing flats and homes. It used to be owned by the Greg family who had Styal Mill, in Cheshire.

Villagers in 1803 discovered a 6ft high Roman milestone near Gresgarth marking the five miles distance from Lancaster.

The most beloved village landmark is the Old Oak Tree at Town End. Legend has it that monks sold their salmon catches from the Lune on the granite slabs, called the 'Fish Stones', which encircle the ancient oak. It survives yet with little more than a single bough, nevertheless braving each spring with new leaf. Visitors are also shown the 'Plague Stone' at Bull Beck bridge, Brookhouse, where in the hollowed basin of sandstone payment was exchanged for provisions to sustain the sick who lived outside the village and came to collect food and goods.

Rotten Row is an enchanting narrow slope of cottages dating from Queen Anne's reign. Rising above them is St Paul's church. A church has existed on the site from the 12th century and a doorway arch of that time was built into the wall adjoining the church tower. The church was rebuilt or extended in 1537 but in the 19th century it was in such disrepair that it was all taken down (except the tower) and rebuilt. The new church was consecrated and given the name of St Paul in 1865.

The railway was essential to Caton's economy in the late 19th century but the line up the Lune valley to Wennington was axed in the 1960s – now the disused line is a country walk nature trail. In the 1930s village eccentric Dick Walling, a walrus-moustached gentleman who favoured a black cloak, was fond of cycling the road alongside the railway between Caton and Hornby and took delight in furious pedalling to race the steam trains! Lawn tennis was also fun in the 1930s. The Ball Lane courts were an exclusive venue drawing Wimbledon names for knock-about practice! Now the club draws a wide membership and there is also village football, cricket and bowling.

Stone-built cottages and manor houses survive to show the character and attractiveness of Caton and Brookhouse as a home for workers and wealthy industrialists of bygone times. Grassyard Hall, later known as Gresgarth, has vaulted cellars of Furness iron-red sandstone, revealing its origins as a monastic retreat in the 11th century. Now it is an MP's country retreat.

The village flower show is one of the main events in the local calendar, another is Caton Gala. This was a renowned North Country sports event earlier this century but lapsed in the 1950s until it was revived with vigour in the early 1980s as an indication of thriving community spirit.

Cherry Tree 🍒

The estate belonged to the Boardman family before 1730, at which time it was a hamlet of two or three cottages and included a few acres of Feniscliffe. Robert Boardman built his large house in 1802 and, having planted cherry trees in the grounds, he named it Cherry Tree House. The estate was sold in 1841 when James, the last male of the line, died but as it developed the name Cherry Tree had been adopted. A doctor's house and surgery for many years, the house was demolished in 1976 and a new crescent of apartments set back off the road has been built on the site.

The Georgian mansion Woodlands House was built in the mid-1800s by George Whiteley the cotton mill magnate, who left Witton Bank House because of the pollution of the river Darwen. His sons lived there for some time after his death but later sold it to Frank Longworth, another cotton magnate, who lived there from 1902–1932. He deemed Cherry Tree to be 'too common a district' as the ribbon development of housing began from Blackburn through the village, extending to Feniscowles. The house had various tenants over the years – not least the Home Guard in the Second World War, but is now a 'Home for Retired Gentlefolk'.

The 'Woodlands' United Reformed church was originally 'Cherry Tree' but changed the name after Mill Hill church closed and the two congregations were combined. Built in 1887 by Cherry Tree's great benefactor Joseph Dugdale the millowner, it is a Gothic stone structure with hand carved pews of different designs.

Of the 903 population in Feniscowles and Cherry Tree 500 were Church of England people and Cherry Tree parishioners wanted a church of their own. A mission church held in the day school was founded in 1888 and by hard work and sacrifices, and the generous gift of £1,000 from Lt Gen Feilden, St Francis' church was consecrated in 1893 – albeit fractionally over the village boundary, in Feniscliffe.

In 1858 Joseph Dugdale acquired Cherry Tree cotton weaving mill, built by the Polding brothers in 1847, and by 1865 he had built Bank spinning mill. As the new Immanuel/Cherry Tree school was inaugurated at the same time, Sir Joseph deferred putting the machinery in so that the 400 children present could be 'comfortably accommodated' for their celebratory tea!

Sadly, the decline of the cotton industry led to the closures of both mills in 1959/60. Bank Mill was demolished in 1987 and a mini-industrial estate was developed and a small estate of attractive private accommodation (Hunter's Lodge) – all tastefully landscaped. The cotton mill is being used as a trading warehouse. Of the houses and streets built for the workers, only the long-gardened Feilden Terrace remains with two or three houses lower down – the rest having been converted into shops. On the opposite side Bank Villas, built for the management, have also survived along with the pretty Cherry Tree terrace.

The Cherry Tree Machine Company was founded in 1880 and has developed from what the older people refer to as the 'Mangle' or 'Wringer' works into a leading manufacturer of sophisticated laundry equipment. A small refrigeration company operates from the old day school.

The shopping area, divided by the railway, is referred to as 'the Village' on the older side and 'the Terminus' on the later-developed side, which *was* the terminus for the tram from Blackburn. It includes every kind of shop – a post office, chemist, hairdresser, ladies outfitter, a barber and a dentist, with a small health centre and the modern library.

Chipping ✿

Chipping, surrounded on three sides by fells, lies in the area of outstanding natural beauty known as the Forest of Bowland. The origins of the village go back over a thousand years, its name deriving from Old English 'Chepyn' meaning 'a market place'. In 1350, the Abbot of Whalley described the inhabitants of Chipping as 'few, intractable and wild'. Today, the throngs of visitors who arrive by coach, car, bicycle or on foot obviously have a very different opinion as they are welcomed with real Lancashire hospitality.

What memories do these visitors take home? Perhaps they remember its famous chairworks, cheese manufacturers, water wheel, home-made ice cream or its delightful 17th century buildings. How many are aware, however, that Chipping is not just a picture-postcard village but a thriving, working community with many amenities and numerous social activities?

The welfare of its people has always been part of the tradition of this caring community. In his will in 1683, John Brabin, a prosperous cloth-dealer and dyer, left money to build a schoolhouse and to pay for a schoolmaster, books and clothes for the poor children of the village. His presence is still felt as his house, dated 1668, is now the post office and

Maltkiln House, Chipping

the school, now a private residence, stands at the entrance to Windy Street alongside the almshouses he also endowed. Since 1789, the Chipping Brothers' Friendly Society (Oddfellows) has supported needy families, and was also responsible for bringing the first resident doctor to Chipping. The caring continues with meals on wheels and the Happy Days Club.

Traditionally an agricultural community, in 1801 Chipping had 827 inhabitants, 75 per cent of whom worked on the land. By 1831, the population had risen dramatically to 1,334. The Industrial Revolution had arrived and with it a diversification of employment which continues to the present. Then, water power from Chipping Brook was harnessed to provide at least eight sites for important industries such as cotton spinning, corn milling, brass founding, chair making, spindle and fly manufacturing. The chief remnant of this period is Kirk Mill, built about

52

1780 as a cotton mill but owned by chair manufacturers H. J. Berry and Sons since the 1890s. Nearby stands Grove Row, built as a workhouse for the poor in 1824 and used for this purpose till 1840 when it became cottages for the millworkers. Otherwise there is little to show that the beauty and tranquillity of Chipping was ever touched by those grimy times.

The new housing on the former site of Tweedy's brass and iron foundry is one of a few small developments built in post-war years, but compared to urban areas little expansion is apparent. Incomers are welcomed and many play an active part, alongside members of the older-established families, in the strong community spirit which won the fight to retain the village's traditionally-styled street lighting. Many participate, too, in the wide variety of recreational activities.

Older Chippingers can recall the nine wells which served the village with water before it was piped in 1913; electricity arriving in 1935; Pancake Tuesday visits to local farms where children were treated to oranges; walking three miles to school in all weathers and a caning for being late.

Memories still linger of the ghost of Elizabeth Dean, the boggarts of Wolfen Hall, the Club Day processions and of the all-male 'Henpeck Club' which elected a 'Mayor' who was wheeled on a watercart to visit every pub in the village. On one occasion, 30 members were arrested! The long tradition of the biannual livestock fairs continues even today in the Chipping Agricultural Show and the September sheep sale.

In the past, the everyday needs of the villagers were amply supplied by various shops – grocers, toffee shops, bakery, fish and chips, a barber, a tailor, a bank and the carters who brought in coal and other commodities. Now Chipping has two well-stocked grocers, a butcher, a sweetshop, a wool and craft shop, a hairdresser and a post office with furniture, crafts and 'bygones' on sale.

Despite the changes it has undergone throughout its long history, Chipping's essential peace and beauty remain.

Churchtown (near Garstang)

All roads led to Churchtown. Narrow paths, bridle paths, tracks traced by the hooves of a thousand horses, even a ley line. Yet the world now passes Churchtown by. The bustling village of the past, where once there were eight shops, is now a quiet backwater.

But Churchtown is still very much alive. Youngsters still meet, talk and lark by the ancient cross but the cottage where they could buy humbugs, treacle toffee and parched peas has gone. It is left to the post office to meet the tastes of today.

A village with three vicarages can reasonably be said to have been the centre of a certain amount of religious fervour, even if two of them are now private houses. Visitors to the area are often startled to be told that St Helen's was once the parish church for Garstang, about two miles away, which meant quite a walk for the faithful.

A stroll along Fylde road, the old route to Blackpool, gives only a clue to what went before. There stand three whitewashed cottages, but not so many years ago, they were thatched and were one storey lower. Apart from the church, they are the oldest buildings in the village.

It is hard to appreciate the number of small cottages, now demolished, which gave trade and support to those eight shops; two grocer's, a post office, a clogger's, a butcher's and three which sold sweets!

If you come on a certain Saturday in August, there will be teas to tempt and the sight of locals going back in time, dressed in the style of years past, marking the Patronal Festival. Flowers deck the 13th century church in honour of St Helen.

When tea is insufficient to restore flagging spirits, the ale house calls. Sup at the 'Covered Cup', today called the Punch Bowl, but once named after a device on the heraldic arms of the Butler-Cole family who, until the 1930s, owned the village. The Horns Inn lies where the traffic to and from Blackpool is funnelled away from the heart of the village on the bypass.

Once that roaring, rushing river of metal is left behind, Churchtown becomes a haven, for the old who were born there, for those who have become 'locals' through decades spent there, and for the young families who cherish its calm.

Claughton on Brock 🦚

Claughton is beautifully situated in the foothills of the Bleasdale fells, on the banks of the river Brock. It is a widespread settlement, still almost exclusively agricultural. It is well-wooded and many of the farmhouses are mellow with age and very well kept. Among the most picturesque buildings is the house called The Street, three-storeyed and with the date

1689 carved over the front door. It owes its name to the fact that it stands at the corner where Smithy Lane joins the old Roman road.

On one side the Roman road skirts the extensive parkland around Claughton Hall, the home of Major and Mrs Fitzherbert-Brockholes. Their family connection goes back to at least the 15th century, when the Brockholes were lords of the manor. A Fitzherbert relative inherited the estate in the 18th century and added his surname to the ancestral one. Mrs Fitzherbert and the Prince Regent visited the Hall and their names appear as sponsors at a local christening in 1797.

The present Hall is modern, replacing the old one. Horse trials are now held in the park and are attended by the foremost horsemen and horsewomen of the day.

Claughton has long been a Roman Catholic centre, visiting priests ministering to the mission when public worship was forbidden. A local farmhouse housed priests in hiding, sheltering them in a small hidden 'priest's hole' when the authorities were searching for them. The Catholic church of St Thomas was eventually built in 1792, thanks to the efforts of an eccentric and determined priest called Father Barrow who had served for some years as an officer in the Navy, into which he was press ganged. The Anglican church is Garstang St Helen's, which is at Churchtown.

A restored preaching cross in the centre of the village was erected by Thomas Fitzherbert-Brockholes in 1920 in memory of two of his sons and of those men of Claughton who gave their lives in the First World War. The Memorial Hall was rebuilt a few years ago and serves as the social centre of the neighbourhood.

Clayton-le-Woods

Clayton-le-Woods, first recorded in 1194, was a farming community dominated by Clayton Hall, a moated manor farm.

The river Lostock meanders through the village and was crossed by a very narrow bridge carrying a rough road of loose stone chippings. This road formed part of the London post road and Clayton-le-Woods had a thriving coaching inn. Market gardeners with laden horses and lorries passed through on their way to Blackburn market.

Earlier this century the village shop dispensed paraffin from a trap and sold all household items including corn feed for the hens. A well provided the only drinking water and rainwater was collected in butts for washing purposes.

The linen weavers' cottages with ground floor loom shops had large, low windows facing south for maximum daylight hours. They still stand in Sheephill Lane.

Built in 1744, the village school was a single room with a coal fire. Children brought their dinners to school and the teacher, Miss Ashworth, who always wore a long black dress, warmed them up by the fire.

May Day was the highlight of the year when scholars walked to the top of the hill to be taken by horse-drawn waggonette to attend the service at St Andrew's church in Leyland. This custom, instituted by the will of Samuel Crooke who died in 1776, still continues but now only one class of children take part, travelling by car from the modern school with its 200 pupils.

Exit 28 of the M6 motorway is very close to Clayton-le-Woods. The narrow bridge has been widened considerably and forms part of a very busy thoroughfare linking the A49 and the A6. Non-stop traffic travelling to Preston, Chorley, Leyland, Wigan and further afield on the motorway takes inhabitants away to work, leaving Clayton-le-Woods as a dormitory town with a regular turnover in its population. There are hundreds of houses where once there were fields.

The largest shop is a supermarket and there is now a library, garden centre, leisure centre, hotel, two more schools and several new pubs and restaurants.

Yet Clayton-le-Woods still has its woods and it is still possible to take a walk among the trees in the Cuerden Valley Park or to stroll along Shady Lane and admire the view across the valley.

Clifton ✺

Bonny little Clifton,
Never such another,
Houses on one side,
Shippons on t'other.

Clifton (a settlement on a cliff, just as the name implies) was built on high ground due to the surrounding terrain.

Lund, meaning 'sacred grove', is where the parish church stands in the village of Clifton. Records mention a chapel in 1349 but the present church was rebuilt in 1824. In 1688 a font was installed in Lund chapel. The stone trough used for the font is thought to be of pagan origin. In 1840 the church was made a parish church, so creating the parish of Lund.

Clifton National school, built in 1837 and rebuilt in 1887 to commemorate Queen Victoria's Jubilee, was the main centre for the community. It was a National school until 1933, Sunday school until 1950, and used for numerous activities. Now refurbished it is mainly used by the Girl Guides and Brownies.

Clifton Hall, built in the 1860s by Thomas Clifton, was originally a farm, which was sold to the Birley family in 1916. They, and all the subsequent families in the Hall, played an active part in the parish. A farm was built in the grounds of the Hall which continues to be worked today. The Hall itself is now a nursing home.

Clifton windmill is situated close to Lund church. It was originally a six storey windmill, which was unusual. Its age is not known, but it is probably 300 years old or more. During the late 1970s the mill was restored and extensions added, when it opened as a restaurant. Now it is a public house.

Some of the oldest houses in the Fylde are in Clifton, on Preston Old Road, at one time the only road with houses. There were farm buildings dating back to 1724 (a stone over the doorway read 'T & M R 1724') until the 1950s when they were demolished.

The expansion of Clifton began with British Nuclear Fuels building homes for its employees in the 1940s and the council building two estates. Three small developments of private housing and a 100-house estate have taken place since the 1970s.

Clifton was known as the village without a pub – but that had not always been so. One of the cottages still standing had a brewery attached, and the horse-tether ring can still be seen on the building.

Clifton Cross dates from July 1913 when it was erected in the memory of Edmund Birley, JP, of Clifton Hall. This cross was erected where the 'weeping' cross was situated, at which funeral parties, carrying the coffin of the deceased to Kirkham for burial, would pause.

The toll road running from Lea to Freckleton went through Clifton Marsh and what is now Clifton Marsh Garage was a cafe and toll house. The marsh still flooded in the 1950s and even today with heavy rainfall the fields surrounding the main roads will be covered in water.

Savick Brook Farm just on the border of Clifton and Lea, is said to be the oldest farm in the Fylde, of wattle and daub walls inside a brick shell. The front of the house overlooks the marsh, as the old toll road ran to the south of the farm. The bridge on the A583 over Savick brook is the marked boundary.

There are three garages, three shops and a hairdresser in Clifton and a nursery. Some still farm and there is work at British Nuclear Fuels at Salwick.

Cliviger ❧

Cliviger is said to be the second largest parish in England. In 1196 it was named Clivercher, and in 1246 Clivacher, which means 'sloping acre'. The parish consists of four hamlets – Walk Mill, Mereclough, Overtown and Holme Chapel. Cliviger Gorge is renowned for its natural beauty.

Village activities are centred on the village hall, St John's church and Mount Zion chapel. There are seven inns, the most notable being the Ram Inn with its interesting sign, the painting on which is thought to represent a prize-winning ram from one of the Lonk sheep breed shows.

The present St John's church was erected in 1788 at a cost of £870, which was defrayed by the Whitaker family, who lived at The Holme for six centuries. The church replaced a chantry chapel built about 1533. The churchyard contains many interesting gravestones, one of which is that of General Scarlett, the hero of the charge of the Heavy Brigade in the Crimean War.

Beside the lychgate, in an enclosure at the corner of the graveyard is the war memorial, which was erected on the site of two old cottages. When the memorial was erected the village stocks were placed at the back of the enclosure. Previously they stood next to the lychgate.

An annual event in the village is the Holme Sheep Fair, which is reputed to be one of the oldest village fairs in England. This dates back to the reign of Elizabeth I, although its character has changed over the years. It is now held in the field adjoining the Ram Inn. The Lonk Sheep Breeders Association has made the fair their annual breed show, and the Holme Sheepdog Trials Association now hold their championship trials in the field in front of the old manor house of The Holme. In mid afternoon there is the Thieveley Pike fell race of three and a half miles through 850 ft. This attracts top class athletes from many parts of the country.

Another annual event is the Sports Day which is organised by the

Cliviger Sports Association. Football and cricket are enjoyed by younger members of the village.

During the 18th and 19th centuries the village had different types of work within its boundaries, but nowadays it is principally farming.

In 1750 the handloom weavers of Cliviger produced 3,597 worsted pieces for use in the textile industry in the neighbouring town of Burnley. The large upstairs window of Berrils Green farmhouse is a handloom weaver's window, and is one of the finest of its type in East Lancashire.

Walk Mill in Victorian times was supported by two collieries. The coal produced was of a high quality, and supplied to the Queen's household. The mine owners built a brewery, which failed after a short time. There was also a stone quarry, a corn mill and a smithy. A cotton shed was erected too.

Mereclough, Overtown and Holme Chapel were inhabited by farm labourers, quarry workers and handloom weavers. Farmers had hill sheep, and cattle were kept in the valley bottom. There was a market for milk and butter etc in Burnley which was only a few miles away and which had a rapidly increasing population due to the boom in cotton weaving.

Pot Oven farm was one of the centres of the Cliviger pottery industry. Cliviger earthenware can now be seen in the museum at Towneley Hall.

There are a few old legends connected with Cliviger. The Towneley boggart of 'Boggart Bridge' was attributed to the restless, remorseful spirit of Sir John Towneley, who enclosed 194 acres of land illegally and forcibly ejected local tenants. The legend grew that the boggart could be heard reciting: 'Be warned! Lay out! Lay Out! Around Horelaw and Hollinghey Clough. To her children give back the widow's cot; for you and yours there is still enough.'

The Holme is said to be haunted and it is believed there are two friendly spirits in the house. One wears a monk's habit and is said to be Milo, one of two Whitakers who served at Whalley Abbey. The other, a young girl with fair hair, is 'The Lady in White'. She has recently been seen to walk across a room and pass through an enormous cupboard which blocks off a doorway leading to the main staircase.

Cliviger today is a thriving community, the population steadily increasing due to the building of many detached and semi-detached houses. Most villagers work in the neighbouring town of Burnley. There are 47 people over 80; village life must agree with them.

Cockerham 🦢

Cockerham is a small peaceful village lying on the shores of Morecambe Bay between the estuaries of the Lune and the Wyre, comprising several rows of mellow sandstone cottages, and many scattered houses and farms.

In the 19th century, however, the villagers of Cockerham were very self sufficient, with two inns, The Manor and The Plough. The attractive tin-roofed cottage with unusual church-like windows on the main street was a toffee shop, and a blacksmith, wheelwright, bootmender, tailor, fishmonger, butcher and postmistress all had flourishing businesses within the village. In the early years of the century Cockerham was known as a lively place with entertainment provided by horse racing, bowling, cockfighting and coursing.

Looking back to even earlier times, Cockerham was mentioned in the Domesday Book as 'Cocreham', belonging to Roger de Poictou. A boundary stone dividing the County Hundreds of the Amounderness and South Lonsdale can still be seen on Cocker-House bridge. The old Roman road from Walton-le-Dale to Lancaster crosses the present Cockerham to Bay-Horse road, probably on the rise beyond the river Cocker.

St Michael's church, Cockerham

Cockerham actually means 'a homestead adjoining the river Cocker', and it was not far from the mouth of this little river that the original village was first established. Frequent flooding soon forced the villagers to resettle on higher land near the present church, and in the early spring when the sun is low in the sky, the faint line of the old village street can still be seen. Sadly, fire destroyed the old village in the early 17th century and the present street was established soon afterwards.

Thus the church of St Michael, once in the centre of the village, now stands solitary amidst green fields. The interior is elegant with dark oak pews and a beautiful stained glass altar window depicting the four evangelists. There has been a church on the site since 1153, and the tower reputedly contained a peal of bells from nearby Cockersand Abbey.

From medieval times the vicar of Cockerham enjoyed the rights to salmon caught in the skear baulks in the Lune estuary on the first morning tide following each full and new moon. Sadly, in the 1960s the baulks fell into disrepair and the River Authority bought out these rights.

The village school, founded in the late 17th century, was first situated in the north-east corner of the churchyard, but moved to its present site in Main Street in 1829. Records provide a delightful insight into the seasonal structure of village life in the early years of this century, with absences explained by 'away haymaking', 'picking fruit', or 'getting up potatoes', and half-day holidays were given 'to gather blackberries'.

Cockerham once boasted a water mill at Mill-Houses on the Moss, and a windmill sited just above the present Rectory Gardens was in such an exposed position that a gale in 1802 turned the sails too quickly and friction set the mill on fire. It was rebuilt but gutted again in 1849.

Farms were first established on the marshland soon after the erection of a protective sea wall by the monks of Cockersand Abbey in the 14th century. Shepherd's Farm, built in 1705 as The Wheatsheaf Inn, was a welcome resting place for travellers on the coach route across the treacherous sands of Morecambe Bay. Cockerham Hall, now a farm-house, has many interesting archaeological features and a history stretching back to early medieval times.

The country mansion, Crookhey Hall, designed by Waterhouse, was built in 1874 by Colonel C. H. Bird whose estate covered a large part of Cockerham, and who reputedly made his money from the slave and cotton trade. The Hall stands in 17 acres of park and woodland with a beautiful walled garden. It was one of the first buildings in the country to generate and use electricity.

Copster Green & Salesbury

The oldest known version of the name is Copthurst, 'cop' meaning pointed hill and 'hurst' a clearing or settlement.

In the 19th century and the early part of this century, geese were kept by some residents on the common, making use of the then existing village ponds. As Copster Green was a much used picnic area, the residents supplemented their incomes by providing food and jugs of tea for their visitors. This is when Copster Green obtained the nickname 'Goose muck Hillock'. Sadly there are no geese kept on the common now.

Handloom weaving was a thriving industry here and in the neighbouring district. The cottagers carried their cloth for sale to Blackburn and Great Harwood and on the return journey brought back yarn needed for weaving.

Many cottagers kept a cow and a pig. The cow grazed the common and the pig was fed by corn ground at the local mill by the waterfall. Now the mill is gone.

The oldest house on the green is Copster Hall, dated 1615. The older part now forms the cellar of the present house, and is also incorporated in some of the farm buildings. In the stable can be seen the top half of an inglenook fireplace, and on a storey higher a Tudor fireplace. The outer walls have been built up enclosing the fireplaces and the roof extended to cover them. A little bit of the oak panelling is left under the stairs.

Bolton Hall, built in 1655, has a baffle entry and two back to back fireplaces. The date was once carved over the entrance.

Lovely Hall is the largest house. Its site is of great antiquity. Its name was originally 'Luftas Lea' and is probably of Saxon origin.

A number of attempts were made to enclose the commons. Some succeeded, others didn't – at night time the villagers would push the walls down. Some enclosures can be seen on Lovely Hall Lane. A few years ago villagers were given an opportunity to register their common rights, which they did. One person had turbary rights, others had pasture rights. A well known rhyme originated during the attempted enclosures:

'Great is the sin of man or woman who steals the goose from off the common,
But who for him shall make excuse who steals the common from the goose.'

People now commute to work, very little building has taken place in the village and the population has not increased very much.

Cragbank 🐿

You've never heard of Cragbank? Well, probably not. No church, no pub, no school, no prestigious buildings. In fact, just an outlying area of Carnforth with a population which has increased tenfold as estates have mushroomed.

A smart stone house on Lancaster Road gives no indication that one step backward in time it was a workingmen's club – a couple of steps back and it was the Travellers' Rest, recorded as a beer house run by William Sarginson in 1881 when it was a welcome resting place for weary travellers in pre-motorised days.

Gone are the swanky tennis courts and croquet green along Cragg Bank Lane advertised in a Carnforth brochure of 1920. Gone and unreplaced by any form of outdoor sport.

Early in the 20th century children raced to the bridge over the LNWR and screamed with delight as expresses whooshed below, enveloping them in clouds of steam. They hung over the bridge looking down at the rails which ran in long straight lines to a spot on the horizon – Hest Bank. This stretch of the old Lancaster–Carlisle Railway had presented few problems to the navvies who around 1844 built the railway which replaced canal packet-boats and stage-coaches.

In Stoney Field over the bridge, Territorial soldiers often camped in their bell-tents. Enjoyable events were their Open Days!

Around a grassy area in the village of 1920, an open square was formed by three terraces – The Grove, The Drive and the famous Dolly-tub Row which had large tubs by the cottages to collect rainwater from the roofs. Behind some homes were square brick 'humps', also used for the collecting and storing of rainwater which was pumped into kitchen slopstones. The only source of drinking water in Cragbank, apart from the springs and wells, was a pump at the top of The Drive, and there villagers gathered to gossip and exchange news.

During the First World War, soldiers of the Liverpool-Scottish Regiment were billeted with Carnforth families so they could practise on Cragbank's rifle-shooting range. The 5th King's Own Regiment at Lancaster's Bowerham Barracks continued to use the range after the war.

The flying of a red flag signified when the range was too dangerous to be used as a short-cut to the shore. Then clusters of children, off for a seaside outing, had to take the long trek along Shore Lane, which lives in the memory as a very peaceful place. Wild flowers in profusion painted the hedgerows with brilliant colours, sky-larks sang overhead, and the air was heavy with the scent of wild roses and honeysuckle.

Happy chatter ceased as a roadside tin hut was neared. It was the local fever hospital where, in two wards, victims of diphtheria and scarlet fever were nursed for six long weeks – or sometimes, sadly, for less! They had been driven there by old Jim Byram in a horse-drawn cab, one of Carnforth Station Hotel's fleet of taxis.

When Shore Lane was left behind, a long meadow led to Marsh Farm. 'Hot Water. 1d per jug', announced a chalk board to anyone interested. A farmyard gate opened on to Cragbank's grassy shore where the tiny river Keer joins the waters of Morecambe Bay.

Times have changed! Gone are the famous dolly-tubs, the pumps, the grassy green, the Army hut, the shooting range, the fever hospital and the right-of-way to the shore. Now Cragbank's tiny platform is the terminus for the old steam trains chuffing along from Carnforth's 'Steamtown'.

Crank ✖

The hamlet of Crank is situated on a hill overlooking a beautiful fertile valley to the east of the South West Lancashire plain. It is good farmland providing grain and vegetables of excellent quality for the towns around.

Take a walk down Red Cat Lane and on to the road leading to Shaley Brow, stop at the top of the hill and gaze down at the panorama before you; if you have any feeling for the countryside at all its sheer beauty must surely bring a lump to your throat.

The village itself is of long standing. The little Alder Lane Mission was built in 1857 and still flourishes as the Methodist chapel. The school was built of solid granite in 1868, and part of the school in those early days was consecrated and used for church services. The old lectern is still in use for school purposes today.

Crank used to boast numerous public houses, but today only the Red Cat still survives. Of course with such a strong farming community a thriving blacksmith's down Red Cat Lane catered for all the shire horses that were the backbone and powerhouse of farm life in those days.

Crank was also renowned for its caverns, extensive excavations that produced fine quality deep sandstone. Several of the older cottages in the village are constructed of this fine stone.

There are two reservoirs in the area supplying Crank itself as well as neighbours St Helen's and Rainford.

'You might see the White Rabbit' is a remark which is still heard amongst today's villagers. It refers to Crank's legend, a tragic story of a bygone era.

An old lady who lived in a cottage at the foot of the hill on which Crank now stands had a little granddaughter about six years old and known as Jenny. Jenny had a large white pet rabbit which she absolutely doted on. Not far from the cottage lived a farmer who was known locally as 'Old Nick', a miser, quarrelsome, morose and rich. He came to believe that he had been bewitched by the old woman, and he and a local ne'er-do-well called Dick Piers plotted to break the spell by spilling her blood.

When they entered the house one night, Jenny, the granddaughter was awakened by all the crashing and shouting, and grabbing her white rabbit which always slept with her she escaped unnoticed through the broken door and raced up the hill towards the chapel. Dick Piers followed her and, angry at losing her, kicked her white rabbit to death.

The following morning a local monk going to the little chapel found Jenny on the doorstep. She had died from a nasty bang on the head sustained by falling against the chapel wall and sheer exhaustion from the terrible happenings of the previous night.

A month after the burial of Jenny and after one of his alcoholic binges Dick Piers was confronted one night by Jenny's white rabbit and with a cry of stark fear he turned and ran into the night. His body was found the following morning at the bottom of a quarry on the local Billinge Hill.

So remember if you see the white rabbit in Crank, do what all country-born folk would do, be friendly!

Cronton 🌿

Cronton is a very old village. Stone Age axe heads have been found in fields at the bottom of Pex Hill (our country park) and are now in Liverpool Museum. It became a Norse settlement under the leadership of Crawenga, hence the name Crawenton, Crohinton and now Cronton.

There are some lovely old houses and in Town End conservation area there are three listed buildings, a listed ancient cross and a listed pair of iron gates all within the space of 200 yards. Sunnyside Farm is of cruck construction and one of the walls is still of wattle and daub.

The very old smithy is still working, and was very important in the days before refrigerated transport. Cattle and geese coming from Ireland into the port of Liverpool were driven along the lanes into the inland towns. Cronton smithy was one of a chain of smithies along the road which put shoes (clips) on the cattle and put tar on the feet of the geese to enable them to walk more easily on the rutted roads after the soft fields. Otherwise the animals and fowl would have had sore feet which, if infected, could have caused the death of the animal, or at least slowed up the delivery.

The village stocks are unusual in having five holes instead of the more usual two or four. There are said to be only three such stocks in England. No-one knows what the extra one is for, but there have been many guesses!

Cronton was the birthplace of a notable man – Charles Leadbetter. He was born in a small cottage, son of a sundial maker, and became an eminent mathematician and astronomer. He became a gauger for the Customs and Excise in London and his book of regulations and weights and measures was standard for the shopkeepers of the 18th century. He wrote several books of astronomy and navigation, some of which are still used today. He also taught and is said to have taught navigation to Captain Cook. One of his books gave the geographical reference to the principal cities of the world and listed after Cracow came Cronton!

The quarry was working in 1604 and several local men worked there as quarrymen. The stone for the Methodist chapel, which was built in 1845, was from the quarry. There were also miners working in the colliery, which was opened in 1914 and closed in 1984 due to a geological fault.

In the past though, most of the inhabitants worked as watch-part makers. They would also have farms which their wives ran and if they didn't, the wives took in washing to supplement the income. This was all very good until the chemical industry came to Widnes. Then the ladies had to see which way the wind was blowing before they hung out their washing! The watchmakers were augmented after the 17th century massacres in France and Switzerland when Huguenot families fled to England. A lot of them made watch parts and knowing that Cronton was a watch part making centre they came here and settled. The watch parts, when finished, were sent by coach to the big watchmakers in London and Liverpool. When Princess Alexandra of Denmark came to Britain to marry the future King Edward VII a watch among her presents was supplied by McCabe of London who ordered the movement from James Glover of Cronton. The movement had to be extra-jewelled and where possible to be made of gold. The last workshop making these small tools etc, was moved to Liverpool Museum when the owner died.

Cronton remained a sleepy, lovely village until about 1960 when the village became the target of builders and several estates were built. Several old buildings, lovely fields and woods were sacrificed to the developers and the village trebled in size. The newcomers have settled happily and Cronton seems to have kept its independent spirit and individuality. Long may it continue!

Croston 🌿

Croston is situated on the banks of the river Yarrow, ten miles south of Preston.

The aptly named, narrow, cobbled Church Street leads to the door of the graceful old church of St Michael and All Angels; it is a fine example of an 18th century Lancashire street, in fact some of its houses bear the date 1704. At the other end of the street is the building that once housed the smithy, and the ancient base of a preaching cross.

The river passes by the church and through the village under a perfect example of a packhorse bridge, dated 1682.

The boundaries of the parish were at one time extensive and included the surrounding villages and even Chorley.

The village green is near the site of a medieval 'faire and market' which was allowed to be held each year by a charter granted in 1283 by Edward I.

Great controversy was caused when it was proposed that houses be built in Castle Walks, thought by some to have been the site of a castle. A castle is marked on an ancient map of this area but there are no signs of a stone edifice, and it is believed that the original castle could have been a wooden structure.

Croston has always been an agricultural community. Small tenanted farms have long been in existence, but comparatively few villagers are now involved in the land.

The population has slowly increased from 1,500 in 1851 to over 3,000 today.

Up until the Second World War Croston was self-sufficient; employment was provided by two cotton manufacturers, the De Trafford estate, the Glebe Farms, the brick works and the animal feed and corn millers. There was a magistrates' court, where matters of debt and petty crimes were dealt with; offenders were kept in the cells underneath the police station. There was a gas works and the village had gas lighting; a cinema; a fire-cart; an ambulance; ten public houses, and most important of all a railway station. The railway gradually caused the biggest change in people's lives; this, coupled with easier transport has made Croston into a dormitory village. People are able to go to work in Preston, Liverpool and other towns; the cotton mills have shut down and apart from a caravan and wood-working business and a few shops there are very few jobs to be had locally.

The squires of Croston Hall had a great deal of influence on the development of the village. The de Traffords were an ancient aristocratic family dating from Norman times. It was due to the foresight of the 'old' squire Sigismund, that Croston did not become a small town. He always said he preferred 'trees' to 'chimneys' and doggedly refused to sell his land for industrial use.

The last squire, Captain Geoffrey de Trafford, was a well-respected figure, a gentle, shy man who dealt kindly with his tenants and became one of the impoverished gentry, living with his sister in the dilapidated Hall which was demolished after their deaths, much to the consternation of the villagers. All that remains is a beautiful little Pugin chapel in a peaceful setting in the old Hall grounds.

The medieval 'fayres', the Wakes, maypole dancing and donkey rides may have gone but exiles are still drawn back for family reunions on Coffee Day (derived from the old 'Feoffing' day when tenants paid their fees or dues to the squire). On that day all the village turns out, and the decorated farm horses and carts take pride of place in the procession led by bands and morris dancers.

As with all ancient places rumours of ghosts prevail. One of these refers to a tiny neglected grave in the far corner of Croston cemetery. A stone cross is said to have recorded that Mary Ellen Hudson died friendless. The grave has become dilapidated and the cross has crumbled away but it is on record that a little girl of that name, a resident of Croston Industrial Home, died in 1890. In 1976 a school teacher came to live adjacent to the cemetery and caused quite a stir when she said a little girl in a red shawl was a frequent visitor to her garden. The red shawl was the uniform in the Home so it was assumed the wraith-like figure was Mary Ellen Hudson.

There is a story of an unusual dispute in the High Court in the 1580s. Potatoes were brought by Sir Walter Raleigh from Virginia to plant in his estate in Ireland. The ship which carried them was wrecked off Hesketh

Bank. Local farmers 'rescued' and planted these strange tubers, thus initiating potato farming in Lancashire. The rector of Croston claimed a tithe, because the land then belonged to Croston parish. The farmers refused for they already paid a tithe for corn. The rector then took the case to the High Court and was awarded the verdict. The farmers had to pay up!

The 20th century has brought many changes to Croston. New houses have sprung up around the village. Only the older folk are nostalgic for the old days when everyone knew everyone else, the days of clogs and shawls, the squire, the old dialect, when people came from miles around for Norris's own recipe ice cream and Hackforth & Seddon the chemist's secret cure for certain illnesses.

Croston itself has changed very little; it is still an attractive village with a friendly welcome for all.

Dolphinholme 🐚

Dolphinholme is a small village of about 600 people nestling in the foothills of the Pennines at the edge of the Forest of Bowland. It is divided into two, the main part clustered close to the parish church of St Mark, the Methodist chapel, the Church of England primary school and the single remaining shop. The remainder of the village, known as Lower Dolphinholme, lies close to the river near the relics of the worsted mill.

Until the end of the 18th century Dolphinholme consisted of little more than a farm, from which the village takes its name, a corn mill and a large house, Wyreside Hall, then the seat of the Fenton Cawthorne family. The village, as such, developed with the establishment of the worsted spinning mill which used the power of the fast flowing Wyre. This factory provided employment for several hundred spinners and outworkers for whom houses were built by the millowners, first in Lower Dolphinholme and later in two rows along the road in what is now the main part of the village.

The wheel providing the power for the mill was 68 ft in diameter and 12 ft broad, the tallest in Britain after the Laxey wheel, built much later, and was capable of generating about 200hp. Unfortunately, after the mill finally closed the wheel was blown up and nothing remains to be seen of it.

The remains of an early gas holder can however still be seen. The village street was lit by gas, perhaps as early as 1806, and if this is the case, Dolphinholme was probably the first village to have such lighting. One of the old street lamps which had survived was restored in 1984 and linked to a bottle gas supply by the Gas Board, although the village has no mains gas supply as yet.

The mill finally closed in 1867 but many of the cottages built for the workers are still occupied, as are the millowner's and the manager's houses. The old warehouse was converted in 1921 to be used for social purposes as a memorial to those who had died in the First World War, but was abandoned when the New Memorial Hall was opened near the church in 1971.

In the 19th century the terraced cottages in the village were surrounded by scattered farms. Between and after the two World Wars more houses, both local authority and private, were built and a number of the farmhouses were absorbed into the village. Their buildings, like that of the old warehouse, have now been converted for residential use. The land around the village is still farmed but has been amalgamated to form larger units. Some of these farms are part of the Duchy of Lancaster estate, the rest being worked by private owners. Employment, which earlier this century was largely agricultural, is now more diverse since many people now living in the village commute to work in Lancaster and further afield. The establishment of the University of Lancaster in 1964 has contributed to the diversification of employment here as several members of staff live locally.

In spite of its changing character there is still a strong community spirit. In 1987 the village fought – successfully – to keep open its primary school, established last century by the millowner. This same spirit led to the establishment, in the early 1970s, of the New Memorial Hall itself and a Men's Club with its own building and, in the 1980s, a Bowling Club with its carefully tended green used by villagers of all ages. Recent efforts have produced a multisports area and an extension to the New Memorial Hall has been built to help accommodate the many activities of the village. The Village Show has recently been revived and the Annual Field Day is always enthusiastically supported.

Downham 🦢

If any village could qualify as the perfect mirror of Blake's 'Jerusalem' then it should be Downham, where the 'green and pleasant land' is seen at its most beautiful even if the 'dark satanic mills' are not too far away.

The history of Downham has been linked to that of the Assheton family since 1558 when they bought the lordship of the manor from the Dyneleys.

Their Hall, in clean-lined Georgian style, was rebuilt over a Tudor farmhouse which, like many other houses in the village, probably overlay much earlier foundations. It stands amid green lawns and ancient beeches commanding a magnificent view across the valley to mysterious Pendle.

This prospect is shared by the adjacent church of St Leonard, where only the tower remains of 15th century origin. Though there has been a church on this site since at least the 13th century, the present building dates largely from 1910 when much village reconstruction, including the present-day post office, was undertaken. Earlier, in 1869, as proclaimed in the Latin inscription, Ralph and his brother Richard Assheton had designed and built the east window with their own hands.

Most of the picturesque grey stone cottages were built in the 18th and 19th centuries, many in the heyday of the handloom weavers, but Downham is thought to have been settled in the 8th and 9th centuries. There is evidence for the Saxon foundation of the church in the field name Kirkacre and at the time of the Norman Conquest the village was under the leadership of Alfred the Saxon. By the time that a thriving medieval village was being recorded in the manor court rolls circa 1400, it is probable that the pattern of dwellings had been long established.

This basically comprises two groups of cottages; the first clustered around the church, the stocks and village inn along the limestone ridge near the Roman road, joined by the steeply sloping village street to a second group around the village green where the road from the south crosses the brook at the foot of the hill.

When, during the improvements of the mid 18th century, the top road was moved to its present position, further from the Hall, the remains of two Roman soldiers were found and reburied in the churchyard. There is also a legend that a large stone near the gates moves of its own accord in the middle of the night. At least two Tudor houses remain, bearing testimony to the prosperity of the yeoman farmers of the day whose descendants, in some cases, can still be traced to families resident in the parish.

The present school building, now used for a flourishing playgroup since enforced closure in 1985, was built in 1839 but a school, kept by the priest, is mentioned as early as 1653.

It is possible that the old sycamore tree by the stocks is on the site of the Pilling or Pillion tree mentioned in the court rolls as a village meeting place, or moot, where the population gathered to administer local justice, check weights and measures and, annually, to beat the bounds of the parish.

Rent days are still held at the Assheton Arms (formerly the George and Dragon) as they were in the 17th century when Nick Assheton, whose famous diary inspired Harrison Ainsworth's *Lancashire Witches*, hunted, fowled and fished through the Bowland streams and coverts and rode over Pendle moors in search of game and ale.

The Assheton family have a long tradition of responsibility for the welfare of the village. Among many charities instituted by them are St Thomas's day dole, started in 1670, which provided for the poor from the produce of certain fields, and also the stipulation in Sir Ralph Assheton's will of 1679 for the preaching of sermons on a chosen text and provision for the poor.

Cricket is still played regularly on the Barley Field, so called because it was planted with this crop in 1812 in response to the food shortage caused by the Napoleonic Wars. The blacksmith's forge near the stocks has vanished almost without trace, as have the butcher's and the baker's shops. The three-wheeled motor bike has replaced the shepherd and his dog just as tractors earlier replaced working horses.

Downham is no longer a working agricultural community but is quietly adapting itself to its late 20th century role as a tourist attraction.

Dunsop Bridge

This small village is built around a picturesque hump-backed bridge. Its amenities include two churches, St Hubert's and St George's, a primary school and the village hall. In the centre of the village stands Leedham's Garage, formerly the smithy, a post office and shop, and by the side of the bridge is the small workingmen's club.

St Hubert's Roman Catholic church is situated on Lancaster Road, Trough of Bowland, on the outskirts of the village. It was built by the Towneley family when their racehorse *Kettledrum* won the Derby in 1861. In the grounds of the church stands a huge white angel as a memorial to Richard Henry Towneley which cost £1,000 to erect.

Thorneyholme residential hotel stands in its own grounds on the banks of the river Hodder, and at one time was part of the Towneley estates. It was inherited by Sister Marie des Saints Anges on the death of her father, and inhabited by the sisters of the convent at Blackburn.

The two major landowners in the area are the Duchy of Lancaster and the North West Water Authority. This is a designated area of natural beauty where most of the land is used for agriculture. Farming is mostly hill sheep or beef, with dairy herds on the lower pastures. The NWWA have this as a main water collection area, giving employment to several families.

The Forestry Commission has its own area office sited here, and manages the vast area of Bowland Forest. Tosside is the production forest for pulp and small logs for the paper and saw mill industries.

The Duchy of Lancaster employs a maintenance staff for the upkeep of their farms, cottages and woodlands.

Grouse and pheasant shooting takes place in the area throughout the season. Gamekeepers manage the shoots and control vermin.

One of the few pieces of private land houses Dunsop Trout Farm Ltd, which originated through compensation from the NWWA after the natural spawning grounds were flooded to make Stocks Reservoir at Slaidburn. Today the farm breeds brown and rainbow trout to stock rivers and reservoirs.

Every third year Dunsop Bridge is the venue of the Hodder Valley Show, rotating with the neighbouring villages of Newton and Slaidburn. This takes place on the second Saturday in September.

The 'Old Man of Bowland' is an outstanding natural feature, which can best be sighted from the war memorial. This 'Old Man' is created by a hill formation on the sky line of Mellor Knoll.

Village life largely depends on community spirit and beneath the quiet sleepy picture postcard views, this spirit thrives in Dunsop Bridge.

Eccleston

Eccleston is a village about six miles from Chorley, and was a Celtic settlement. The name is derived from the Latin 'Ecclesia' meaning church and 'tun' meaning town. The Anglo-Saxons had a church here and the first church record is for 1094.

The present St Mary's church, standing on the banks of the river Yarrow, probably stands where the early church did, and dates back to the 14th century. It is to the north of the village boundary. The church was restored in the 18th century, and not much of the original building remains. From 1883 to 1978 three members of the Bretherton family, father and two sons, were rectors of St Mary's and for most of the time lived in the rectory now called Eccleston Hall, but in 1956 a new rectory was built near to the Hall.

There are two other churches at the opposite end of the village to St Mary's. One is the Methodist church which was built in 1900. The original chapel, built in 1863, stands behind the present church and is used as a church hall. The other church is St Agnes', the Roman Catholic church. It was completed in 1922, but services had been held in a local fish and chip shop since 1920, on the same site.

One Sunday, in June, the three churches join together and hold a Procession of Witness through the village, and they also unite in raising money for Christian Aid and other charities.

There are two schools, St Mary's primary school, and the County primary school. Before St Mary's was opened, children attended a school on Towngate, locally called 'The Old School', which at present needs repair and is not used. But meetings used to be held there and during the Second World War it was an A.R.P. centre.

Farming was the chief occupation during previous centuries. There are several old farmhouses in the village. One is Whalley Farm on Towngate, where it is said that monks used to live and that there was a tunnel from there to St Mary's church. On the porch is inscribed '1669', so probably there was a building there before the present one. Another old farm is Manor House Farm, near to St Mary's church, and Bradley Hall, which used to have a moat round it. Ingrave Farm on New Lane is also moated.

Weaving had been a cottage industry in Eccleston for a long time, but in 1884 factory weaving came to Eccleston when Carrington, Woods and Company purchased Grove Mill, which had previously been a printing works. The first manager was Mr I. Sagar. In 1895, a partnership was formed between Mr A. Carrington and Mr J. M. Dewhurst. In 1925, artificial silk began to be woven and the weaving of cotton was abandoned a few years later. In 1928, the New Mill was acquired by the same firm. During the Second World War, millions of yards of fabric for parachutes, balloons and utility uses were woven so the people of Eccleston helped a great deal with the war effort. Three shifts were worked and men and women were seen cycling or walking to the two mills, while locally owned buses brought in workers from the villages around. Automatic looms were installed at the New Mill and here, in the 1960s, workers were trained to man a mill at Tarleton, which had been purchased by Carrington and Dewhurst.

In 1970, the firm joined the big textile firm of Viyella International and became known as Carrington-Viyella. New materials, including Crimplene were researched, developed and woven in both mills in Eccleston. Sadly, business declined and in the early 1980s, both mills were closed, with many redundancies in Eccleston and surrounding villages.

Now the two mills are again flourishing in a different way. The New Mill is called the Carrington Centre, which houses several shops, a supermarket and a library. Behind are light industrial units. The Old Mill now houses 'Bygone Times' which is a collection of old implements, clothes, toys etc and there are stalls selling antiques.

During the last 30 years, there has been a great increase in population with four new housing estates. The M6 and M61 motorways are very near to the village which makes it very convenient for business people living in Eccleston to commute to work.

Edgworth 🍃

The village of Edgworth, with its companion village of Turton or Chapeltown, lies in a valley almost surrounded by moors, about five miles north of Bolton. Besides the village centre there are groups of houses and farms, such as Entwistle, Quarlton and Broadhead, scattered over a wide area of moorland, all in the parish of St Anne, Turton. The beautiful parish church stands in the village of Chapeltown.

In pre-Christian times, men looked down into the valley as they met to worship at the stone circle on the moors, or to bury their dead in mounds, and well over 3,000 years ago one of these men lost his bronze palstave or axe head, which was found again in the 19th century and is now in Manchester Museum. The Roman legions also marched through the valley on the road between Manchester and Ribchester, parts of which are still used.

Simple farming was carried on, with quarrying of the good local stone, and this went on into the 20th century. Spinning and weaving were done in the home, and the finished pieces were either collected on teams of packhorses or taken to market, and at least one local family, in the 18th century, took theirs to Preston. After a time John Horrocks realised that he could do much better for himself by being on the receiving end of this trade, so he moved to Preston, and in 1792 opened one of the early mills. The firm of 'Horrocks's, the greatest name in cotton' became known all over the world for fine cotton goods.

As the Industrial Revolution spread, mills came to the valley, first of all powered by the good water supply, then by steam, and there were mills for spinning, weaving, bleaching and dyeing. Now there is just one mill weaving towels in Chapeltown.

Another local family who opened mills in the valley and in Bolton was the Barlow family. A son, born in Edgworth, became a doctor, and as Sir Thomas Barlow was physician to Queen Victoria, King Edward VII and King George V. He was a frequent visitor to his native village, and died just a few months short of his century.

The Barlows were responsible for opening a branch of the National Children's Homes on the moors, where needy children were well looked

Edgworth from Quarlton

after in a healthy atmosphere and taught a trade. One of the sights of the village on a Sunday morning until a few years ago was the crocodiles of children walking down to the Methodist church – and back up the hill again. Now Crowthorn school is a special school both for residents and local children.

It was Miss Annie Barlow, Sir Thomas's sister, who was hostess to Edgworth's most famous visitor. Well known for her help to all in need, her care extended to the people of India, and when Mahatma Gandhi visited Lancashire in 1931 she arranged a meeting at her home, on the

JULIA · H · BAGGLEY

evening of 26th September, so that he could meet with men involved with leading the cotton industry. The meeting was kept secret, but when the police descended in force the news got out, and he was given a good send off by many villagers.

When more water was needed for the growing town, Bolton naturally looked to the streams up in the moors. In 1831 a dam was built across a brook high in the hills, and Turton and Entwistle Reservoir was formed. Thirteen years later the valley lower down was also dammed, and the Wayoh Reservoir came into being. These are now areas of great beauty with a wide range of wild life and wonderful open views, so it is not surprising that the valley is very popular with walkers.

There are many attractive old houses and cottages built of local stone, including Turton Tower, the old manor house, now a museum. There was some building in brick before the Second World War and more since, though some are stone-faced. The private developments are of a high standard, and old cottages and derelict barns have been made into 'desirable residences'.

There are fewer farms today because of changing land practices. They are still run by local families, but many more sheep are seen where previously there would have been dairy cows. Few of the villagers are involved in agriculture or work in the village at all, though there are some small engineering and building firms. One modern primary school has replaced the three older buildings, and many of the older children attend the comprehensive school two or three miles away.

The older people are well catered for with various activities, including a well-attended Christmas party for the over 80s, run by the WI. There are a number of sporting activities including a successful cricket team, and a football team which was originally founded in 1871 and was the forerunner of Bolton Wanderers.

Elswick ♧

To many people town planning is a modern phenomenon. However, Elswick, a small village nestling eight miles inland from the Fylde coast, is a very early example of organised layout with a row of farmhouses regularly spaced along the High Street, each with a barn alongside and fields behind.

Elswick, recorded in the Domesday Book as Edeleswic, has always been primarily a farming community, although there were handloom weavers in the village until the 19th century weaving flax, wool and then cotton.

The Fylde area was a centre of nonconformist religion and in Elswick there is one of the oldest independent chapels. The foundation stone was laid by Ann Smith in the 17th century and the church hall was renovated by Tom Hall in 1906. Because the Fylde is relatively isolated, worshippers were generally unaffected by the laws that were in force against nonconformists. That did not save one Quaker preacher, however, who was seized at a meeting at Hurdles Farm and put in the High Street stocks!

In 1643 the Roundheads camped near Elswick, presumably in pursuit of Lord Derby who marched from the coast to support the King during the Civil War. It has been claimed that cannon balls were dug up in the village during the last century, a reminder of those troubled times.

Elizabeth Hoole, who died in 1727, endowed a field in her will which was to be rented out and the proceeds (£3 a year) divided between the poor of Elswick. This is called the Hoole Charity and a committee still sits to distribute the endowment – still fixed at £3 a year!

The isolation of Elswick and its remoteness from the larger towns made it ideal for the building of a smallpox sanatorium in 1902. The patients came mostly from the ships docked in Fleetwood and travelled to Elswick in closed carriages. At one time a chemist from Garstang, Joe Thomas, contracted smallpox from a tramp who had called at his shop. While he was recovering in the sanatorium, he asked if he might have rabbit for his evening meal. A rabbit was obtained but, unfortunately was never cooked as a nurse was found trying to pluck the hapless creature!

Later, when the threat of smallpox began to wane, the buildings were given over to tuberculosis sufferers and some of the older village residents worked at the sanatorium at this time. In 1951 there was a waiting list of over 1,000 people wanting treatment but by 1969 there were none. The building, which is now known as Hoole House, is currently a probation hostel for men.

Ernest Smith operated his Pilgrim Motors bus service from Garstang to Blackpool and had his garage in Elswick. His was one of the first motor services to start operating in 1923 and he was very obliging. Parcels were delivered, he would stop anywhere along the route for people to get on or off the bus, and would wait outside people's homes for them if they put a shopping basket on the gate post as a sign. It must be wondered how the journeys were ever completed!

Entertainment in the village once consisted of magic lantern shows at the chapel. There was also a bowling green in Lodge Lane which was built in memory of local men who had died in the First World War. Elswick nowadays has a gala, as do many of the surrounding villages but, in earlier years, there was a 'field day' which was attended by people from miles around as it was reputed to be one of the best in the area. The oldest village organisation is the Brownies who were established in 1928.

Elswick is now in all respects a modern village, with its post office and village store in modern buildings. New housing has increased the size of the village and people from far afield have come to settle. A major change has been the introduction of gas in 1988, which may not have caused such excitement as the erection of the first three street lamps in 1956 followed by the sewers in 1964. However, all this has done nothing to diminish the charm and friendliness of this delightful Fylde village.

Euxton 🦢

Pronounced 'Exton', strangers betray themselves by saying 'Yooxton', as the German propagandist Lord Haw Haw did during the Second World War. It has had various forms of spelling, being Euckeston in the 13th century.

There was a population of 8,000 in 1989, against a population of 803 in 1801. Euxton was mainly agricultural until the massive Royal Ordnance factory was opened in 1938, employing over 35,000 day and night. The ROF was built in Euxton because the land was subject to field mist, hoping to make it invisible to enemy aircraft. It is now owned by British Aerospace and the work force has been drastically reduced.

Euxton Hall, ancestral home to the Andertons (buried in St Mary's Roman Catholic church) is now an independent hospital. The inn, The Anderton Arms (formerly a farm), is now a restaurant.

The oldest house, Armetriding (1570), is a working farm. Armetriding is in the Pincock area, by the river Yarrow. As did most habitations, Euxton began life by its river. Methodism had its roots in Pincock.

Euxton's paper mill, 1611–1766, was the earliest in England. Still standing are two well-preserved cottages, Riverside where paper was made, and Waterside where it was dried. It is referred to in a document of 1615, a copy of which is in the WI scrapbook, housed in the local library.

Industries included a bobbin mill, nail factory, corn mills, weaving and spinning sheds. We had 'treacle mines' where surface mining took place for cannel, a bituminous coal which looks like treacle toffee. Present industries include rubber manufacturers, concrete products, printers and suppliers of building materials, tiles and auto-spares.

A lady, resident here for 80 years, remembers skipping down the centre of the A49. 'The only traffic was my dad's horse and cart, and we knew what time he was coming.' In those days meat was delivered by a man walking round with a basket. Now there are excellent shops and the fish van calls weekly. A dentist has settled here and there is a medical centre. Forty years ago there was just a visiting doctor who held weekly surgery in a local parlour.

The oldest building is the parish church, one window of which is dated 1322. It made headlines in *The Times* in 1854 when part of a whiskey still was found beneath the pulpit.

There was a railway station at Balshaw Lane and it is hoped to restore it as a 'park and ride'. Until 1965 oil lamps were in use, and the porter's wife delivered parcels by pram. There was another station behind the inn now known as The Ordnance (previously The Railway Tavern or Old Mother Eccles), where the trade was 'jug and bottle'.

Farming has altered and is now mostly grazing. Foxes seek sanctuary in the old ROF grounds. Here is Buckshaw Hall, where priests sought sanctuary. The present building (1654) is on the site of a more ancient fabric. A nearby lane is said to be haunted by a hooded figure!

Building may disturb these shades, but they return. Dawbers Lane indicates the old craft of wattle and daub, while one of its dwellings houses a modern day builder.

Washington Lane was renamed from German Lane for American airmen stationed here during the Second World War. Washington Hall, once a farm, is the site of the Forensic Science Laboratories and the International Fire Training Centre.

Farington & Farington Moss

The villages of Farington and Farington Moss are situated south of Preston and close to Leyland, separated geographically and historically by the Industrial Revolution.

In 1801 Farington had a population of only 382. It was mainly mossland, called Charnock Moss and Farington Moss. At Newgate, one piece of unenclosed land was called 'turbary', denoting land turf or peat which might be dug for fuel. Turbary Farm is now a garden centre.

Naptha Lane can still be found, a reminder of the process of dipping turf in naptha for fuel.

Agriculture remained the chief occupation until the 1830s, supplemented by spinning and weaving in the home. Every farmhouse had one or more looms until the Industrial Revolution led to production in factories.

The first cotton mill was built by William Boardman in 1835, situated in Mill Street. This eventually split Farington into two communities. With the coming of the East-Lancs and North Union Railways (now the London–Scotland line) the population increased by 1851 to 1,932.

The cotton famine of 1861 to 1863, caused by the American Civil War, brought distress, poverty and starvation to many families. In April 1864 Messrs Bashall and Boardman's mill had been stopped for a year and a half, when news came that cotton was on its way from Liverpool. Records from the time report: 'All day the villagers looked anxiously for the arrival of their cotton. Next day a couple of wagons of cotton were deposited in the mill sidings. Soon the villages began to rejoice. A large number of women preceded by music, went down to the railway sidings, and with hearty vigour pushed the wagons with their welcome freight up the steep and curved incline into the factory yard. This done, the crowd sang the doxology to the tune of the Old Hundred.'

To offer thanks for continuing work, the churches of Farington held a Walking Day on the last Saturday in August, always known as 'last Saturday in Farington'. The tradition is still upheld. St Paul's church, built by public subscription, was consecrated in 1840, and a school had been built earlier in Farington Moss. William Boardman, millowner and benefactor, built a second school nearer to his mill, in 1843. His mill, eventually Dewhurst's, was closed in 1963.

The industrial development meant that Farington and Farington Moss grew separately. Farington houses what is now Leyland DAF, the descendant of Leyland Motors, originally the blacksmith and engineering firm of Elias Sumner whose son, James, inherited the business in 1892. He fitted a power unit to a lawn mower and never looked back. His works in Leyland are now demolished, but his Farington expansion goes from strength to strength. Vehicles for both world wars were built here, including the famous Churchill tanks. Later, many hundreds of Centurion tanks rolled out of the gates on to the appropriately named Centurion Way. The Sumner firm has gone a long way in a hundred years. Other industrial concerns are housed on this thoroughfare, some large, like the British Tyre and Rubber Company, many small, created during the last 20 years.

At Farington Moss the forest land of years ago is now well-drained to a black peaty soil. It has seen changes from the arable use which provided a living for families farming the moss for generations, to the intensive horticulture of today.

The soil was once tilled with horses and seed sowed by hand. Now seeds are sown in blocks and the making of these blocks is a new industry on the moss. The blocks of young plants are planted with electronically controlled tractors and some growers have their own irrigation systems. Eighty per cent of the crops are lettuce and celery, with potatoes, barley, green vegetables and tomatoes making up the rest.

From across the Moss the new assembly plant for Leyland DAF may be clearly seen. The Farington Link road and the Western Primary roads were built to accommodate the increased traffic. Major housing developments have raised the population to almost 6,000. The face of Farington is changing. But it is still true, as it was many years ago, that 'the Moss is a grand place for giving one an appetite'. It is still a healthy and invigorating place in which to live, even with the encroaching industry and increasing traffic. Farington Moss still keeps to its rural community and its village life.

Fence-in-Pendle

The origin of the name Fence dates from the time of William the Conqueror. Most of what is now Pendle Forest was waste land and so readily available for hunting. In those far-off days it was a custom for the King and nobles to hunt deer in the Pendle Forest and an enclosure was made to preserve the herd to provide sport for the nobility.

Fence is regarded as a street-village. Wheatley Lane Road is the principal thoroughfare, and the agricultural exploits of our ancestors are recalled in the names 'Wheatley' and 'Barley'.

In 1618 Sir Jonas Moore, to whom we ultimately owe Greenwich Mean Time, the most distinguished son of Fence, was born at White Lee. He interested himself in astronomy, and it was through him that the Royal Observatory at Greenwich was built.

The area gained national publicity when the so called Pendle Witches were tried and hanged at Lancaster in the 17th century. One of these 'witches' was a Fence lady, Anne Whittle, also known as Old Chattox, who lived at Greenhead Farm.

Hoarstones, Fence-in-Pendle

Cuckstool Lane, in Wheatley Lane, is a reminder of the ducking stool, one of the forms of punishment in use at that time.

Local industries centre on the Green Slate Company, Holgate's joiner's shop at Field Top, Chris Nutter's car repairs and Cloverbrook textile warehouse which was once a flourishing weaving shed in the village. A spinning mill had existed for some time at Field Top: it closed down in 1880.

In recent years the village has grown considerably. The construction of the bypass and of the motorway have encouraged residents to commute.

For years the social life of the village has centred round the three churches. St Anne's, Church of England, was opened in August 1837. The Wheatley Lane Methodist chapel was built in 1824 and restored in 1867. The fine and well equipped school dates from 1859. The Inghamite church at Wheatley Carr dates from 1750. Benjamin Ingham was in close association with George Whitefield and other itinerant preachers, and it is quite likely that on one of these expeditions the foundation of the Cause at Old Wheatley was laid. The chapel was originally built of rough unhewn stone and acquired its present appearance in 1897. In its early days many travelled long distances for the Sunday worship.

Captain H. Astley made a gift of land to the village for the purpose of establishing the Pendle Forest Sports Club, which has facilities for football and cricket and a club house for billiards and other indoor games. The Lancashire County Council established a branch library in the village, situated near the flats in Wheatley Close. The Wheatley Court Hostel provides accommodation and care for about 20 elderly people. The Over 60s club members meet at the hostel for whist and dominoes.

Among the interesting buildings in Fence, 'Hoarstones' was referred to in 1547, though the present house was restored in 1895. An iron cross, said to have been a safeguard against witches, was found in a wall. 'Ashlar' or 'Hewn Atchelor House', originally known as 'The Fence', was finished in 1594. 'Greenhead' is a good example of early architecture. The great fireplace and the front door bolt – a solid oak beam – are particularly noteworthy.

Feniscowles ⬥

Located south-west of Blackburn, Feniscowles was a hamlet of about 60 people within the township of Pleasington. It was bought by William, one of the two Feilden brothers, from Thomas Ainsworth in 1800–1.

Sir William built Feniscowles New Hall in 1812 and lived there until his death in 1850. From 1854/55 his son Sir William Henry made repeated complaints about the serious pollution of the river Darwen, culminating in his suing the Corporation and Over Darwen Health Board in 1872. The proceedings failed and in 1877 he left the Hall and died two years later.

Succeeding tenants tried, without success, to develop the house and grounds into a recreation centre and it eventually fell into sad disrepair – accelerated by the removal of the roof-lead during the Second World War. The ruins can still be seen from the Old Road to Preston.

The smithy tollgate house stands unchanged at the junction of Preston Old Road and Livesey Branch Road. Originally owned in 1835 by Ned Pickup it has since housed a variety of tenants and is at present an antiques shop.

Moulden Brow tollgate house stands further along at the junction of

Finnington Lane. Although the gardens have been developed, the house remains – externally – the same as the original. Cottages built for the handloom weavers still survive near the end of Pleasington Road, albeit somewhat changed.

Due to the generosity of Sir William Feilden, building of Immanuel church began in 1835 and it was consecrated in 1836. It is in a beautiful setting on the hillside by the river Darwen. The money for the war memorial cross (£400) was raised within three weeks!

To celebrate the wedding of the Prince of Wales on 10th March 1863, a grand procession went all round Cherry Tree, Pleasington fields and back to the church where an oak tree was planted. Known forever as Albert's Oak, it is now a sturdy reminder of that special day.

St Paul's Roman Catholic church and school was built as recently as 1973 to serve the needs of the expanding population, whose nearest place of worship was Pleasington Priory. It is of a striking new design but aesthetically very pleasing.

In 1832, Sir William Feilden built a local schoolroom and school house in which both his daughters taught religious studies. In 1836, this became a fee-paying school and was the only educational establishment until, in 1865, the National school was built at Cherry Tree, catering for both villages. The original schoolroom was given upper rooms and is now Immanuel Sunday school and the school house is now the home of the verger. In 1902, Feniscowles County primary school was built and as the population grew it was enlarged and then the new infants school was built in 1974.

In Feniscowles, industry has literally developed 'astronomically'. The 'Sun' and 'Star' paper mills were established in 1874 and 1875 and are still operating successfully today. The 'Moon' was a corn mill on the river Darwen in the 1830s, opposite Immanuel church. It was completely burned down in 1864 but remains of walls and window openings can still be seen. It was only logical that the new cotton mill built in 1913 should then be named 'Eclipse'. It survived until 1967 and is now used for supplying textile accessories.

No account of Feniscowles village industry would be complete without a reference to the 'Jam Works' which, although located in Stockclough Lane (Jam Pot Lane) was strangely enough called 'Cherry Tree Jam Works'. It began as a thriving cottage industry and during the First World War people walked from Witton to have their own jars filled for 1d. Whenever fruit and sugar were scarce, jam was made from turnips with plum juice added and sold as 'Red jam'. The daughter of the owner

(Mr Walmsley) was appointed forewoman but throughout her life she was never known by any other name than 'Cissie Jam'.

Groups of streets and houses were built for the mill workers (East Street is still known locally as 'Star Row') and these well-maintained terraces are still attractive. The Park Farm and Beechwood estates are of the modern style and Lingfield sheltered housing complex has a very pleasant aspect above Immanuel church.

Villagers' requirements are amply catered for, with a variety of shops, a hairdresser, post office and doctor's surgery. The Feilden Arms hotel was built in the early 19th century, the Hordern Rake and the Beechwood are hotels of more recent times but all three are very congenial hostelries.

Although the railway is closed, there are excellent road links for shopping in several main towns.

In spite of peripheral development, Feniscowles retains its original village flavour and many of the villagers have lived there all their lives as did their forbears.

Fernyhalgh ❧

If you asked in the centre of Preston today how to get to Fernyhalgh, I doubt if one person could tell you correctly. It isn't located on any Ordnance Survey map, yet this secluded well-wooded spot situated in the eastern part of the township of Broughton, about four miles north of Preston, has played an important part in the lives of the local community for many centuries. It consists only of scattered farms and cottages over a few square miles. But the legend of Fernyhalgh goes back to the 14th century.

It is said that a wealthy and virtuous merchant, in danger of shipwreck on the Irish sea, promised to perform some conspicuous act of piety if his life was spared. Landing safely on the Lancashire coast he prayed his thanks and asked for guidance to fulfil his promise. His searching led him to a remote spot near to what is now called Squire Anderton's wood, where he found the spring and well, and statue of the Virgin Mary he had been seeking. Here he had a chapel built in 1348 beside the well, which is called Ladywell to this day.

The first authentic records are in the writings of Rev Christopher Tootel, parish priest of Fernyhalgh from 1699–1729. He tells that the Archbishop of York granted a licence to Thomas de Singleton, then lord of the manor of Broughton, to hold Divine Service at oratories at Broughton, Fernyhalgh and Farmunholes. And so another chapter in the life of Fernyhalgh began, with many instances of persecution throughout the 17th and 18th centuries, when Roman Catholic chapels were burned and pillaged, but still the staunch and devout community struggled on, until times improved and in the 1790s the new chapel was built about a quarter of a mile to the north of Ladywell. This church of St Mary serves the scattered parish of Fernyhalgh today.

Beside it stands the school built in 1836, but there are recordings of a school in the area from much earlier times, known as Dame Alice's school. Alice Harrison continued her school until she was 'very advanced in years'. This school was probably in the house now called Haighton Top Farm, and must have been a boarding school as the census of 1851 records 25 names in that house.

In spite of the close proximity of the M6 and industrial buildings encroaching on the rural scene, Fernyhalgh is still a 'hidden gem' and any stranger can so easily lose his way along the twisting lanes and byways, searching for the Ladywell which the merchant found so many, many years ago.

Forton 🌿

The name of Forton will be familiar to many who travel along the M6, as the distinctive mushroom-shaped building of the Top Rank service station comes into view. Fewer will know the village of Forton that lies beyond; a place with a long history and a thriving present.

Forton is mentioned in the Domesday Book as an ancient township under the name Fortune. In the 15th century the whole of Forton belonged to the Abbot of Cockersand Abbey, and stayed so until the Dissolution of the Monasteries in the reign of Henry VIII. In the 17th century the land was divided and sold to existing tenants and has remained in individual ownership to this day.

The village is divided by the A6 road between old and new Forton, the old being to the east of the main road and called Hollins Lane. There the village post office and shop stands amidst the little stone cottages along with the Methodist chapel. Opposite the post office there used to be engine sheds, housing all the steam rollers which worked on the roads in the surrounding areas. These buildings are now converted into houses for first-time buyers.

Hollins Lane was once the main route for coaches travelling north or south. A pretty little group of cottages known as The Square was originally a coaching inn called the Holly. When the A6 was built the coaches bypassed the Holly, so a new public house was built a little further south on the new road, and named the 'New Holly'. It was rather surprising that within half a mile of each other there were two other coaching inns, the Old Holly and Middle Holly, and the latter was said to be one of the oldest coaching inns in the country. It is now a farmhouse.

Changes were slow in the village until 1953, when to celebrate the coronation of Queen Elizabeth II, Coronation Avenue was built on the west side. With growing prosperity, and the increase in car ownership and mobility, further development took place west of the A6. Many more houses and bungalows were built in the 1960s, which brought a great influx of young people to the village. Locally however, farming and horticulture are the chief occupations.

The old village school was already in need of major expansion, so following the increase in children of school age, a new school was built. The old school after many years of planning and fund raising has now been converted into a very successful village hall. Opposite is the village shop.

One of the highlights in the village is the annual Forton Field Day, when the Rose Queen is crowned and a procession parades round the village led by a band, and followed by children in fancy dress. Teas, stalls and many attractions all add up to a good day.

The Anglican church of St James celebrated its centenary in 1989, but there is an older church of St Paul which was erected in 1805 on a site where there is a record of a building for worship since 1520.

The United Reformed church is of considerable historical interest, built as an Independent chapel in 1707 under the Five Mile Act, which stated that all dissenters who refused to conform to the Established Church, with obedience to the King and Bishops, would be banned from teaching their doctrine within five miles of any town. Nowadays, while still belonging to the United Reformed Church it is also used for worship by the local Roman Catholic community.

The biggest landowner in this part of the North West is the Duke of Lancaster, ie HM the Queen. The administrator responsible for these Duchy lands lives in Duchy House, Forton.

Within minutes of the village itself one finds oneself amid very peaceful country lanes, farms and footpaths, or along a beautiful stretch of canal, where wildlife abounds in the reeds and a profusion of wild flowers delight the eye.

Freckleton 🦩

Freckleton is the largest village in the Fylde. The population in 1801 was 561, and up to the early 1920s it was a truly rural community of under 2,000 inhabitants. Today the population is more than 7,000.

Situated as it is at the mouth of the rivers Ribble, Dow and Douglas, Freckleton was used by the Romans as a port serving their fort at Kirkham.

A watermill was in existence in 1199, owned by Sir Richard de Freckleton. In 1615 a new mill and house was built, and in 1699 was sold to the Earl of Derby. It passed to the Clifton family in 1850. Farmers from all over the Fylde brought their corn to be ground and the mill was in full working order until 1915. In hard winters the villagers would skate on the mill dam to violin and melodeon music. The mill was demolished in the early 1960s.

Sailcloth had been made in the village for many years, for the early boatbuilding industry. Balderstone Mill, erected in 1880, was the first organised factory system in Freckleton. The weaving shed contained 320 looms, and the cloth sold on the Manchester Cotton Exchange. It was closed in 1980.

The brickwork of the quay can still be seen just below the Naze. Cargoes of wood, grain and slate arrived, mainly from Connah's Quay on the Dee and occasionally in an Irish freighter. Coal was brought daily from Wigan via the canal, the river Douglas and thence to Freckleton. In 1814 Freckleton Shipyard was established and the first ocean going vessel was built in 1871. Six schooners were built, 18 sharking boats, one sailing yacht and five barges. In later years the yard serviced all lifeboats in the north west of England.

The oldest building in Preston Old Road has a facing wall of wattle and daub construction and was used as a gaol. In the 1920s the road across the marsh to Preston was a toll road and the toll house is still in existence although the road is now a busy dual carriageway.

Freckleton was one of the earliest villages in Lancashire where Quaker meetings were held. In 1689 the first meetings were held in the village, one of the meeting places being Fold Side Farm (opposite the Plough Hotel), now demolished. The last meeting was held at the old Hodgson Institute. The Quakers opened their burial ground at Quakers Wood, Lower Lane, in 1725. Trees were planted where a member of their group was interred. There is one stone (now vandalised) commemorating

Joseph and Sarah Jesper who founded the Quaker group in the village. This can be seen today and is said to be haunted.

Live eels and elvers, which swam up-river, were caught by local men and sold in the street with the cry of 'snig fra'.

Holy Trinity church was built in 1837 and the Methodist church in 1814. The Ship Inn in Bunker Street dates back to 1777 and was the centre of local smuggling activities.

Club Day, one of the highlights of the village year, is held on the third Saturday in June. It was started in 1874 by the Friendly Societies and is very well supported by the four churches, Freckleton Band and other village organisations.

On a hot, thundery day in August 1944 an American Liberator plane took off from Warton, but due to the bad weather conditions decided to turn back. As it flew low over Freckleton it clipped some trees and as a result ploughed into the village school, killing 36 children in the infants class and 36 adults. As a result of this tragedy various funds were set up. There was a lot of disagreement in the village about how the money was to be spent. The Parish Council decided to invest the money until the bitterness had died down. Thirty years later the money had still not been used. Although the investment had not been as lucrative as had been expected the fund was boosted by government grants and in 1977 the Memorial Hall was finally achieved and is a very valuable asset to the village.

Galgate

The village of Galgate is situated within the parish of Ellel, to the south of the city of Lancaster. The silk mill, which was reputed to be the oldest in the country, dating back to 1790, closed down production in the 1960s. At one time the workforce was around 400, but at the end of production there were only about 80 workers. The building is now used for small works units. There was another factory to the west of the village, known as Low Mill, which was used for flax and cotton, then later silk. There were two small schoolroom buildings dating back to 1733, built with money left in a will by a local person. A new larger modern school was built in recent years, the former being sold off for private dwellings. There is also a Roman Catholic church.

The village over the years has been divided into the old and the new part, separated by the A6 road and the London to Glasgow railway. The

Preston to Tewitfield canal also goes through the village and there is a marina for approximately 100 boats, and a well-looked-after pathway for local walks, leading through locks to Glasson Dock.

During the summer months there are regattas which are quite popular. The local Horticultural Club's 'Gaslight Show' has a popular following in the village. It started in 1865, to pay for the gas bought from the mill to light the village streets, hence the name. Another annual event is the 'Galgate Treat' for all village children. A Queen and retinue are chosen, and a parade goes round the village to the playing field where a crowning ceremony takes place.

Garstang ❧

Garstang serves as a nucleus for the surrounding villages and has all the characteristics of community and cohesion which characterise a village. It has had a Thursday market since 1314 when King Edward II granted a charter to the Abbot of Cockersand Abbey, which then largely owned Garstang. Two horse and cattle fairs were a feature for many years into the present century. The markets and fairs gave the country folk an opportunity to sell their stock and produce.

In the Domesday Book Garstang appears as Cherestanc and was one of the larger townships. The meaning is not clear but the favoured interpretation is the curious one of 'triangular plot of land with a pole on it'.

On the outskirts are the ruins of Greenhalgh Castle, built by Thomas Stanley, Earl of Derby, in 1490. He was afraid of reprisals by outlawed nobles whose estates had been given to him by Henry VII. Later it was one of the last two Royalist castles in Lancashire to hold out against Cromwell, but it eventually surrendered when the Governor died in about 1649. Many of the nearby farms have incorporated its stones into their buildings.

The parish church of Garstang was at Churchtown, and Churchtown's church is still officially 'Garstang St Helen's'. There was, however, a chapel of ease at Garstang from the 16th century and in 1769 the present church of St Thomas was erected and was restored in 1848 as the parish church. The Roman Catholic church of St Mary and St Michael is just over the river Wyre and is strictly in Barnacre with Bonds. It was built in 1858, though there had been a Catholic place of worship in Garstang from 1784. The Wesleyans had a chapel from 1814 and the United

Reformed church has celebrated its tricentenary. The Free Methodists have a modern chapel.

On the coaching route to Scotland, Garstang was also on the route of the Jacobites coming south from Scotland in 1715 and 1745. Four men were hanged for supporting the Old Pretender after the 1715 rebellion.

The May Bank Holiday children's festival has superseded the Whit Monday processions, once the highlight of the year. The event attracts many visitors and maintains its popularity. So too does the Garstang Agricultural Show founded in 1809, held on the first Saturday in August. There is a modern sports centre and a swimming pool, and the Lancaster Canal, near the centre, attracts boating enthusiasts. The occasional wild duck may be seen exploring the town! An Arts Centre occupies the old grammar school, founded in 1756.

There is still a Thursday market, but it is not exclusively for farm produce by any means. A bell is still rung at 10 am to mark the opening of trading. A bell used to be rung on Shrove Tuesday by the town crier as a signal for the children to run from school to go 'pancaking' to the shops where they would be given fruit or sweets. Gone are the days of hop scotch, skipping, and whip and top played in the main street. But the river Wyre still invites exploration of the Wyresdale Fells and Bleasdale and the Trough of Bowland do not change.

Glasson Dock

Glasson Dock, near Lancaster, or Glasson as it was called originally, and still is to the locals, was formerly a farming settlement. The first thing that strikes one now, however, is the vast number of boats, both leisure craft and commercial, which use Glasson.

The dock was built in 1787 after the demise of Sunderland Point and is now once again a busy working port after going through a period of decline.

The canal, which is popular with boaters, walkers or naturalists, was built in the 19th century. A railway link followed but was closed in 1964 and the disused line is now a popular footpath with a picnic area at Condor Green. The path runs alongside the Lune estuary which provides habitat and feeding grounds for many species of wading birds and is a site of special scientific interest. The path leads to Lancaster and is itself rich in flora and fauna.

The housing is a mix of 18th and 19th century houses built when the shipyard was thriving. The Graving Dock, thought to have been the first of its type in England, was designed by Jesse Hartley who designed the Albert Dock in Liverpool. It has been filled in, although many people hope that one day it can be restored. There is also an estate of modern bungalows.

The main road through the village 'disappears' when the swing bridge is opened to allow boats from the freshwater basin through the locks to the dock and thence to the open sea through the new dock gates, which were installed in 1987. The old Custom House is dwarfed by industrial buildings and the Sailing Club is on Fishnet Point.

Employment is provided by the port-based companies at the boatyard and shipping companies, at the large factory complex where silencers are made, at the three pubs, plus the cafes and shops which cater for the tourists. Agriculture is also still one of the primary industries.

There are spectacular panoramic views of the Lakeland hills and Bowland Fells from the top of Tithebarn Hill with the University of Lancaster, the Ashton Memorial and Heysham nuclear power station all prominent landmarks.

Goosnargh & Whittingham

This thriving community is seven miles north of Preston and three miles from the busy M6. Goosnargh is thought to be the second largest ecclesiastical parish in the country, though much is fell land and the inhabitants cattle and sheep!

Well farmed, picturesque and rich in historical interest, the area includes Beacon Fell within its boundaries, the first country park opened in Lancashire.

The historian Atticus in *Lancashire Chantries and Parish Churches* refers to Goosnargh as a goose green or field – 'argh' in Scandinavian means a field. The central feature of the village was and still is the 'field' now embracing the summer football league, the children's playground and the tennis courts with pavilion. The Council keeps the green well trimmed, sapling trees have been planted to replace old oak and ash, whilst round the boles the WI planted daffodils.

In June the fair comes to the green to help celebrate the Festival, the beginnings of which are lost in time, and which attracts hundreds of people. The Queen is crowned in the grounds of Whittingham Hospital where the patients enjoy the spectacle too.

The two ancient hostelries, the Grapes Inn and the Bushell's Arms, still offer hospitality as they have for 300 years. There are still typical village shops far removed from superstores and you can buy traditional Goosnargh cakes, though only a few farm families claim the original recipe!

There is a splendid village hall paid for partly by public subscription and well used by local organisations. Another hall belongs to the school, still partly governed by the Church, and which celebrated its 150th birthday in 1989. In the 1960s Sir Robert Lloyd, a shipping millionaire, returned to Goosnargh where he had grown up and presented gifts, a bursary and the lychgate.

The centre of any medieval village was the church – and so it has remained in Goosnargh. Every current organisation owes its origin to St Mary's, St Francis' (Hill Chapel), the Methodist or the Congregational churches. St Mary's church has a record of priests since 1333.

Chingle Hall was built by the Singletons in 1260 and boasts its own ghost, St John Wall, the martyr, still searching for his head. There is Middleton Hall too, owned in the 17th century by the Rigby family. Sir Alexander was one of Cromwell's colonels involved in the storming of Lathom House, home of the Earls of Derby. The Lady Chapel in St Mary's bears his initials carved in oak – A. R. Cromwell's signature on an ancient manuscript found in the school is now in the care of the Record Office. In the square stands Bushell House, bequeathed by William Bushell in 1735 to be a home for 'decayed gentlefolk' within a six mile radius of Preston. The present 27 residents are anything but decayed!

At the present time the future of Whittingham Hospital, once the second largest psychiatric hospital in Europe, is at stake. Forward looking firms are targeting the attractive 200 acre site now on the market – the time scale for ultimate closure being 1994.

Great Eccleston

Great Eccleston, in the heart of the Fylde, lies between the sea and the hills, eight miles from Blackpool and six from Garstang, bypassed by the A586. It has always been something of a centre. Even in the Domesday Book, where it appeared as Eglestun, it was of greater area than the surrounding villages. Although the name means 'church settlement' there is no record of a Saxon church.

Until the Second World War it was a self-contained community, serving a wide hinterland of farms, with trades of all kinds servicing the country people while a blacksmith and a saddler looked after the horses. To the end of the 19th century, there was a flourishing rush-light industry, imported rushes augmenting local supplies. In earlier years there had been a corn mill, a tithe barn and a pinfold (still extant) for stray animals.

The focal point of the village is the Square, once cobbled, now macadamised. It is flanked by buildings both old and new, on the whole blending together and keeping the true village atmosphere. Some date back to Elizabethan days, some are post-war constructions on old sites. The Black and White Bulls confront each other, no doubt reminders of former barbaric sports.

The Square has always been a convenient gathering place. It was once the site of three annual horse fairs. The pre-1914 Club Day assembled here and until 1939 it accommodated the fair which came each September at the time of the Agricultural Show. Today it is the setting for the crowning of the Gala Queen, and the assembly point for the Gala procession. Carols are sung at Christmas at an ecumenical service and every Wednesday there is a market, patronised by customers from a wide area.

The Show is now held on two days in July. Founded in 1853, the Show is one of the oldest and, in its hey-day, was one of the most prestigious of the Lancashire shows. Its new format attracts many visitors, and there is still a good entry of farm animals and of shire horses, but only three or

The Square, Great Eccleston

four of these gentle giants appear nowadays caparisoned in their finery, lovingly tended by their grooms. Gone, too, are the tents full of farmhouse cheeses or piled high with the banks of vegetables we marvelled at in our youth.

Leckonby Street is called after the Leckonby family. Richard Leckonby is perhaps the most colourful character the village has produced. He exhausted his inheritance, and his wife's considerable fortune, borrowing heavily and spending recklessly, ending his days in 1783, imprisoned for debt in Lancaster Castle. His initials are on the craft shop and on the wall of the present Leckonby House, a part of the original edifice.

Leckonby Street leads to Copp Lane, where an 18th century dovecote, one of the very few in Lancashire and a scheduled ancient monument, may be seen. Almost a mile further on is the parish church of St Anne, Copp, sturdy and reassuring, enlarged a century ago from the 1723 original. The Roman Catholic chapel of St Mary was built in 1835 and is of graceful proportions and is suffused with light.

Great Eccleston Hall itself is a farm, once moated, on the site occupied by the Stanley family, a branch of the Derbys, until 1714 and purchased from the Ecclestons in 1592.

The village was known as 'Little London' in the 18th century, suggesting a centre of social hospitality. Thomas Barrow, a pupil of the artist Romney, lived here and Peter Newby, the recusant poet, ran a private school.

Certainly the village has long been a centre for those making excursions into the country. Aunt Ann's Tea Rooms ministered to the horse-drawn char-a-bancs, and Mrs Cutler catered for the Cyclists Touring Club. Today, caravan parks attract seasonal visitors, and mystery tours include the village in their itinerary.

The village schools, both Roman Catholic and Church of England, are expanding and a splendid health centre serves the neighbourhood. There are many flourishing organisations. The more intimate village general shops have gone, but two small supermarkets, run by families long connected with the village, provide something of a substitute. There are other shops and enterprises, from DIY to legal advice. The village values its post office and resident policeman, even if the telephone is no longer operated by the postmaster and his wife, and even if some remember the time when both a sergeant *and* a constable lived here.

In the last 30 years the village has grown from 600 inhabitants to over 2,000. The extent of the new houses and estates is not noticeable from the main street and this has enabled the village to keep its identity. It may no longer be Little London, but it is still a thriving community.

Great & Little Mitton 🍃

The old county boundaries of Lancashire and Yorkshire split the village of Mitton; Little Mitton being in Lancashire and Great Mitton in Yorkshire. This boundary was on the bridge over the river Ribble.

By the school stands the ancient All Hallows church, the nave of which dates from 1270 and the tower from the 15th century. The chapel was added in 1594 by Sir Richard Shireburne of Stonyhurst, whose ancestral home is now a famous public school on the outskirts of the next village of Hurst Green.

Present WI members can remember their fathers attending the Court Leet of the manor. This relic of feudal times was an annual event for men only, held in the local hostelry The Three Fishes Inn. The court room was the upper floor. After a dinner a jury and officers would be sworn to ancient appointments. The Archdeacon F. G. Ackerley once held the title of Ale Taster, and his fame even spread to America! Other appointments were as constable, hedgers and ditchers and pinners and pounders, these latter being responsible for catching stray stock and enclosing it, then fining the claimants.

Today Mitton is still a farming community, the main landowners being Mr J. Aspinall of Standen Hall, and the CWS.

Mitton's farthest boundary is marked by the Edisford and the Higher Hodder bridges. A nearer boundary is the famous Cromwell bridge spanning the Lower Hodder. Cromwell actually crossed this Tudor relic in 1648 to rest at Stonyhurst before taking Preston. Macadam replaced the old bridge in 1826 although it still stands as a picturesque ruin against a wooded backdrop.

The name of Mitton comes from the Saxon word 'Mythe' which means a farmstead at the junction of two rivers. Hence a local rhyme:

'The rivers Ribble, Hodder and Calder and rain,
All meet together at Mitton demain'

Greenmount 🍃

Greenmount, a community of 1,200 houses, is situated three and a half miles north of Bury. The name Greenmount came into existence in 1848 when the Old School was built, on the outskirts of Tottington. At first, people who lived near to the Old School included the name of Greenmount in their address, and gradually this was extended to the surrounding area and so Greenmount became a village.

Greenmount remained primarily an agricultural area, with a residential community, until after the Second World War when a massive demand for new houses entirely changed the area. The first estate was built in 1960 and others followed.

A well known village character was Samuel Horrocks, known as 'Sammy Kite' because of the kites he made. He died in 1958 at the age of 75. One kite had a wing span of 13 ft 6 ins and was 8 ft 6 ins high. It was flown on a wire leading to a pulley on the ground, at which the operator sat. He took the first aerial views of Greenmount at the beginning of this century, by sending a camera up with the kite after working out a mechanism to take the photographs. He usually flew his kite from a field near the Nailor's Green.

Billy Shaw, the village barber and newsagent, who worked for the *Daily Despatch*, decided as a prank to write an article about Doctor Rigby of Whitebirk and Samuel Horrocks of Brandlesholme Road, having a flying contest.

A short time afterwards, two men came by train from Manchester. They enquired at Billy Shaw's shop as to where Samuel Horrocks lived and where the hangar for the aeroplanes was. Later Samuel Horrocks was surprised to learn that the two men were the Roe brothers, founders of A. V. Roe & Co Ltd, constructors of Avro planes. Although they had been led on a wild goose chase, they were very interested in his kite.

Gregson Lane 🪁

In the opening years of the 20th century, Gregson Lane was a thriving self-contained village. Two mills as well as farms and quarries kept local people employed, though trains also brought in workers, stopping at the halt at Bournes Mill, from where the rail tickets were sold.

The Co-operative Store supplied the bulk of household goods but several bakehouses replaced the burden of the bread-baking day for those women who worked in the cotton mills for five and a half days a week. Small grocers and confectioners dotted the village and one shopkeeper used his upstairs room as a refreshment hall for such events as Sunday school parties. There was a chip shop, a butcher and a clogger, a slaughterhouse and a blacksmith as well as the joiner and undertaker. A milliner kept the ladies properly attired – with grosgrain ribbon and hat pins for imaginative fashion adaptations.

Several doctors' surgeries, held in various parlours, ensured the best medical attention and medicines were brought in and left for collection from here as late as the 1960s.

A Pot Fair was held every year down the side of the Black Horse, as well as an annual sale of haberdashery and linen at the back of Cross Cottage. This was the home of Matt Worsley, the general trader who supplied the surrounding villages from his horse and cart. One of the first to progress to a motor car, he continued to serve the area up to his death in the 1960s.

Preston tradespeople sent out regular roundsmen, but a carrier could be hired at the Farmers' Arms, next to the covered market, to fetch items bought in town like mangles or wash-boilers. They were often delivered home before the customer, who either walked or travelled on the wagonette, was back. Mr Eddie Bagshaw's wagonette plied this route but at Preston Brow passengers were obliged to alight when the strain on the horses was heaviest. Mr Hodson, an enterprising local man, began a bus service which later flourished into the Ribble Motor Company. The first bus came to Gregson Lane on 17th February, 1912.

The Methodist chapel allowed the Council school to share its building but Sunday school was as much an obligation as was day school. Many Church of England members chose to worship at the chapel rather than walk to either Brindle or Higher Walton, but the Roman Catholics strode out the long mile to their school and church, rain or fine. Because people lived, worked and worshipped in the village, the community was always alive with constant bustle and children played their age-old games in the lane. All this in a settlement of only a few hundred people, living mainly in a few rows of neat terraced houses – each row separated by and overlooking open fields. A happy life!

Modern life has imposed its changes: the slaughterhouse has gone, the Pot Fair is held in Preston, the doctors no longer hold surgeries in the village but a chemist is now established. There has been considerable housing development, with two large estates and other smaller areas built up. One cotton mill, which had become a corn mill, has been replaced by sheltered accommodation. The other is divided into smaller units catering for a number of commercial ventures.

The area is rural; almost all the houses in Gregson Lane have reasonably-sized gardens and there is obvious pride in keeping these well-stocked and colourful. Within minutes even a slow walker can be in open country with pleasant walks along quiet lanes and footpaths where the farming is mainly in pasture for cattle and sheep.

Grimsargh 🪶

Once a little hamlet half-way between Preston and Longridge, Grimsargh is now a sizeable village. Historically, it has always been 'passed through' en route to somewhere else, but it is thought that a Norseman named Grim claimed a tract of land (or 'argh') and settled here.

Much later Cromwell and his armies probably passed through after his victory at Preston in 1648. In the next century, skirmishes in the area were between the Catholic Jacobites and Protestant supporters of the new Hanoverian King. Perhaps these armies marched past the newly built farmhouses, Wood Top with a 1724 date stone and Grimsargh Hall built just a year or two later.

Before recorded history, Grimsargh features in legend. A disastrous drought affected the area and the country folk were starving. A mysterious and enormous Dun Cow was roaming the fields now known as Cow Hill. This cow had a seemingly unending supply of milk. She provided milk for all who milked her in the open field. But a wicked witch, who wished to cause distress, came and milked the cow into a sieve, her purpose to milk the cow completely dry. The poor thing collapsed and died exhausted. Her skeleton was venerated for generations and to this day an enormous rib is mounted over the door of a house on the outskirts of Longridge built in 1616 – the 'Owd Rib'. Grimsargh Hall has its own portion of rib mounted over its front door.

The coming of the railway to the quarries of Longridge really put Grimsargh on the map. This was in 1848 and Grimsargh had its own level crossing and railway station, now beautifully transformed into attractive bungalows for the elderly, called 'Old Station Close'. A footpath marks the route of the old railway lines and provides a pleasant stroll into the heart of the village itself.

Grimsargh today is a delightful, rural village community with a population of about 1,400, within easy reach of farmland and fells as well as cities and towns. The old church of St Michael and its vicarage, together with the traditional public house, built from local gritstone, keep Grimsargh in touch with the richness of the past whilst the new homes and the splendid new village hall add diversity and freshness.

Most people in the village, apart from the farming community, travel to work in all parts of Lancashire. A few local shops provide essential services and there is also a Grimsargh Club. The village fete, held each year on the green, is a major event which brings people together. There is a village football team and cricket team, both of which contribute to the quality of life in this flourishing little village.

Grindleton

Grindleton nestles on the slopes of the Ribble valley, the river below and the fells rising to 1,000 ft as its backdrop. Its houses face this way and that, back to back, front to front, with short rows of interesting cottages, pretty gardens and allotments. Back Lane is still a rough thoroughfare, linked in ladder-like fashion to Main Street by narrow ginnels and tracks, and provides a safe passageway to school and to the post office and shop.

Two pubs, The Buck and The Duke of York, are situated at the junction of the Sawley and Slaidburn roads in the centre of the village. The Duke of York is a reminder that Grindleton has changed counties since the reorganization in 1974, now being wholly in Lancashire. Refreshments are provided at both the hostelries for walkers, cyclists and

View of Grindleton village

others who come to explore this lovely area. The Ribble Way skirts the river down in the valley, and the village itself is on a recognised cycle route.

Both the Methodist chapel and St Ambrose Church school, situated adjacent to the church, have excellent facilities for local groups. As well as the primary school with 40 pupils on the rolls, Grindleton boasts a secondary modern school, Bowland School.

The almshouses on the Sawley Road were built in 1860 as a memorial to the brother and sister of Mary Brown of Rathmell, who founded them. Also adjoining the Sawley Road is the playing field, of which the village is justifiably proud.

In years gone by, the 'Hen-Pecked Club' held its annual demonstration and fete on the second Tuesday in June. A procession through the streets followed a sumptuous meal at the Duke or the Buck, and each character attempted to portray by dress or action how he thought he played second-fiddle at home. A local brass band led the parade. Nowadays it is the annual village sports day which provides fun and entertainment for all ages.

Villagers remember the days of the felt hat works, the jam factory, and clog soles stacked in circles to season. Some of the cottages still show evidence of handloom weaving. One hears tales of the ferryman who plied from bank to bank until the 1860s, when the bridge was constructed, and of children who visited the woods and waited for the fairies at Cat Steps. The beneficial effects of the sulphur and lime springs could be enjoyed at the Hydro Hotel, and the well at Wortwells, by Whitehall, which was used by weavers for shrinking tweeds, also had medicinal properties.

As handloom weaving ceased and the villagers moved away to the towns to work in the mills, the population dwindled. The highest recorded census for the village was 1,125 in 1821. The present number on the electoral roll is 568. Grindleton has no major housing developments. Barns within the village are being converted into private dwellings, and the few modern properties are scattered unobtrusively.

The curlews call in spring, and the damson blossom whitens the hedges and gardens, later in the year providing the fruit for which Grindleton is famous. The general air of tranquillity and quiet activity remains.

Halewood 🦋

Halewood is situated in south Merseyside, a few miles from Liverpool. There used to be a large wood in the village, rich in beautiful trees and flowers, wild raspberries and winding paths. It belonged to Hale manor; hence the name of Halewood.

St Mary's church was built in 1967, burned down by vandals in 1972 and rebuilt in 1974, re-dedicated by Bishop Blanche. St Nicholas' church was built in 1839.

Mr Billy Grace, who once owned a farm down Court Avenue, was considered the 'Squire' of Halewood. He bequeathed land for the village hall and recreation field and was known as the man who played music to his cows to encourage them to give more milk.

The house at the corner of Church Road and Hollies Road named The Hollies, used to be the village blacksmith's before the establishment of the smithy across the road adjacent to the Eagle and Child. Later The Hollies became a private school run by Miss Hilton and Mrs Lowcock. The privileged pupils used to arrive by pony and trap.

In 1938 a Wellington bomber crashed near the village, the four occupants escaping unhurt by parachute from 3,000 ft up. In the 1950s a Frenchman attempting to fly with wings from Speke Airport was not so lucky. He fell to his death in Higher Road. The first bombs of the Liverpool blitz during the Second World War fell in Halewood churchyard, making a huge crater and damaging some gravestones. Numerous incendiary bombs fell on the village and the surrounding area in subsequent bombing.

The village has grown considerably in post-war years. A new school has been built, and the Eagle and Child has added a steak bar which has brought quite a number of motorists and visitors to Halewood. One policeman used to walk the beat, now there is a police station and a full force of officers.

The inhabitants today are employed mainly by the Ford Motor Company and local shops and public houses. Others travel to Garston and Liverpool to work.

Halsall 🦢

Halsall extends from the pretty hamlets of Primrose Hill and Bangors Green on the outskirts of Ormskirk, west to the Southport boundary at Ainsdale, and has a population of about 1,920.

Much of the rich fertile farming land in Halsall has been won after many years of draining from the extensive Halsall Moss. In the Domesday Book Halsall is named Haleshale, which means rising ground near the edge of a great bog or moss.

The parish church of St Cuthbert, one of the oldest and most beautiful in the Liverpool Diocese, dates back to the 12th century. It stands majestically on rising ground on the edge of a broad stretch of level land which was once Halsall Moss. It is, as it must have been designed to be, a conspicuous landmark for miles around. The first school in Halsall was founded by Edward Halsall in 1593, situated in what is now the choir vestry of St Cuthbert's church. In 1861 the school was transferred to a site adjoining the graveyard known as St Cuthbert's Hall, and later in 1904 to its present site on New Street.

With the Industrial Revolution and the introduction of the Leeds–Liverpool Canal, Halsall and the western parishes found themselves on the thoroughfare from the docks at Liverpool to the towns and villages in the North West. When the Leeds–Liverpool Canal was dug, the first sod this side of the Pennines was cut at Halsall Hill.

In 1887 Halsall saw its next step forward with the introduction of the Lancashire and Yorkshire Railway Line. The 'Altcar Bob' was introduced; a one carriage loco that offered locals a train service to Southport. This stopped at every little nook and cranny on the way, giving more freedom to the villagers than they had ever had before. Sadly, the 'Altcar Bob' no longer runs, and the only craft on the canal are pleasure cruisers.

Local characters are always a feature of small hamlets. The 'Goose King' was John Harrison, farmer of Mill House Farm. He bought hundreds of geese each autumn and fattened them on the stubble fields after the corn was cut, ready for the Christmas market. The village craftsmen must not be left out: Knowles (the wheelwright), Wilson (the saddler), Cores and Mellings (the blacksmiths) and never-to-be-forgotten Nurse Bond (the local doctor-cum-nurse-cum-midwife).

Hughie Sharrock, who was the landlord of the Saracen's Head, started a bus service from Formby to Halsall, and later extended it to Ormskirk on a Thursday and Saturday only. This was very popular with the farmers, especially on Thursdays. They travelled to the Corn Exchange in Ormskirk, and discussed prices of all their farm produce. This bus service has never improved over the years. The service still only runs on Thursdays and Saturdays.

Halsall past and present has been to the fore with its sporting activities. Between the world wars Halsall was the venue for sports held annually in Halsall Park, where there was a running track and all facilities. These sports attracted competition from a wide area, not just local talent. Alas, during the Second World War the park, and the running track, had to be ploughed up to 'Dig for Victory'. They were never re-introduced.

Halton ✤

The village of Halton is situated on the north bank of the river Lune about three miles east of Lancaster.

Present-day Halton has become a rather sprawling village as a result of the housing built since the 1950s, but there are still 17th and 18th century houses remaining and a friendly village atmosphere still exists.

There are two popular annual events in the village, with a rather nice, slightly old-fashioned air about them – the Halton Gala Day with sports, Rose Queen and decorated floats, and the Horticultural Show with lively competition to produce the best flowers, vegetables, home cooking and various crafts.

The village school is St Wilfrid's and is housed in two buildings, the 'new' school built in 1966, and the 'old' school which was originally a tithe barn. In years gone by, the children often had a rather unusual start to their school day – they were sent into the woods to collect fuel to keep the old cast iron stove going. This old building has served the village well but is soon to be closed and the new school extended.

Halton has three churches: United Reformed, Roman Catholic and St Wilfrid's, which has a long and interesting history. There have been four churches on the site of the present St Wilfrid's, which was consecrated in 1877. From ancient relics found in and around the church, Christianity must have come to Halton long before the Norman Conquest. In the churchyard is the Halton Cross, carved by Norsemen about 1,000 years ago. On the east side of the cross are pagan scenes and on the west side scenes of Christ's crucifixion and ascension. Also in the churchyard is an impressive mausoleum built to house the remains of William Bradshaw, lord of the manor from 1743 to 1775, and his family.

A little distance from the church is Castle Hill, showing earthworks of the motte and bailey castle erected by the Normans.

Near Castle Hill is an old well, now almost completely choked up, but long ago believed to be good for eye troubles:

O come with us to St Wilfrid's Well,
Its waters carry a kindly spell;
Bathe your eyes and the charm will be
That you with clearer sight shall see.

Also close by the church is the White Lion public house. There is no record as to how long this has been a public house but one of the earliest references to it was in 1792, and in 1829 three men were found guilty of passing a forged £5 note to Mrs Redhead of the White Lion and were sentenced to death. The sentence was not carried out, as all convicted prisoners were reprieved at the close of the Assizes. There is another hostelry in the village – the Greyhound – but, so far as we know, none of their customers have ever been sentenced to death.

Another interesting story from Halton's past concerns the Halton Moor find. When Halton Moor was enclosed in 1797 a man digging his allotted portion found a silver cup filled with more than a thousand coins of King Canute (1017 to 1035) and a gold necklace. This treasure may possibly have been buried there for safety by the lord of the manor before he set off on his journey to help King Malcolm of Scotland. They are now in the British Museum.

The river Lune has always been important to Halton, providing power for the mills on its banks and employment for the village. The old mills are now gone, but there is still some employment provided by small factories located by the river. There is also good fishing to be had in its waters, particularly around the local beauty spot, the Crook o' Lune. It is popular with boating enthusiasts too, the Lancaster Regatta being held here annually. The Lancaster to Leeds railway line which ran along the south bank of the river is now a country walk from Lancaster to beyond Halton, and the one-time station building is now a boathouse used by Lancaster University.

The bridge across the river which was the link between Halton and the railway station is still a great asset to the village, giving easy access to the motorway, which, although quite close, passes by high over the river and leaves us to enjoy our pleasant village with its lovely views.

Hambleton ✤

Hambleton, the village on the bend of the river, perhaps dates back to Roman times, when soldiers may have crossed the river at Shard just as villagers do today over the now famous toll bridge, opened in 1864.

Traditions blend with modern trends as the clattering of clogs mingles with the skateboards and stereos, but no doubt most of the residents would agree with an old rhyme:

> Pilling for praties
> Pres'll for pluck
> 'Amleton for bonnie lasses
> Stalmine for muck

One of the best kept traditions is Gala Day. Centuries ago May Day was celebrated in Hambleton. With the passing of years this celebration became a field day, later a Gala Day and due to the uncertainty of spring weather the date was moved to July.

Village life has changed greatly over the years and the once small farming community has rapidly expanded. Now villagers frequently commute to their work in Blackpool, Preston and Poulton. Although farming is still important it is no longer the main source of income for the residents.

As boats bob on the river bank and animals graze in the green pastured fields, Hambleton provides an ideal setting for rest homes and restaurants, many of which provide full and part time work for the ladies of the village.

As long ago as 1563 there was a tavern or public house at Wardleys Creek, once famous for smugglers and 'Amleton 'ookers, which were mussels caught on hooks in the mud back in the 1930s and renowned to be amongst the best in English waters. The Wardleys pub still stands to this day as well as The Shovels Inn, dating back to 1760. A new sports and social club and the Shard Hotel also stand here so the villagers need never go thirsty.

As in the early days the churches have had an important role to play. Hambleton has three; the parish church of the Blessed Virgin Mary, the United Reformed church and the very recent Roman Catholic church of St Francis of Assisi, all of which help with the organisations, coffee mornings and flea markets, etc.

The Peg Mill was situated in Mill Lane near to Mill Garage and was known throughout the Over Wyre region for its high quality milling. After the death of James Baron in 1902, the last miller, the mill was demolished.

Hambleton is very rapidly becoming a commuter village, but it can still boast a reasonable selection of shops. The fishmonger still visits on Thursdays. He now arrives in a car and caravan instead of on foot with baskets; but even time cannot transform the smell!

Hapton 🌿

The village of Hapton is to be found at the foot of Hameldon Hill, overshadowed by Pendle Hill to the north and the towns of Burnley and Accrington to the east and west. It is a typical Lancastrian industrial village with its streets of terraced houses, corner shops and industrial premises. In addition there is a council housing estate, several new housing developments, a school, two churches and four drinking venues in which to quench your thirst.

Flowing through the north of the village is the Leeds–Liverpool canal. By the side of the canal is the chemical works which was started up in 1844 by John Riley and is still a thriving industry today.

Signposts depicting 'Picnic Area' lead to one of Hapton's tourist attractions, an area of superb natural beauty, where a narrow stream meanders through a deep gorge, filled with trees, ferns and flowers, beneath overhanging massive rocks. This is called Castle Clough, so named because it was once the site of Hapton Castle, which was a fortified residence belonging to the lord of the manor. Reynor-de-Arches was the first lord in 1242 of whom there is a known record.

Hapton Castle was one of the many private fortresses which lined both sides of the Calder valley in the reign of Stephen, when the border between the kingdoms of England and Scotland was the Ribble. The fortresses were used as retreats in times of danger, particularly during the raids of the Scots which occurred quite frequently. The manor passed into the hands of the de-la-Legh family at the beginning of the 14th century. The last occupant, John de-la-Legh, married a co-heiress of Towneley and on their deaths their son Richard succeeded to the whole inheritance of Hapton and Towneley. He adopted his mother's name, Towneley, and became the ancestor of the line of Towneleys of Towneley Hall, Burnley.

Hapton Castle became uninhabited and fell into decay. All that remains now is a low wall 2 ft high between two trees in Castle Clough and an Elizabethan coin which was found on the site. It is now displayed in Accrington Museum. So it was that Hapton lost its castle.

In 1510 Sir John Towneley built Hapton Tower on a magnificent site on Hameldon Hill, from which elevated position could be seen the Calder, Ribble and Hodder valleys and the Pennine Hills from Longridge Fell to Cliviger Gorge. He enclosed the tower in 1,100 acres of the surrounding land and thus Hapton Park became, next to Knowsley, the largest in Lancashire. While hunting his red deer he was able to keep a wary eye on the vast area of land stretching out below him for any sign of the marauding Scots. Sir John died at his Hapton Tower in 1541 having spent the last nine years of his life as Sheriff of Lancashire. He was probably the most powerful in the long line of Towneleys.

The Tower became empty in 1637 on the death of Jane Assheton who had been married to Richard Towneley. She had continued to live there with her infant son after the death of her husband. The tower was then used as poor tenements until the 18th century when it was dismantled and the materials used to rebuild the Towneleys' farmhouses at Hapton. A search of the area by Titus Thornber in 1984 revealed a low section of straight dry stone wall, which included a slip window, and a jumble of ground level foundations of rectangular buildings. However, at Dyneley Hall, the house of Simon Towneley, three ornamental stone waterspouts can be seen which were once part of the Tower buildings and they give some idea of the grandeur of the place.

An event in 1887 brought the people of Hapton much pleasure and pride. The Simpson brothers had wired up the streets of Hapton to their dynamo and Hapton became perhaps the first village in England to be lit by electric lights. People came from far and wide to see this 'wonder of the world'.

Today new industries are taking the place of the derelict coal mine, the cotton mill and engineering works.

Hawkshaw

Hawkshaw is on the edge of the West Pennine Moors, though only six miles from Bolton and six miles from Bury, and is surrounded by beautiful countryside, with the moorland of Bull Hill and Holcombe Hill a short walk away – it is a marvellous place for walkers.

Hawkshaw Lane

The original village was one mile from its present position. There the old farms and cottages built of local stone still stand largely unaltered after 200 or more years. Hawkshaw then stood on a busy packhorse route, now known as Hawkshaw Lane, which ran from north to south but in 1820 the main road was built, east to west, linking Burnley and Bolton, crossing the old lane, and a new community came into being at what was then known as Hawkshaw Lane End.

Three mills were built providing local work; Rigg Mill wove cotton sheeting, Kenyons Mill wove towels and Two Brooks Mill bleached the material. Two Brooks Mill was demolished about 30 years ago but its tall square cream stone chimney still stands on the hillside, built above the mill so that smuts would not spoil the finished cloth. The other two mills still provide local work, one is used for dyeing and finishing material, the other for sewing and packing of curtains for mail order suppliers.

The lodges or small reservoirs, constructed to supply the mills with water, filled by the many streams and springs in the area, are still much in evidence, some stocked with fish, others left for wild life. Herons and kingfishers are frequently seen.

111

Hawkshaw has some fine tennis courts originally made by a mill owner for his employees. These have been much improved and installed with floodlighting and a club house. A playing field was also provided and it is here that the Annual Gala is held. A Gala Queen and her attendants are chosen and over two days in summer a variety of entertainments are organised, together with stalls run by various local organisations. Sports are held for all ages with the Fell Race being the most gruelling.

Long before the mills, weaving was done in some of the cottages and work was also provided on the farms and at the local quarry at Quarlton, where coal was also mined. During the miners' strike in 1927 the coal seam was re-worked, which meant the village was never without coal.

Hawkshaw has had some interesting inhabitants, one being Roger Worthington, a Baptist preacher who lived in the 'old' village. He ministered to the local people despite persecution and it was his wish to be buried near his home. The original tombstone of 1709 was broken by a harnessed horse in the 19th century, but in 1935 a new stone was laid beside the old so that the inscription can be clearly read. Today the little grave is set in a walled garden tended by the village schoolchildren and local residents. It is a very peaceful spot in which to rest and look down over the village.

Then there was poor Ellen Strange who was murdered by her boy-friend, a pedlar, on her way back home across the moor from Haslingden Fair. The pedlar confessed and he was hanged at Lancaster and his body hung on the gibbet on Bull Hill. Local people brought stones to build a cairn there and later a memorial stone was erected in her memory.

There are two other memorials on the moor near Hawkshaw, one being the Pilgrims' Cross. A stone monument was erected where the cross once stood, recording its history. The original cross was in existence in 1176 and was a resting place for pilgrims on their way to Whalley Abbey. Vandals destroyed all that remained of the plinth in 1901 and the new monument was placed there in 1902.

The other monument is Peel Tower which was built in 1852 to the memory of Sir Robert Peel, who was born in Bury, to commemorate the services he rendered in the repeal of the Corn Laws. Now that it is restored, it is possible to climb to the top and admire the view.

Times have changed in Hawkshaw. Two small housing developments were built in the 1960s but the stone cottages remain. Many shops have gone but the village stores, the post office, a Methodist chapel and an Anglican church, and two pubs, The Waggon and Horses and the Red Lion provide local needs. The small homely village school is flourishing.

There is a village football team, a Women's Institute, Brownies and Guides, Cubs and Scouts. The Waggon and Horses pub's bowling green is frequently in use and their quiz teams and darts and domino teams are kept very busy.

So Hawkshaw with a population of about 1,000, some of whom work in the village while others travel to Bolton, Bury and Manchester, is still a busy thriving and friendly community of both young and old, in a beautiful corner of Lancashire.

Hesketh-with-Becconsall 🦚

There are differing opinions on the origins of the names of the two hamlets which combine to form the parish of Hesketh-with-Becconsall. However, since the coming of the railway in 1878, the village has become known in common parlance as 'Hesketh Bank'.

The parish is bounded in the north by the Ribble estuary, in the east by the river Douglas and in the west by drainage ditches at Hundred End, so-called because the hundreds of West Derby and Leyland meet here. An ancient boulder known as the Snotterstone stood on the Ribble Marsh to define the northern end of the dividing line. The southern boundary is not as clearly marked near the village centre because housing development intermingles with that of the neighbouring parish of Tarleton.

Parishes bordering the Ribble estuary form an area which is blessed with a temperate climate and is second only to Worthing in Sussex in enjoying the highest quality of light and the most hours of sunshine in this country. This factor joins with others such as top-grade soil to make the parish a most productive farming and horticultural area, though drainage difficulties arise because of the flatness of the land and the high water-table. The Outmarsh at Hesketh Bank links up with the Nature Conservancy Wetlands at Banks so there is an abundance of bird life on the banks of the rivers. Wild fowling used to be a popular pastime but since the Wildfowl Trust established a sanctuary at Martin Mere, bird watching has taken its place. Skeins of geese fly over in their characteristic 'V' formation in the winter months to feed on the Outmarsh during the day and to roost at Martin Mere at night.

The soils of the parish are mainly of three types: heavy clay, alluvial and peat or moss. Heavy clay borders the river Douglas which flows in a northerly direction to join the Ribble and also forms low cliffs along the original shoreline of the Ribble estuary. In addition to giving rise to a

113

brick-croft (now closed), this band of clay prevented water from escaping from the hinterland which was, for ages, an area of marsh, woodland and fen. With time it developed into peat moss and, when drained in the early 19th century, became an ideal soil for the production of salad crops both on open ground and in the many acres of glasshouses erected in recent years. Later, the local landowner, Lord Hesketh of Rufford, reclaimed 2,000 acres of land from the Ribble Marsh by causing successive earth banks to be built. Recently, a further 500 acres have been enclosed. The marsh is now a very productive area devoted mainly to arable crops. Sheep and cattle are pastured here too, as they are on the permanent grassland of the heavy clays. Most of the farmsteads are built on the low ridge bordering the original shore line and look out over the marsh to Lytham St Annes and Warton. Sadly, there are no woods in the parish but there are some precious groups of trees.

An ancient highway, Guide Road, goes in a northerly direction from Shore Road across the marsh towards Guide House at Freckleton on the far bank of the estuary. Prior to the dredging of the river to create a port at Preston, a guide with a horse led travellers, including armies of the Civil War, across the sands and the river thus keeping an important north/south route open. A guide in the 17th century, William Tomlinson of Warton, petitioned the Lancashire Justices of the Peace for financial help to purchase a horse as he had lost ten in the course of his duties and was impoverished.

Many Hesketh Bank residents earned their living on the river or at sea. Fishermen caught dabs and salmon and gathered cockles. Mariners plied their boats along the coast to Ireland carrying coal, slates, iron, bricks and even gunpowder. The rector still receives £2.82 per annum to say prayers for mariners. At Becconsall, beside the old church which is a Grade II listed building dated 1764, lies the Douglas Boatyard which provides berths and services for ocean-going yachts and pleasure boats but originally had a more mundane purpose. Here also is Ferry House in which the ferryman or woman lived. They rowed travellers across the Douglas for the princely sum of 1d. Nearby, Becconsall Hall stands in the fields. A stone over the door records that 'John and Lucy Milineux built this house. Anno 1667 TH'. When she became a widow, Lucy married Robert Hesketh and her property became part of the estate of the Hesketh family at Rufford. In 1915 the Hesketh Bank estate was sold by auction, mainly to the sitting tenants.

To replace Becconsall church, which became too small for the needs of the parish, a new All Saints' church was built in Station Road in 1925. It adjoined the Old Rectory which is now a residential home for the elderly. The Hesketh family donated the church tower which is surmounted by a weather-vane, a golden dolphin. Annual services were held in Becconsall Old Church but since deterioration in its fabric made it unsafe, they have been held in an adjoining field.

The Parish Council manages a field known as 'The Poor Marsh'. It was bequeathed to the parish to enable poor people to support themselves by cultivating an allotment. There are 24 allotments which are seven ridges wide and stretch the length of the field, about 80 yards. This generous provision enabled local families to begin their farming careers on the Poor Marsh and to gradually establish themselves on viable holdings.

Since the closure of the Southport/Preston railway line in 1964 and the installation of mains sewerage, there has been much residential development. The railway station situated near the Tarleton boundary became the village 'centre'. The line still divides the parish in two. Three large housing estates and seven or eight smaller ones and many single infill houses have been built. This increase has placed a strain on all the services, especially the roads which become congested at school and commuter times.

There is a musical tradition in Hesketh Bank which is reflected in church services, the rousing hymn-singing in the two Methodist chapels and in the concerts given by Hesketh Bank Silver Band. Clubs abound and cater for every interest and all ages and the parish has a church primary school.

Higham

Higham is a village three miles north-west of Burnley. Up to 1930 it was regarded as the metropolis of the Pendle Forest area, with nearly everyone connected with either farming or weaving. At one time there were three mills and there is still one flourishing in the centre of the village. The variety of shops has shrunk to just one combined post office and general stores.

Over the years the village had decreased considerably in size but with the building of a bypass, which opened in 1968, and two housing estates soon after, the village expanded again – and changed in character. New houses meant more children and a new school was built. In 1988 the old school, a listed building, became the village hall, which is run by a

115

committee drawn from the many flourishing organisations within the village.

Higham is also famous for its public house called the Four Alls with an unusual sign depicting a parson: 'I pray for all'; a king: 'I govern all'; a soldier: 'I fight for all'; and a worker: 'I pay for all'. The Four Alls was the centre of the glorious myth of the Balloon Juice Company which was originated by Martin Cook, the landlord for many years, who was noted for his sense of whimsy.

It was Mr Cook, otherwise known as Signor Martini, who launched the Higham Balloon Juice Company together with a small group of close friends and tap-room regulars, as a sort of 'in-joke'. Among the illustrious 'board of directors' was the local paper's Pendleside correspondent at that time, Mr Rennie Lawson.

Word of the miraculous balloon juice soon spread round the village. A local worthy named Billy Cook soon became better known as Monsieur Flashpot Johnson than by his real name. He was a salesman for a mill and always wore spats and a bow tie.

Outrageous claims were made for the balloon juice, the constituents of which were never made quite clear, and members of the manufacturing company were rapidly elevated to a zany sort of elite.

What started out as a private bit of fun in a country pub in the 1920s had reached enormous proportions by the 1930s. News of the company, of new members and new inventions was regularly appearing in the local paper – the *Nelson Leader*. People from far and near journeyed to the headquarters at Higham seeking membership of the company.

The exploits of the company, some of them completely mythical, some of them with more than a grain of truth, some completely true, continued to make news until the 1940s. On the death of the founder the whole magnificent spoof was consigned to the cellars of history, until the Women's Institute started doing some research. Once again Higham is full of memories and stories and discussion about the Balloon Juice Company.

Higher Walton

Higher Walton, as the name suggests, is higher than Walton-le-Dale, its older and much more historical neighbour. It was only after the 'New Road' built in 1809 was completed that Higher Walton really got its name. Previously it was a small hamlet at the foot of Kittlingborne Brow known as Moon's Mill, after an iron foundry owned by a Mr Moon.

Later two cotton mills were built nearby and also terraces and streets of houses for the workers.

The whole village lies astride the A675, three miles from Preston and eight miles from Blackburn. The river Darwen which supplied the water power for the mills, augmented by the 'Manybrooks', flows through the village, under the Cann Bridge on its way to join the river Ribble at Walton-le-Dale.

The cotton mills which gave employment to the majority of the villagers have been owned by various people and companies but among the most generous were the Rodgett family, who met the whole cost of supplying and building All Saints' day school in 1864 and who gave the land and £1,000 to build All Saints' church in 1862, as well as providing many beautiful items for the interior. The church with its high steeple and large white-faced clock stands proudly on the hill overlooking all the village.

The Dewhurst Company which followed the Rodgetts was equally keen on following the tradition of social welfare for their employees, and provided a reading room where daily newspapers including the *Times* and *Manchester Guardian* were available for all. In addition hot baths could be had for a charge of 6d or a game of billiards, snooker, dominoes or cards. Also boating and swimming were allowed in the Mill Lodge. The company even supplied a pavilion to be used as changing rooms and summer galas were organised and prizes offered to both ladies and gentlemen. The ladies had their own bath-house near the mill gates. All these buildings still exist, used for different purposes, but alas the lodge has been filled in and is now a car park for the foundry.

Another place of employment for the men was Bannister Hall Works where cotton cloth from Spinners (Crown Agents) next door was dyed either khaki or blue. Khaki (Urdu for dust) dye was first produced by Mr F. A. Gatty who owned the works and a Manchester businessman who discovered that iron oxide made the dye permanent. In 1890 khaki was adopted as the official colour for British Army uniforms. Many other countries soon followed their lead.

The former Moon's Mill Foundry is still used for the same purpose with a much expanded and thriving business. The cotton mill, the existing building erected in 1860, is now an industrial estate being used by many and varied small businesses. The Bannister Hall Works closed in 1964 and has been partly demolished. The area is now used by an animal feeds firm and a large haulage concern.

Higher Walton is best known for the fact that the internationally famous contralto, Kathleen Ferrier, OBE was born here in 1912, the second daughter of the local headmaster, and baptised in All Saints' church. Plaques to mark the events appear both at her former home and near the font in the church.

Another claim to fame is the Higher Walton hand bells, first purchased in about 1906 but not used from the First World War until 1962, when they were restored by a dedicated band of ringers who now perform at various venues throughout the county and also at rallies much further afield.

Osbaldeston House, built in 1661 for William and Dorothy Osbaldeston is still inhabited, although it has changed hands many times during the ensuing years. Bannister Hall, built in the same period, became a farm and is now reduced to the ground-floor level and used as farm buildings. Was it haunted by the Bannister Hall Doll? Strange noises and footsteps have been heard and door latches have opened without human hand upon them!

Hoghton ✎

The history of Hoghton can be traced back to the Saxons, the word meaning literally 'the township at the foot of a hill'. The name first appeared in a deed dated 1160, when it was spelled Hoctonam.

Hoghton village has no centre as such, but the Boar's Head pub could claim the central position, lying midway between Quaker Brook Lane and Dover Lane. A road which has linked Preston and Blackburn from ancient times, passes through the length of the village and travellers in past centuries would have passed through an environment almost identical to that which we see today, a lovely pastoral area, varied with woodland and stream.

Hoghton Tower, a 16th century fortified mansion, stands 560 ft above sea level, and being visible for miles around, is the dominating feature of the village. Much has been written of the ostentatious entertainment which Sir Richard de Hoghton gave to King James I in 1617, when it was reported that the King knighted a particularly delicious loin of beef. Sir-Loin it has been ever since. Following three days of lavishly entertaining the King and his retinue, Sir Richard found himself in a debtors' prison. The motto of the de Hoghton family 'Malgré le tort' 'In spite of the wrong', seeming particularly appropriate for the occasion.

Facing the impressive half mile drive to the Tower is the Hoghton war memorial, which remembers the villagers who gave their lives in the 20th century. The original drive to the Tower ran alongside the 17th century Royal Oak pub, the present drive only being opened in 1901.

In the 18th century the population mainly consisted of yeoman farmers and their labourers, together with tiny communities of handloom weavers in Hoghton Bottoms, Riley Green and other small hamlets. A rocky gorge leads down to Hoghton Bottoms and this area is a reminder of how closely weaving and agriculture were combined. The river Darwen powered two mills by water-wheel and yarn was produced for the weavers working from their pretty cottages in Chapel Lane. The mills originally operated as cotton spinning mills, then were later used as weaving sheds, only closing down in 1971. Weaving was not the earliest industry in Hoghton, Alum Scar, Alum Wood and Alum House being reminders that the de Hoghton family had an alum mine, on licence from the King. The Tower quarry and the Duxon Hill quarry provided stone for buildings and local houses and roads; both quarries are now closed.

The East Lancashire Railway runs through Hoghton and the three arches of a fine viaduct, erected in 1826, tower 116 ft above the rocky bed of the river Darwen. Hoghton railway station was closed in 1960. Modern commuters travel by road to their city jobs, motorway links making quick and easy connections from a rural area to the town centres. Another village pub is to be found on Station Road, aptly named The Sirloin and dating from the 17th century. Small housing developments have taken place around Station Road, Gib Lane and Quaker Brook Lane, pleasantly varied modern houses and bungalows. In Chapel Lane a small number of contemporary houses contrast with stone cottages. These cottages are known as 'The Barracks' following some Roundhead troops being billeted there in 1651.

Hoghton Tower, a 16th century mansion

In the hey-day of canal traffic, a boatyard was opened on the Leeds–Liverpool canal, giving employment to the local men in the building and repairing of barges. The last launching was in 1958 and it is now a marina for pleasure cruising.

The Anglican parish church, known as Holy Trinity, was founded in 1823 by the Parliamentary Commissioners and then given a completely new structure in 1887, by the generosity of the de Hoghton family. Prior to the church being built, the chapel or the Grand Hall in the Tower were used for services for the villagers, many of them travelling considerable distances by traps, gigs or on horseback. Some of the de Hoghton ancestors are buried in a modest plot in a corner of the churchyard. Close by is a headstone bearing the name 'Gatty', a gentleman who perfected the khaki dye for use in warfare uniforms.

The de Hoghtons financed a school for Hoghton children in 1883, which was built across the road from the church. The children paid 1½d per week for the privilege of attending school, as well as paying for their books, slates and pencils. Boarders were also accommodated for a while at the school. The old school house is now a private dwelling and the children attend new schools in Coupe Green and Gregson Lane, both short distances from Hoghton.

The oldest Wesleyan chapel in the North-West is to be found in Chapel Lane. It was built in 1794 from local stone from the Tower quarry, and houses the pulpit taken from Clayton St Chapel in Blackburn, from which John Wesley preached during one of his visits to Blackburn.

Hoghton is fortunate to have a post office/shop and a petrol station/shop to serve the immediate needs of the villagers. The village hall, built in 1976, is the meeting place for most of the activities in the village today and is well used by villagers, as well as outside organisations. Hoghton boasts a sports field and pavilion and enjoys facilities for cricket, football, bowling and tennis, the keen and enthusiastic teams being well supported.

Hoghton Tower has recently been chosen as a top tourist attraction, winning an award for being an outstanding example of the very best in attracting visitors in Britain today, and the villagers are justly proud of their heritage.

Hoole

Two adjacent parishes – Much Hoole and Little Hoole – combine to make the village of Hoole, straddling the A59 south of Preston. The name is derived from the Old English for 'shed' or 'hovel'. The river Douglas (or Asland) borders the village on the west, rising in the moors around Wigan, and was used extensively at one time by shipping engaged in foreign trade, including conveying coal from Wigan to Ireland and the north of England. It is known that there was trade with Holland, the supply of 'Hollands' (gin) and Dutch lace not always being 'official' – thus accounting for tales of smuggling and secret passages. Legend has it that there was a castle at the south (Much Hoole) end of the village, Manor House Farm (once moated) being in this area.

One of the most notable buildings is the parish church, dedicated to St Michael. The most certain date available for the building of the present church is 1628, although it is believed there was a chapel at Hoole in 1280. Built of what is believed to be Dutch brick, an interesting feature is a wall-sundial proclaiming 'Sine Sole Sileo' ('Without the sun I am silent'). Inside the church is a hatchment of the Rothwell family, land-owners and lords of the manor of Much Hoole, Richard Rothwell receiving the title of Count de Rothwell from the future King of Italy in 1860. Their estate was sold to tenant farmers as recently as the 1950s.

There is also a memorial to the memory of Jeremiah Horrox (or Horrocks) who was curate during 1639/40. At the age of 21, during this period, he calculated and witnessed the transit of Venus across the sun, thus achieving a place of fame in the history of astronomy and a tablet to his memory in Westminster Abbey. Horrox's success led directly to Captain Cook's voyage to observe the transit again in 1769 in Tahiti, from where he went on to discover Australia and explore New Zealand. Horrox paved the way for modern space travel and one of the craters on the moon is named after him. Buried in St Michael's churchyard is John Stananought, who was also acclaimed as a mathematical genius; whilst in London during the Napoleonic wars his eccentricities and learning caused him to be suspected as a French spy.

Methodism commenced in Much Hoole in the early 19th century, when a local preacher opened a granary over his own home for worship, progressing to the use of a weaving shop for services, and in 1848 they set out to build a chapel.

Hoole has always been a farming community, embracing dairying, beef, poultry, horticulture and, latterly, mushrooms. Some of these producers are traders at the local markets. For more than 100 years there has been a joinery business and woodyard and a more modern industry is that of manufacturing swimming pools. Many of the present day residents commute to the towns of Liverpool, Manchester, Southport and Preston to work. In the 1950s the landlord of one of the village's three traditional old inns – the Rose and Crown – was Albert Pierpoint, official hangman.

Time was when cockfighting took place in the village, youths from neighbouring villages challenged Hoole lads to fights on Club Days, and people went 'May Walking' on the first Sunday in May, washing their faces in the dew. The churches still hold Walking days and memories extend to the times when the procession would finish round the lawn of the rectory, children being given presents of nuts. At weddings it was customary for a rope to be tied across the road leading from the church, thus halting the carriage of the bride and groom who would throw coppers (or 'scrumps') to the waiting children. Games had their seasons (and still do to a certain extent). In the days before roads were so congested with motorised traffic children played many seasonal games, such as skipping, marbles, hopscotch, whip and top and bowling hoops.

The original Lancashire dialect is still used by some of the older people and, although with the influx of new residents speech is becoming 'urbanised', there are those who try to keep the dialect alive – so . . .

> We're fain to 'ev remembered th'owden times,
> Wi' thowts o' legends, places, folks and ways;
> We've putten news o' wod we're doing now
> An' end wi' gradely hopes for future days.

Hornby 🌿

The picturesque village of Hornby lies in the Lune valley, nine miles from Lancaster and seven and a half miles form Kirkby Lonsdale. The name Hornby is of Danish/Viking origin.

Today it boasts a fine castle, an unusual church – facing its Catholic counterpart across the road, an early castle site at Castle Stede, two schools, two public houses, a bank, a post office, three shops, a garage, a fire station, a police station, a bowling green and a tea room.

The village naturally divides into two halves, the bridge over the river Wenning forming the divide. Most of the older houses lie to the south of this bridge. To the north, the castle and its estate buildings, together with the two churches, tend to dominate, although much of the new housing also exists here.

Station Road is named from the old railway station which was demolished in 1968. This is actually part of a much older drove road

Hornby Castle

leading up to the high fells of Roeburndale. The roads meet at the fountain outside Lambs Garage where a natural spring wells up. Above the basin is the crest of Mr Pudsey Dawson depicting a cat holding a rat in its mouth, dated 1858. The story goes that during the 19th century the castle was left empty for several years and became infested with rats. The owner, Mr Pudsey Dawson, brought in a large number of cats to help rid the castle of them.

Hornby owes its origin and very position to the owners of the castle and their predecessors. The castle itself has an imposing site, standing on a high mound overlooking the river Wenning. The present castle is mainly of 16th and 19th century construction, but the lower parts of the tower are thought to date from the 13th century.

Further up the road St Margaret's church has a most unusual octagonal tower, built by Sir Edward Stanley, Lord Monteagle, in the 16th century. The tower was built in fulfilment of a vow, that if he returned victorious from the war against the Scottish invader, he would honour his patron saint, St Margaret. Thus the church tower can be seen as a thanksgiving for the victory of Flodden Field in 1513.

The church contains two fragments of pre-Norman crosses decorated with loaves and fishes which originally came from a monastery on the site now occupied by Priory Farm.

Across from the church is the war memorial, which has been erected on the base of the old market cross, the site of a market under the protection of the castle during the Middle Ages.

Just down from the war memorial is the Catholic church of St Mary. From 1811 to 1851 the eminent historian Dr Lingard was Catholic priest at Hornby and here he wrote his *History of England*. We get a more personal glimpse of him from the fact that the shell of his pet tortoise *Moses* is still lovingly preserved in the presbytery.

Just on the edge of the village to the south is a large stone building which was once the workhouse. Built in 1894 it was capable of accommodating 87 people, although the average number was 18. It contained its own hospital and mortuary. One of the last residents who lived there as a child speaks of the cruelty and beatings meted out to inmates. The workhouse later became offices for the Rural District Council, but now it has been converted into private houses.

Hornby today is a thriving, close-knit community with activities catering for all interests and age groups. Today many of the villagers still follow traditional rural occupations, but both the university and the power station at Heysham have brought newcomers into the village.

Hurst Green ✤

The lovely village of Hurst Green lies in the 'green and pleasant' Ribble valley, between Preston and Clitheroe.

In 1647 Cromwell passed through the area to engage the Royalist army at Preston. Many stories are told about him, but it is a fact that he crossed the Hodder and encamped his army in Stonyhurst Park because he issued a pamphlet describing his movements. The stone bridge at Lower Hodder however, is popularly called Cromwell's Bridge even though the bridge had already existed for more than 80 years before that time.

Some of the most important benefactors of the village were the Shireburns. Richard Shireburn built the almshouse and school and it is recorded that his son, Nicholas was a man of great humanity, sympathy and concern for the good of all mankind.

In 1794 the Jesuits came to Stonyhurst and used the Shireburn stable as a chapel until the present beautiful church of St Peter was built. Stonyhurst College is a well known public school, still providing employment for many of the village residents.

Many years ago, in addition to farming, the main industry was handloom weaving and there were three bobbin mills in the village. The only one of these still in use has turned its activities from bobbin making to plastics.

The village has had its share of 'characters' over the years. One was Joe Walmsley who was the village blacksmith and an excellent craftsman. Children were fascinated to watch him in action. There has been a village policeman for over 130 years and one claim to 'fame' is that the last woman to be hanged at Lancaster was from Hurst Green – she poisoned her husband with arsenic.

Tourism came to Hurst Green long before the councils promoted it. Waggonettes brought visitors, and cycling enthusiasts stayed in local wooden chalets. Various cottages provided teas. There were two ferries across the river, one at Trough House which has now been replaced by the bridge at Dinckley, and another one was Hacking Boat near Winkley Hall farm. Prospective users would stand at the river bank shouting 'boat' until the farmer ambled his way down to take them over the river on their way to Whalley.

Hurst Green Brass Band was a joy to listen to and existed for almost

100 years. Many families were proud to wear the blue and silver uniforms but it has sadly not been heard for many years.

Club Day has always been a special day in the life of the village. Organised by the members of St Peter's Guild, it used to be a great day for the children of St Joseph's when they had a holiday from school and there was all the fun of the fair in the village. In addition to all the excitement there was the delight of seeing coloured lights before many of the children had electricity installed in their homes. The day is still recognised by the men from the Guild walking up to the church, accompanied by a brass band, for a special Mass at St Peter's tide.

St Joseph's RC school is believed to have the longest unbroken tradition in the county. St John's Anglican church has celebrated its 150th anniversary, being established in 1838, and the whole of the community share most activities.

The highlight of the past few years has been the installation of a bowling green, which is now a very popular meeting place on warm summer evenings.

Inglewhite & Whitechapel 🎋

The village of Inglewhite is situated off the main A6 road between Preston and Garstang. Its chief feature, perhaps, is the triangular green on which stands the market cross. The green is divided by five lanes and the main Inglewhite Road, and is surrounded by a few gracious 17th century houses, a smithy and the well known Green Man Inn. The cross is some 10 ft high and inscribed on the stone is 'H.C.I.W.1675', the initials being those of the lord of the manor.

Famous annual fairs were held at Inglewhite. A toll-bar stone can still be seen, and Lord de Tabley, another lord of the manor of the 17th century, claimed the tolls – 2½d a head for cows and the same price for a score of sheep! An early 19th century vicar of Goosnargh stopped the holding of fairs on a Sunday, not surprising as the practice of bull-baiting was active on the green.

Where Sanderson's the joiner's now stands, there was once a workhouse. The present Congregational chapel of Inglewhite was built in 1826 over a pit known as a chucking pit, a form of punishment.

The site of the former holy well of St Anne, famed for its healing properties, was on land belonging to Longley Hall.

Going along Button Street and Trotter Hill (the latter so named because horses were trotted there prior to sale) one comes to Whitechapel. The parish, which includes Beacon Fell, forms part of the greater parish of Goosnargh. The Knights of St John of Jerusalem owned property here, the present Lichurst estate once belonging to them.

There are several houses of historical note, still occupied and the land farmed. Bullsnape Hall was once part of a greater Elizabethan manor, whilst Whitechapel Farm occupies the site of a small Franciscan monastery. Here lived the Heskeths who helped finance the building of the present Hill Chapel of St Francis, visited by Cardinal Basil Hume during its 150th celebrations in 1988. Ashes Farm still stands where one John Threlfall lived in Tudor times. Nor was it all farming in past centuries, for Button Street and Silk Mill Lane are a reminder of the industrial past of Inglewhite.

Today Whitechapel church and school are the centre of much activity in a fairly sparsely populated area. The original school was established in the church in 1705 by a linen weaver from Goosnargh. The present school accommodates some 60 to 70 children, and is a short distance from the church, a busy place where in addition to learning, the children and staff are valued members of the community.

Inglewhite and Whitechapel villages are still small as regards population. Nearby Goosnargh has more development. Farms and dwellings are more scattered in the two former hamlets. A few choice dwellings have been built or extended and barns modernised, but both remain essentially rural communities, where one can still find solitude and the wonderful peace of the countryside, magnificent views and rolling fells.

Ingol 🌿

Ingol has never been a typical village. It has developed from a scattered rural district to an active community within an urban area.

The records of the area are few, the first being a mention of the land in a report of the Commissioners for the Domesday Book in 1086. Part of the old Roman road from Ribchester ran along what is now known as Cadley Causeway, Tag Lane and across the Cottam Brickcroft and behind St Margaret's church. For several centuries it was sparsely populated with just a few farms and two or three more substantial dwellings.

The religious troubles of the 16th century brought Richard Haydock's family and home at Cottam Hall to public notice, as information was given that he practised the Roman Catholic religion there. It is recorded that in 1745 the chapel at Cottam Hall was destroyed, and the priest, Reverend Father Harrison, was found hanging from an oak tree in Cottam Hall Lane. Older residents link this incident to the name of 'catch meadow' given to a field nearby. The Haydock family still lived here in 1774 when George Haydock was born in Tag House. He became a distinguished biblical annotator and after a chequered career he retired, as Father Haydock, to Ingol where he died in 1848.

But still there appears to have been only a few scattered farms, a few cottages and larger properties such as Tanterton Hall. People were probably fairly self-sufficient, or travelled to the market in Preston for any other needs.

After the First World War, soldiers returned to settle down to a new life and Ingol became a poultry-keeping district. Gradually more houses were built, though still rather scattered and with no focal centre. By 1925 some residents felt there was a need for a communal meeting place and St Margaret's mission church was built. This was a dual purpose church and village hall, built from asbestos-type sheets and internally boarded with wood. For many this was the start of community life and Ingol really became a village at last. Sunday school was started, and in 1928 Ingol Women's Institute was formed.

The brickcroft, originally founded at the time of the construction of the Preston to Lancaster canal in 1797, now restarted to satisfy the local demand for bricks. A shop and a post office were opened. A small library, run by volunteers, was held in one of the rooms at St Margaret's mission church. Six boxes of books that had been collected from the County Library were placed on card tables. Library night also became a social occasion when the men of Ingol met and discussed poultry keeping and tomato growing. Some years later a small collection of books was kept permanently in St Margaret's hall and the County Library provided staff for it.

With a population of about 900, the community paid for a District Nurse (who was also the midwife), by collecting 1s 6d a quarter from those families who wished to belong to the Nursing Association. Her help and advice must have been very welcome but her round of visits must at times have been hard work. Tag Lane, much narrower than it is now, was the only paved road. All other lanes were cinder tracks that often became impassable after rain, due to the heavy clay soil.

Methodists, who previously had met in a private house, opened their church in 1937; but Ingol did not have a Catholic church until the Holy Family was built in 1964. The Mother's Union started in the late 1950s, and the modern St Margaret's church was built in 1966.

128

After the Second World War, social life flourished, and a drama group was formed in 1949. Rural Ingol began to fade away. Ingol now became an urban district and began a steady expansion with the building of council and private housing estates. Surprisingly, the first school was Tulketh High (a secondary school), opened in 1964. It was another four years before the Ingol County primary and Catholic primary schools were built. There is a row of shops and an attractive small library. In 1978 HRH Duke of Edinburgh arrived by helicopter to open the Rehabilitation Centre, which provides facilities found in only one other establishment in England.

For many people who may never have known the old rural Ingol, social life now centres on the two social clubs and the pub. Perhaps the only trace of Ingol's former green fields to remain will be the golf course constructed in 1981, and its many associated public footpaths.

Inskip with Sowerby

The name Inskip defeats the experts. The most favoured suggestion is that it may mean the island where wicker baskets are made. There is certainly a field of willows at Sowerby and many willows in the hedgerows. As the area is marshy, and Sowerby itself means a village or farmstead on marshy soil, Inskip may have been an 'island' of drier land. Both villages appear in the Domesday Book.

Between Elswick and Catforth, Inskip is still predominantly an agricultural village. Though post-war housing developments have brought in commuters working elsewhere and retired people, Inskip has not increased in population as dramatically as some other Fylde villages.

Relics of the Civil War, in the form of Cromwellian swords, were dug up in the 19th century but no record of local involvement survives.

Rushlight making and handloom weaving once supplemented agricultural earnings and Inskip Mill once ground the oatmeal in which the Fylde specialised. There was also a watermill which ground cereal for cattlefoods and a brickcroft made bricks for repairing the houses on the estate of Lord Derby, a principal landowner. A hooping-stone, used for fixing the ironwork on cart wheels, stood in the village street and was in use at the beginning of the century. In the 1930s a cheese factory was started, later becoming a provender store.

During the Second World War, the Fleet Air Arm set up HMS Inskip, a radar station which still operates. The masts dominate the skyline from almost anywhere in the Fylde.

St Peter's church was built in 1848, paid for by Lord Derby and Archdeacon Hornby, of St Michael's on Wyre. The first record of a school dates from 1848 but the present school, opened in 1953 and twice since extended, had as its nucleus an old radar station given by the Ministry of Works.

The Baptist chapel was opened in 1817 on land provided by Lord Shuttleworth. Until then baptisms had been performed in the mill dam and Baptists had worshipped in a room in an inn in a neighbouring village. Each year since the centenary year of 1917 an annual convention has been held at the chapel, an event still drawing many to hear eminent preachers. It is known as the Fylde Convention.

The Parish Council now owns Carr's Green, the 60 acres of common originally owned by Lord Derby, and on which grazing rights were granted to smallholders according to the acreage of land farmed. The green yields many wild flowers and some rare grasses beloved by flower arrangers.

Today, Inskip has a regular hourly bus service but it once relied on a one-horse bus carrying twelve people and running from Great Eccleston to Preston on Wednesday and Saturday. Once a woman with her donkey was a familiar figure on her weekly way to Preston market. Now transport is somewhat speedier. But there are still families in Inskip who have farmed for generations and although some change has been inevitable there are still many links with the old Inskip of yesterday.

Kirkham 🦜

Kirkham is situated roughly midway between Preston and the coast at Blackpool. There is evidence that the Romans were at Kirkham and that a road connected it with the fort at Ribchester. There is also evidence of even earlier settlement in the Fylde and the Kirkham area, as Bronze age artefacts have been preserved in the peat and mosses.

The first charter was granted in 1296, making Kirkham a Free Borough with the right to hold a market and fairs, and have a prison, a pillory, ducking stool and gibbet. At the Dissolution of the Monasteries, Henry VIII granted the manor and the church patronage to Christ Church, Oxford who are still the patrons of the mother church of St Michael. There has been a Roman Catholic chapel at the Willows since 1809 and Congregationalist worship dates from 1805. It was 1844

130

Kirkham market place

before the Methodists had a chapel, many worshipping in nearby Freckleton before this.

The present lordship of the manor is an interesting survival, with the right to engage a town crier for important occasions, and to hold a weekly market and grant permission for public holidays.

In the 18th century two firms of flax merchants became important employers and the merchants themselves were important in Kirkham, serving on all the committees and holding office. The firms of Hornby and Hankinson and Shepherd Langton and Birley dominated the town for much of the century but after about 1830 only the Birley descendants of the earlier merchants continued in prominence. The firm was now known as John Birley and Sons and as both Langtons and Hornbys had left Kirkham, they had no local competition. The mill finally closed in 1895, but it had altered the face of Kirkham with the workers' cottages and the grander houses of the employers. The families of Langton, Hornby and Birley intermarried and their various branches were influential in the district as well as in the town.

The town boasts a cobbled Market Place in the historic centre, used for markets and fairs since 1296. A feature of this is the Fishstones, which records show have been positioned there since at least 1683; the present Fishstones date from 1829. A lamp stands in the centre of the Fishstones, a gift of Thomas Langton Birley in 1872, and recently restored by the joint efforts of the Local History Society and the BNFL apprentices from Salwick.

Kirkham grammar school came into existence in 1551 and was originally a low thatched building. The school was saved from extinction through the years by various bequests and trusts. Today it is housed in a fine building, opened in 1911, taking both boarders and day pupils and in recent years has admitted girls. In the 18th century some girls were taught in the school until the Master refused to allow them to attend, so their inclusion is not as modern an idea as might seem!

Club Day, which began in the 19th century, is still an event in the town, usually occurring on the second Saturday in June. All the churches combine to take part in a colourful procession, ranging from the toddlers to those whose proud boast is that they have taken part for over 50 years. Relatives return from afar for this important family day in the Kirkham year. In the afternoon there are sports activities and in the evening a carnival procession through the town.

Old towns spawn characters easily. At the turn of the century it was the Muffin Man plying his wares, and the bell-ringer heralding the latest news of losses, fires etc. The tradition is ably carried on today by several 90 year olds. One such, as recently as 15 years ago, housed his two cows in a shippon behind his terraced house and, bringing them in from grazing, held up the traffic through the main street, riding leisurely behind them on his cycle. He claims his longevity is largely due to the fact that he has never had a drink past his lips, never a cigarette between his fingers, and never kissed a woman in his life!

Much development, both in property and business enterprise, has come to the town these latter years, but Kirkham, with its historic past, the friendliness of its people, and its easy access to both countryside and the Irish sea is a truly delightful place in which to live.

Langho ✤

The village nestles at the foot of Langho Fells and extends westwards towards Dinckley Brook, dominated to the north-east by the prospect of Pendle Hill, traditional haunt of witches. The name is Saxon, and thought to come from the battle of Billangho fought here in AD 798.

The original small village, now known as Old Langho, has an old Anglican church built of stones from Whalley Abbey in 1537. Some of the stones are carved and there is some ancient glass in the south-east window. Surrounding it is the old churchyard where the forefathers of the village sleep in peaceful tranquillity. There, too, is the old National school, now a private dwelling. Nearby is Brockhall Hospital where many of the residents of the more modern village work. Others commute to nearby towns.

The 'modern' village has grown enormously in recent years, there being six new estates of houses and bungalows created since the 1960s. This more recent Langho, a little over a mile from the old village, first developed in the early 19th century when the road from Blackburn to Clitheroe was built and, later, a cotton mill opened. The stone terraced cottages which straggle the road were built to house the mill workers. The mill closed many years ago and on its site there is a bright, modern pub, the Spring Mill, named after the factory.

Scattered farms, dating from the 17th century, are still occupied, but the fields belonging to them now house the new estates. Some of the farm buildings are of interest, housing shippon, barn and dwelling under one roof in the typical Pennine style of construction.

Roman soldiers used to march from their fort in nearby Ribchester up what is now York Lane in Langho to visit their rest camp and warm springs in Whalley. Many Roman coins have been found in York Lane. The old Roman road, with its stones and cobbles well defined has, sadly, been covered with tarmacadam. Ghosts of these Romans are said to haunt this district.

The most famous resident of the village was the late Jessica Lofthouse, lover of Lancashire and prolific writer on the countryside and local history. Invariably hatted and scarved, she was a stalwart of tradition, a great raconteur, former president of the Women's Institute and a woman who made the Ribble valley known worldwide.

A colourful character seen around the village some years ago was 'Old Roger', a gentleman of the road. Wearing a number of hats, enveloped in layers of old clothes and carrying a back-pack, he caused no problems at all. It was said that he was an educated man, scion of some noble family, but no-one ever really knew his history nor, sadly, his ending.

In former centuries, social life revolved round the church, school and Black Bull Inn in Old Langho. Children from outlying farms were christened in the church, educated in the school house, grew up, danced in the schoolroom, met their friends, married, reared families, worked the land and were eventually buried in the churchyard. It was a closely-knit community. Likewise, the mill workers of the 19th century formed a close community although the coming of the railway in 1850 from

Blackburn to Clitheroe gave Langho its own station and made travel more easy. There is now a small residential development on the site of the station, which was made redundant with the closure of the line to regular passenger services in 1964.

Social life still centres round the churches and schools, just as the school in Old Langho was used over a hundred years ago. The inns are still very popular meeting places and, happily, all within walking distance of the houses, old and new.

Plans have been made to build a village hall which would serve as a focal point for the community and various activities. Until that becomes a reality, Langho will carry on as it has always done – a friendly, happy village.

Lathom 🌿

Lathom is situated in West Lancashire just north of Ormskirk and almost equidistant from Liverpool and Preston. It is a small rural community which grew around the estate of the Earls of Lathom.

It is an agricultural area and, other than farming, the only local employer is Pilkington Brothers, glass manufacturers, who have a research station there.

Until early this century most farms reared some stock and Lathom was noted for its prize dairy herds. Today most farms are arable and crops include potatoes, sugar beet, rape seed and vegetables for the frozen food market.

At Spa Farm there was once a well with an interesting history. A holy well dedicated in the Middle Ages to St Mary Magdalene, it became known following the Reformation, as a mineral spa. Local people washed in it and brewed beer with it and the water was said to have healing properties. A book written in 1670 by Edmund Borlase claimed the spring water cured asthma, dropsy, gonorrhoea, worms and consumption. It was said that many locals, including the Countess of Derby, obtained relief from 'taking the waters'. In 1850 the well was covered over and drained into the workings of a local colliery (long since closed). All that remains is a slight dip in the lawn at Spa Farm.

The most significant change in Lathom came about in 1924 when the third and last Earl sold off the estate. Fortunately, some farms were sold to tenant families. Until a few years before that, most of the community who weren't employed in farming, would have worked for 'the family'

134

on the estate. The local school was provided by the first Earl for the estate workers' children, and the household sent its linen to the school each week to be mended by the schoolgirls. (There would not have been much mending done on Mondays as the attendance registers show that the girls were kept at home to do the family wash).

The first Lathom House, home of Lord Stanley, Earl of Derby, was besieged by Cromwell's troops in February 1644. It was then bravely defended by the Countess, Charlotte de Tremouille and her household but was finally plundered and destroyed in December 1645. The earl was executed at Bolton for his support of the Royalist cause.

The present Lathom House – one wing only remains – is situated in Lathom Park which is the core or centre of the community. Here also is the ancient chapel of St John the Divine, consecrated in 1509, and ten adjoining almshouses built for the chapel bedesmen. The chapel was slightly damaged in the Civil War, but bears her scars proudly. It is a beautiful gem of a building in a lovely setting and attracts many visitors. Local families have worshipped here for centuries and there are services twice each Sunday.

The first Earl of Lathom, second Baron Skelmersdale, was a family man much loved by his tenants and workers. He was very interested in agricultural matters and instituted an annual Lathom Show, which was the highlight of the year for the community. He entertained on a grand scale and Lathom House provided shooting and theatrical productions for his guests, most famous of whom was Edward, Prince of Wales.

The second Earl appears to have been more reserved and less flamboyant than his father and preferred home life and outdoor sports, but his only son Edward, third Earl of Lathom – Ned to his friends – was said to be obsessed by the stage and theatricals. He had some success in writing plays, but they tended to be too explicit and one, called *Wet Paint* was banned by the censor. In 1920 he provided a wooden building called 'The Lathom Club' to be used by his tenants for social gatherings and functions. He staged concerts there for his own friends, including Ivor Novello, Gladys Cooper and Noel Coward.

The third Earl moved to London after the estate was sold, and died there in 1930 at the age of 35. So passed the earldom bestowed by Queen Victoria on one of her favourite Lords-in-Waiting. Happily, the club, the park and those things unique to Lathom, remain, so far, for us all to enjoy.

Lea 🦢

Lea (pronounced Lee-ah) is four miles west of Preston and north of the river Ribble. Today there is little material evidence of the historical association of this part of the rural district but it is interesting to note that Lea with the present day spelling was mentioned in the Domesday Book.

In ancient times the district of Lea was divided into two hamlets called French Lea (presumed to be through the Norman settlers) and English Lea, the estates of the de Hoghtons. It was divided by the middle course of the Savick Brook. It was mostly agricultural land but many farms have merged or disappeared altogether and flats and houses now occupy the land. There is still a prize-winning farm run by Mr and Mrs Cross of Lea Town. There are three schools, four public houses, a Catholic church, a Methodist chapel and an Anglican church, and there is a very helpful police station. A lot of the land is still owned by the de Hoghton family and this includes the Ashton & Lea golf club.

Along the main Preston to Blackpool road is a listed building known as Old Lea Hall farmhouse. Probably dating from at least the 16th century, part of the original old timber frame can be seen, reaching from the ground to the loft. The farm also belongs to the de Hoghton family, but has been worked for the past 80 years by the Goodier family. The most prominent historical incident of the tenancy of Lea Hall was in 1589 when a Thomas Hoghton was killed in a night 'affray' over a family feud, not uncommon in Queen Elizabeth I's time.

Who would have thought that a 'Will Shakeshaft' (Shakespeare) was named among Thomas Hoghton's singing boys at Lea Hall during the 'hidden years' of the young poet. Or that the way from the Hall to the shore of the river Ribble, which once could be seen from the Hall, had dark secrets, as when a Hoghton in 1568 fled to Flanders with his family, taking a boat from Lea by night and never returning. Or that men landed at Lea, unmarked, to be passed inland by secret ways to safe retreats in penal times, when a papist priest was forbidden to perform his duties.

Part of the 42 mile land-locked Lancaster Canal passes through Lea, but thanks to a lot of hard work put in by members of the Ribble Link Trust, negotiations are being completed to join it to the rest of the canal system by the new Ribble Link. The canal bank is very popular with ramblers and wild life enthusiasts. Many birds such as herons, curlews, kingfishers and blackheaded gulls can be seen and also wild animals. It is also very popular with fishermen.

In Lea Road stands a roadside cross passed unseen by many 'in memory of the pioneer of restoration of roadside crosses of Lea Lodge and Catherine Mary his wife.' This anonymous gentleman was Thomas H. Myres, FRIBA, architect, archaeologist and lecturer. From 1871 he took a very active part in the social and religious life of the town. He was greatly interested in the restoration of roadside crosses and succeeded in restoring 16 throughout Lancashire. It was fitting that a cross should be erected in his memory.

Leck & Cowan Bridge ॐ

As the name implies, Leck & Cowan Bridge are two distinct communities. Cowan Bridge straddles either side of the very busy A65 Skipton to Kendal trunk road, whereas Leck is a hamlet nestling on the lower ground before its rise to the high fell, the northernmost point in Lancashire.

Leck Beck rises out of Leck Fell and flows gently down until it meets the Lune at Burrow, eventually flowing out into Morecambe Bay. Each year the salmon make their epic leap to spawn upstream and make a spectacular sight. Underneath Leck Fell is a labyrinth of pot holes, caves and passages, known as the Lancaster Pot system. For those who prefer the sky as their roof, there are spectacular walks on the fells. Leck Fell House is the highest farm in the parish at a height of 1,300 ft above sea level.

Leck is derived from the Norse 'Locke', meaning brook. Cowan Bridge has a much younger place name – 'Collingbrighe' from a personal name 'Colling'. Both villages have seen minimal housing development in recent years.

Cowan Bridge has always spanned a busy main highway through from Yorkshire into the North West area of Kendal and beyond. As early as 1511 tolls were being gathered from Cowan Bridge but it was 1751 before the Skipton–Kendal turnpike was completed. The turnpike gate just east of the parish (no longer there) was called the 'Wallhead' Gate. Much road widening and straightening out has taken place recently, making an exceedingly fast and busy road, especially at weekends with the flow of traffic to the Lakes. The old road bridge now quietly spans the beck and stands as a reminder of days when there were fewer cars.

The railway through the village was built in 1861 to link the Ingleton line with Low Gill. There was a large construction gang lodging in the

137

village at that time. This must have brought many changes to village life; milk could be sent daily to the dairies, each farmer taking his churns by horse and float to the station, and where daily papers were thrown from the moving 9.25 am train. The line was closed in 1966, but not without a celebration on board the last train when Victorian dress was worn by many.

There has been a chapel of ease at Leck since the 17th century, Tunstall being the mother church, but it was in 1879 that a fine church was built at a cost of £3,000 with money donated by the parish, and dedicated to St Peter. Carelessness caused a fire on the night of 21st October 1913 and the church was completely destroyed. Work to rebuild the church was quickly started and dedication took place on 26th March 1915, now with a spire instead of a tower.

The Methodist chapel in Cowan Bridge was built in 1862, and in 1904 the schoolroom was added, with many children given a holiday from school to attend the laying of the foundation stone.

The Clergy Daughters' School was founded in 1823 by the Rev William Carus Wilson. Amongst its many pupils were the daughters of the Rev Patrick Brontë of Howarth – Maria, Elizabeth, Charlotte and Emily. The Clergy Daughters' School was closed in 1833 and moved to its present site at Casterton.

There is one village shop/post office with petrol pumps, two joinery businesses, two haulage firms, builders, farmers, an agricultural contractor, two private hotels, a gamekeeper, estate workers and an expanding sheepskin warehouse which employs over 100 people from the surrounding area. Parishioners also find employment in Kirkby Lonsdale, Lancaster, Kendal etc. In the past the village has been served by a blacksmith, cobbler, tailor, publican, miller, cordwainer, baker, carrier etc and its own police constable since 1861.

There are some fine old properties, but perhaps the largest and most imposing is Leck Hall, a seat of Lord Shuttleworth. The esate was bought in 1771 by Robert Welch, who was responsible for reclaiming and improving the land, planting trees and generally laying the ground work for the appearance of the area today. The Hall as it is today was rebuilt in 1801. In 1952 the late Lord Shuttleworth and Lady Shuttleworth bought Leck Hall, moving from the ancient family seat of Gawthorpe Hall, near Burnley.

There is a good village hall which is well used by the community. How we wish we could buy ham for 10d per lb as they did for a social in 1908! The village also boasts a new Youth Centre. In the past it had a tennis court, bowling green, billiard room, library, cricket and football teams.

Little Eccleston with Larbreck 🐌

Although less than half a mile separates Little Eccleston from Great Eccleston it has never been closely associated with its larger neighbour administratively. Nowadays it is within the borough of Fylde while Great Eccleston is in Wyre. Until 1849 it was in the parish of Kirkham while Great Eccleston was within the parish of St Michaels of Wyre. It has always been fiercely independent of its greater namesake and guards its separate identity jealously.

In the Domesday Book it tags after Eglestun as 'alia Eglestun' (another Eccleston) and Larbreck is not mentioned. Larbreck is a hamlet some mile or so beyond Little Eccleston.

Little Eccleston Hall was the home of the ffrance family from Elizabethan times until the later 18th century and, now a farm, remains largely in its original form. Larbreck Hall, originally the home of the Molyneux family of Liverpool, was even older but was demolished some 40 years ago and completely rebuilt on the same site.

The Gillows were resident in Little Eccleston, inhabiting Malt Kiln Farm and other property nearer the river. The Gillow charity, founded in 1697 and augmented in 1720, provided from rents for annual payments to the poor at Christmas. A new housing complex is called after this family.

The Cartford Hotel, by the toll bridge over the Wyre, is reputed to have a ghost who interferes with the arrangements of the inn, switching on lights and moving objects.

Larbreck once had a well which was visited for the medicinal qualities of the water. No such pilgrimage is made today, but the name of Well Lane bears witness to the past.

Little Eccleston was a centre of Quaker worship. In 1718 a Quaker meeting house was built on land already used, from 1669, as a burial ground. The house, appropriately named Quakers' Rest, has been modernised from the original building but retains something of the character. This area of the Fylde was a haven for the persecuted of all non conformist sects penalised by the Established Church. Its remoteness from the authorities was much in its favour.

Old cottages and farms, interesting in their atmosphere and individuality, have been joined since the Second World War by houses of some style, making the village an interesting amalgam of the ancient and modern. Two caravan sites have brought visitors, several of whom have chosen to settle in the neighbourhood upon retirement.

With its ghosts, historic buildings and modern houses, Little Eccleston is in no way overshadowed by its greater sister, even though the amenities of 20th century living are largely sited in the larger village just down the road.

Longridge 🌿

Longridge is approximately seven miles north-east of Preston, on the southern edge of the Forest of Bowland, with Clitheroe and the Ribble valley to the east, and Chipping and the Loud valley to the north. It sits on the lower reaches of Longridge Fell, with Beacon Fell and the range of Parlick and Fairsnape forming a beautiful backdrop to the north. As one approaches from Preston, the first sight of Longridge on the hillside is quite impressive. It is said that the Dog Inn (a public house on Market Place) is level in height with Blackpool Tower.

Since local government reorganisation in 1974, Longridge is under the administration of the Ribble Valley Borough Council, with headquarters at Clitheroe. At the last census in 1981, Longridge had a population of 7,151.

The town as it appears today is largely a result of the Industrial Revolution, which made its impact in the second half of the 19th century and centred the community on Berry Lane. Before 1750, the centre of Longridge was near the parish church of St Lawrence on Chapel Hill, but then the population expanded and shifted during the 18th and 19th centuries, first to Market Place and then to Berry Lane in the 1850s. Longridge's first stone quarry had opened on Tootle Heights in 1830, leading to the building of the Preston to Longridge railway in 1840, to transport the stone to Preston. (The Harris Library and Museum, and Fulwood Barracks are two notable buildings made of Longridge stone). The railway in turn led to the opening of four power-loom mills to weave cotton.

Many of the stone-built terraced houses so prevalent in Longridge were built to house the mill workers. Longridge has some fine old houses, especially in Market Place, King Street and Higher Road. In particular, 'Club Row', a row of 20 listed terraced cottages, numbered 4 to 44 Higher Road, was built in the 1790s by some quarrymen who formed themselves into a club, into which each member paid a fixed weekly sum. With the pooled money, they began to build a row of cottages and as each cottage was finished, they drew lots to see who should occupy it. In this way 20 cottages were built at a cost of £138 3s 6d each. Club Row is now the oldest group of Building Society houses surviving today, and is mentioned in the Guinness Book of Records.

Housing development in Longridge has continued over the years, and several housing estates have been built in and around Longridge since the 1960s to accommodate natives and incomers alike. Many of the terraced houses on Berry Lane are now used as shops and offices.

The cotton mills have long since closed, and the surviving buildings house newer industries. The railway has gone, the quarries are no longer worked, and a caravan site has taken over on Tootle Heights. But newer industries thrive, small family businesses, offices and shops provide employment for local people.

An interesting local legend is that of the Written Stone. At Written Stone Farm an 8 ft long stone is inscribed with the words 'Raiffe Radcliffe laid this stone to lie for ever AD 1655'. At a later date it was moved by the farm occupiers, and used as a buttery stone. But the pots and pans would shake and spill and topple off, so the stone was replaced.

Longton

Situated in the borough of South Ribble about five miles south of Preston and the same distance north of Leyland, yet in a quiet rural setting, Longton is a good place to live.

The old village has seen many changes from when the Anglo-Saxons settled in Longetuna, their long village, almost inaccessible through bogs, marshes and frequent floods.

Although by the 17th century most people were still farmers, there were tradesmen and craftsmen, such as blacksmiths, millers, shoemakers, drapers, nailers, fishermen and innkeepers working in the village. Most families brewed their own ale and many were beginning to eke out a living by spinning and weaving on small domestic hand looms.

The shape of Longton was still that of the linear village on either side of the Preston to Liverpool turnpike, but the village was changing socially. In the early 1820s agriculture was in a distressed condition, life was difficult and many had to apply for relief under the Poor Law. In 1821 the Longton workhouse was built, but it was closed in 1839.

In 1837 Longton was described as a desirable place to live – by the end of the 19th century it was a thriving village with the newly built St

Andrew's church, Primitive and Wesleyan Methodist chapels, schools, shops, mills, public houses, brickworks and the new brewery.

In 1882 the Longton Bridge station was built. The railway opened up a wider world to the people of Longton – and also opened up Longton to a wider world. Several middle class families built rather grand solid houses here, using the railway to commute to work in nearby towns.

Like the railway train, the motor car made a huge, but a more lasting, impact on the village as all the traffic between Preston and Liverpool passed through. Eventually, after many complaints and frustrating delays the bypass was constructed – but not until the middle 1950s!

Throughout the two World Wars, and the Depression, Longton remained a rural community, providing its own entertainment in the Walking Days, Club Sports Days, the Folk Dancers, the St Andrew's Brass Band, the Women's Bright Hour, and the WI. The War Memorial Playing Fields were bought and used by local clubs.

In 1961 there were 3,884 inhabitants of Longton – by 1971 there were 8,022! Extensive estates of detached and semi-detached houses and bungalows were built on either side of Longton's Liverpool Road, changing the face and shape of the village almost beyond recognition.

But the increased population brought advantages – a new primary school, health centre, sewage works – and much later, in 1980, a library. New shops and offices were opened as well as residential homes for the elderly.

In the 1970s there were plans for an even larger development of over 700 houses on the derelict site of the Bentley brickworks. The Longton Village Protection Association was formed to fight the proposal, which was eventually quashed. Although some houses are being built on the Bentley estate, the water-filled clay pits have been cleared of rubbish, the immediate area landscaped and made into a conservation area, much appreciated by local inhabitants – including those with webbed feet!

Longton is still surrounded by farms, market gardens, nurseries and chickens, it is still a village, a friendly caring village where people matter.

Loveclough

According to one local historian (Newbigging) 'Luffeclogh' was the spelling in the year 1473. In the reign of Henry VII Rossendale ceased to be a Royal Hunting Forest by Royal decree, and about eleven vaccaries (cattle farms) were set up and rented out to some of the local inhabitants.

Loveclough was one of these vaccaries, and was valued at £5 in 1604.

Surrounding vaccaries were Gambleside, Goodshaw, Crawshawbooth, Dunnockshaw and Constablee. Although in the very early days they were separate entities, they have developed together over the years, and it is now somewhat difficult to write about one without making reference to the others.

There is still in existence a Loveclough Fold situated on the Limy stream between Hameldon Hill and Swinshaw Moor. One of the buildings bears a datestone 1714. This building is being restored, and it is to be hoped that the character of the place will not change, as it did dramatically when Loveclough Textile Printing Works was first built alongside the Fold, discharging industrial effluent into the Limy Brook. Today the brook is much cleaner and is beginning to support fish, but a great deal of industrial pollution will have to be removed before the brook returns to the bright clear stream of bygone days.

Whichever way one looks in Loveclough one cannot help seeing hillside and valley with farms scattered amidst fields partitioned with dry stone walls. Much of the land is still farmed, for cattle and sheep mainly, and milk production.

In the past there were many farms and hamlets engaged either full or part time in handloom weaving, spinning and other textile crafts, but all this came to an end with the advent of the factory system, when many streams were used to power water wheels, and were afterwards superseded by steam power, with the consequent introduction of the factory system.

There is much industrial archaeology in Loveclough and its environs, ranging from lead and coal mines to stone quarrying and textile mills, both early and more recent. But man was here from the earliest times, and evidence of Stone Age settlements has been found on surrounding hill tops.

Present day industry is something of a mixture – plastics, engineering, car breakers and repairers, slippers, cartons etc, and is often located in small units in old mills which were previously used for the manufacture of textiles. Some of these industries are still situated alongside the Limy Brook, others form a part of the strip development alongside the A682 road.

Of the original vaccaries not much is left except perhaps a pile of stones where once they stood. Gambleside has gone, but its location can still be viewed by an ancient track in the fields across Clowbridge Reservoir, marked by a clump of trees and the North West Electricity

Board pylons. Gambleside was a flourishing community in the 18th century, being close to the ancient road from Pontefract to Clitheroe. Higher on the moor within a few score feet from the more recent Comptons Cross are the remains of two ancient wayside crosses which are believed to have marked the junction of two old packhorse trails.

Goodshaw village has now largely gone, but the parish church is still there, built originally about 1546 and rebuilt in Victorian times. Goodshaw was the centre of religion for the area for a long time.

The Baptist chapel at Goodshaw is now part of our national heritage, and is under the care of the Department of the Environment. Its early congregation removed to Goodshaw mainly from the villages of Water and Dean in the adjacent valleys where they had previously worshipped. They decided to bring their chapel furniture with them, together with their musical expertise and accomplishment. The village of Dean earned a high reputation for its choral and musical abilities, a reputation which gave the name still remembered today to 'Deighn Layrocks' (Dean Larks). The tradition lived on, and Rossendale still has a high reputation for music, notably in the Rossendale Male Voice Choir.

Within half a mile to the north of Goodshaw chapel is the old dower house (now a nursing home) of the Towneley family of Towneley Hall, Burnley who featured many times in our turbulent national history, and suffered much persecution for their adherence to the Catholic faith. Nonconformists also suffered persecution and nearby at Crawshaw-booth is the Quaker meeting house, which was built in 1716 at a cost of £60. The Society of Friends still use it. There is also a Quaker burial yard on nearby Chapel Hill, though not now used, where Quakers met in 1663. Crawshawbooth also has an architectural gem in St John's church, built in 1890 by the local Brooks family (Lord Crawshaw), nestling in a wooded glade, and referred to locally as the Crawshawbooth Cathedral.

What of Loveclough now? Many new housing developments are taking place, housing commuters to Manchester and nearby towns. Hameldon Hill has grown radio communication masts and local papers from time to time report sightings of UFOs. However, Loveclough is still a beautiful place, indeed its beauty has been enhanced by the closure of much of the old time industry. It is sad, however, that so much industrial despoilation has been allowed to remain, and many modern industries and farms are blameworthy in adding to the despoilation. It will take a supreme effort on the part of everyone to restore the Limy Brook to a clear unpolluted stream, and the countryside and valleys to the pristine condition of which they are worthy. But come to Loveclough, it will be well worth your while.

Lowton ✒

The name Lowton comes from a corruption of the word 'Llaw' which means hill or undulating ground. So Lowton means 'a high town' and not, as one might expect, a low-lying town. The first mention of the village comes in an old deed which probably dates from the 13th century. It records the conveyancing of land from one Richard Stephen to his daughter and her husband.

Lowton began as a farming village and the women had the reputation for being the best cheese makers in the county. One farmer used to say that anyone who ate the bread and cheese made by his wife 'ud never dee'. Home industry came in the form of silk and muslin weaving. Some of the old silk cottages still stand. Earnings were very low but Lowtoners then, as now, valued their independence and when their cottage industries were threatened during the Industrial Revolution, many joined the Chartist movement. Some of the Chartists were imprisoned and the stocks, which still stand, were well used. However, despite all this, cotton mills grew up in the nearby town of Leigh and the home weaving stopped. Coal mines, too, were opened in neighbouring towns and provided employment both for men as miners and some of the women as 'pit brow lassies'.

Lowton these days has little industry of its own. The inhabitants travel to their work. Atomic Energy, the prison service and the few pits and engineering works are the main employers now and they are all outside the village.

Years ago there were many customs and traditions in Lowton which have now been lost. 'Barring out' was a great occasion for the boys of St Mary's school. On the last day before the Christmas holidays, the older boys would arrive early and fasten up all the windows and doors. When the headmaster arrived he was handed a note saying he would not be admitted unless he promised that there would be no lessons for a fortnight. Of course, a holiday was immediately declared. Royal Oak Day and St George's Day were observed. Any child not wearing an oak leaf on Royal Oak Day would be chased and, if caught, slapped on the legs with a bunch of stinging nettles. On May Day, scholars danced round a maypole in the school playground. The churches and chapels still have their walking days and Rose Queen celebrations.

Lowton was also a sporting village with football and cricket teams. In Victorian days, Lowton men were famous for their running, jumping and skating. They even skated for the Championship of England which was held in the Fen country. Unfortunately, the fen men proved too good for the Lowtoners and they were beaten. Nowadays there is yachting on Pennington Flash and walking in the beautiful Pennington Country Park, part of which is in Lowton.

In 1883 the only Lowton murder occurred. The murdered man had the reputation of being a 'nowty mon'. He was a brutal and hard taskmaster. He quarrelled bitterly with his nephew and his wife who worked for him. One morning the nephew found the farm door locked and when he got in through a window, he found his uncle dead. His throat had been cut. Bank books belonging to the dead man were found at the nephew's home and he was arrested and tried. At the trial one juryman was taken ill and the judge and counsel had a private consultation. The judge advised the jury to bring in a verdict of 'not guilty', so no one was ever convicted. The dead man's ghost is said to have been seen wandering about his fields at dead of night.

There is a very attractive modern church dedicated to St Catherine of Siena and an old church built in 1732 dedicated to St Luke. It is a small pleasant cruciform church and the clear glass windows in the aisles give it a light and pleasant feeling. The east window is of stained glass and is Victorian.

Just within the boundaries of Lowton lies Byrom Hall. Brick built and three storeys high, it was constructed during the 18th century and was once surrounded by a moat, crossed by a drawbridge. The Byroms of Byrom Hall were of the same family as John Byrom who wrote the hymn *Christians Awake*. Lime House was the home of Peter Eckersley who played cricket for Lancashire. It is now a delightful residential home for elderly people.

Housing now fills what was once good farming land and the village seems to grow day by day. But it is still a green and pleasant place and the old Lowtoners still retain their independent and industrious character.

Mawdesley 🌿

Mawdesley is in rich farming country, the soil varying from heavy clay to rich peat moss. It is bounded by the river Douglas, Sid Brook and Bentley Brook, is skirted by the railway and canal at Rufford and is sheltered from the east by Harrock and Hunter's Hills. The land is undulating, apart from the mossland, which is low-lying and there are about 25 miles of twisting, country roads.

There are some extremely interesting properties in the village. Mawdesley Hall, built on an outcrop of red sandstone, was, for many generations, the home of the Mawdesley (or Mawdsley) family. The house is of two storeys, originally built in the 16th century, but much altered towards the end of the 18th or beginning of the 19th centuries. The central hall is Tudor and some of the inner walls are wattle and daub. The south wing is built in red sandstone, taken from the quarry opposite and the north wing is constructed of small, hand-made bricks, from the now disused brickworks in nearby Bluestone Lane. One approach to the Hall is up stone steps, dated approximately 1613, which have a preservation order. A 'white lady' is supposed to haunt the Hall.

Next door is the Black Bull Inn, originally Bamford House, the home of that family. There are a score of amusing tales connected with it. Some used to call it 'Hell' or 'Hell Hob', as it houses a famous poker, 16 lbs in weight. 'Surely big enough to stoke and poke the fires of Hades', to quote Jessica Lofthouse. Opposite, there is a group of old cottages, known as City House, City Cottage and City Farm. They were originally built with small windows, undulating roof lines and low-browed eaves, but are now modernised.

At the other end of the village is Lane Ends House, built 1590, the ancestral home of the Finch family. It was a Mass centre, which helped the Roman Catholic faith to survive in the locality, through times of persecution. The dwelling, with its chapel in the attics, is a three-storeyed building, constructed chiefly of the local hand-made bricks, with tiny-paned windows, now almost covered in ivy. Chief among the heirlooms is a skull, reverently preserved in the chapel. This relic is said to be of William Haydock, monk of Whalley Abbey, executed in 1537. When persecution ceased the old chapel continued in use, until the present Roman Catholic church was built in 1831. Had not the Finch descendants restored this chapel in 1966, it might have gradually sunk into oblivion.

Several other buildings in the village are of early date and are usually named after the original tenants. Ambrose House, formerly Bradshaw House, built 1577, in Bradshaw Lane, Barret House Farm (1695) in Back Lane, Back House Farm (1690) on the edge of Mawdesley Moss and Jay Bank Cottage (1692), to name but a few. Worthy of special mention is Bluestone Farm (pre 1697), situated in the lane of that name. A large blue boulder, reported to have been scored in the Ice Age used to stand at the roadside near the farm. It was removed during road repairs and taken to a tip, but retrieved by a resident of the lane and is still to be seen in his garden.

Mawdesley has three churches today. The parish church of St Peter, Mawdesley with Bispham, which celebrates its 150th anniversary in 1990, the Roman Catholic chapel of St Peter and St Paul, built 1831, and the present Methodist church, built about 1905. An annual event, first started in 1874, is the Tea Party. Members of the parish church, Sunday and day schools attend a short service, walk in procession through the village and then enjoy refreshments on the Rectory field, where a fair is held that evening and on the following Monday.

Agriculture, the growing of willows and basket making were the main occupations of the past. Five generations of the Cobham family were basket makers in the village. The famous Lancashire cricketer, Jack Iddon, who was born here, was the grandson of Robert and Ellen Iddon (nee Cobham), basket makers of New Street. Today, there are several, varied businesses, which are thriving. The village has grown considerably during the last 25 years. The majority of the population are professional people, who commute to the nearby towns, or use the motorway network, which is a few miles distant.

Mellor 🦢

Originally called Moel from the Celtic word for a small round-topped hill, Mellor stands at the top of a 733 ft hill overlooking the panorama of the Ribble valley.

Standing as it does Mellor was ideal for the positioning of a Roman signalling station. Near the ruins of the signalling station, are ruins of early Christian worship. If one places an ear to the ground, especially on Christmas Eve, it is said that the sounds of bells can be heard.

Mellor inhabitants were called 'Mellor Poots' or 'Mellorites' and continued to farm the land during the Industrial Revolution. Handloom weaving and spinning featured greatly in Mellor cottage life, but at harvest time all helped getting the hay in safely. Many children from the workhouse on Mellor Moor were apprenticed to work with the weavers.

As spinning and weaving ceased to be cottage industries and the work went increasingly to mills containing power looms, Mellorites became angry at the change, many joining the Luddite movement. At this time Ralph Miller the village blacksmith not only shod horses but produced pikes for use in the Luddite fight against the installation of these machines, which many thought would take away their living.

Elswick Mill (a weaving shed) employed about 150 village people at the turn of the 19th century, which saw the building of a Wesleyan chapel, the founding of the parish church of St Mary and the building of day and Sunday schools in 1833. Mr Daniel Thwaites, the lord of the manor gave the land plus £500. He also gave St Mary's its first peal of bells. The roof of St Mary's was soon found to contain bees and when opened up yielded several pounds of honey! Attendance of school-children differed greatly in 1835, the day school had 76 pupils whereas the Sunday school had 276 pupils, due to children having to work during the week.

Mellor's poor benefited by a donation of £1,000 by Miss Nancy Hargreaves on her death in 1898. Life now revolved round the land to a lesser extent, the mill and quarry occupying many people in work. Road conditions had improved but water was still pumped from springs and wells around the village. The population in 1901 was 1,111 and there were still 62 farms.

The 20th century has probably seen the greatest changes in Mellor life. Modern conveniences of water, electricity, gas, telephone and tarmaca-damed roads have made Mellor life much easier.

In 1929 a Recreation Club provided cricket, tennis, bowling and football, later the land was sold for building new bungalows. Mellor's only Agricultural Show was held in 1924 providing keen local competi-tion and rivalry. The Women's Institute opened in 1920 with 17 mem-bers (one of the first to be formed in Lancashire).

The adult population in 1989 was 1,897. The school rebuilt in 1883 is now replaced by modern buildings, likewise the Wesleyan chapel has twice been replaced and is now an attractive modern edifice.

Characters like Chocker, Long Bob, Cumberland Dick and Bovril no longer tread Mellor's paths. Mellor is no longer the quiet village of long ago, but a highly desirable village in which to live.

On top of Mellor Moor bubbles a spring which divides into three streams. One, Showley Brook, feeds the river Ribble, the second feeds the river Blakewater, the third runs westwards towards the sea. Here time stands still; like Mellor it is immortal.

Mellor Brook 🌿

Mellor Brook is a small friendly village which straddles the A59. It derives its name from the brook which runs through the village and eventually joins Bezza Brook, which in turn runs into the river Ribble. By no means can it be called a picturesque village but it has a warm and friendly atmosphere. There is no central feature to the village (no village green, cross or war memorial) but it is full of quaint nooks and terraces. It is hard to define just where the village starts and finishes, and although it has grown in recent years the amenities and shops have dwindled.

The Fieldens Arms public house is the only remaining inn. It stands on a blind corner on the A59, it bears the scars and scrapes of traffic mishaps. In the past many more public houses and working men's clubs were features of Mellor Brook, such as Bridge Inn, which contained a gymnasium so that people could either work up a thirst or work out bad blood. Next door was a toll house.

The village used to boast more shops, even though the population was smaller. There was a confectionery shop in Victoria Terrace and a fish and chip shop on the corner just below what was then the Wesleyan chapel, since converted into flats. Just across from the chip shop was a general grocery shop which was run by a 'bit of a character'. As well as running the shop Mr Ashton was the grave-digger and village barber (you could get a haircut at 3 o'clock in the morning). He could also be called on to lay out the dead and he ran a Christmas Club collecting 1d a week.

Victoria Terrace was once the site of a spinning mill and was also the home of another village character, 'Pump Tom', so called because he was said to have invented a pump which the farmers used in their middens.

In the centre of the village, in a building which now houses Hargreaves Agricultural Contractors, stood the Pack Horse Working Men's Club and a farm which was burnt down in the early 1940s. The local Home Guard used to hold their meetings there. A butcher's shop was once on the site of the present day Britannia Picture Framing Shop and a sweet shop and cafe stood on the opposite corner. Where now stands Sanderson's, the local bakery, there was a greengrocer's shop run by a huge man called 'Tootle' who drove a pony and trap and whose weight used to lift the pony off the ground.

A feature of the village is the rounded corner of Sanderson's shop. One icy winter's morning a Ribble bus taking workers to British Aerospace skidded across the road and knocked down the gable end of the building, which had to be rebuilt. Luckily no-one was injured.

In the old mill building at the top of Victoria Terrace, waste paper was collected by the large stores (Woolworth, Marks and Spencers, Littlewoods etc). It was brought to Mellor Brook by the local coal merchant, T. Hull, and sorted into bales by the women of the village, rebaled and sent back to the paper mill for recycling. The local men earned their living by working in the stone quarry situated on Abbot Brow, owned by the Peacock family, but the quarry has since been filled in by the local authority.

As there were no main sewers or water mains, water was carried in 'Yorks', a wooden shoulder piece with a large bucket at each side. Wells were found in Bosburn Wood and on Mellor and Abbots Brow.

Just how hard it is to define the beginning and end of Mellor Brook is shown in its postal address i.e. Preston New Road Mellor Brook and Preston New Road Samlesbury. People of the village today travel to work in Blackburn or Preston or even further afield, or to British Aerospace, Samlesbury aerodrome, whose runways, hangars and perimeter fence run a few yards from the village.

Mere Brow

Mere is situated in the market gardening plain between Southport and Croston. The site of the village was once submerged under Martin Mere which, before it was drained, covered a wide area. Hence the name. Most of the land is now used for agricultural and horticultural farming, and some very good produce is grown, especially lettuce, tomatoes, celery, potatoes and other vegetables.

Bank Farm is built with hand-made bricks fashioned from clay on farmland in the village. The first Primitive Methodist chapel was built in Mere Brow in 1861 and was used as a Sunday school when the new chapel was built in 1902.

Among the characters who have lived at Mere Brow was Alice Banks (nee Wright) who, at 45, built a house on land owned by Lord Lilford and took out a 25 year lease, thinking she would die at 70. As she lived to be 85 she paid rent on her own house for 15 years! Alice Mayor (nee Lea) spoke in very broad Lancashire dialect and was sought out by university graduates interested in studying dialect.

Moss Side 🦡

Moss Side area is, as the name suggests, moss land, and is a very flat landscape. There are still one or two farms but not so many working farms as in the past, when the farmers of the district had cows and horses and they would deliver milk daily by means of a horse-drawn milk float.

There was a blacksmith's shop in Dunkirk Lane and the blacksmiths were the Nelson family. Many an odd half hour was spent watching all the process of shoeing a horse, from taking the old shoe off to making and putting the new ones on.

St James' church, Moss Side, Leyland

During the Second World War there was an army camp in Dunkirk Lane and the Military Police were there for several years.

The local public house is the Black Bull and originally this was the only one in Moss Side, but there is now another at Dunkirk Hall, which was formerly rather a big house but has now been further enlarged. In Slater Lane there is another big house which was formerly owned by Berry's, the local mill owners, and which the present owners have converted into a rest home.

One villager remembers life in Moss Side in the past. 'My parents were market gardeners and had about an acre of land, much of which was occupied by greenhouses, in which they grew tomatoes as the main crop and mustard and cress, lettuce, radishes, spring onions and shallots. We had several vines growing in the passages of the greenhouses and in the summer they provided us with a crop of both white and black grapes. The produce from the nursery was taken to Blackburn market every Wednesday and Saturday for a number of years. Early in the morning they would set off in all weathers to sell the salads to the Blackburn housewives.

'The Walking Day and May festivals over the years provided the highlight of village life and people came from far and wide to watch, to help, and to take part in the processions.

'The venue in the early days was Worden Hall and we would walk all the way dressed in our best dresses and new white shoes. The very tiny children would travel on a decorated farm lorry accompanied by the teachers. We would have bands from the nearby villages playing and on arrival at the park we were greeted by the staff of "The Hall" who would serve us all with as much lemonade as we could consume. We would all go off to have a look at the gardens and the maze and would be reminded it was time to form up again and set off back, by the beat of the big drum. On arrival back at the school we had sandwiches and cakes and tea, all served by the ladies of the parish.'

Nether Kellet

The earliest record of the village was in the Domesday Book of 1086, when it was called Chellet. The name comes from Kelda, old Norse for a spring, and changed its spelling throughout the 13th century from Chellet, Kelled, Keleth, Kellit and to Nether Kellet in 1299.

About 50 years ago people still got their water from the local well, fed by the spring, both of which still exist. Many home-brewers of ale still use the spring water, because of its purity and the absence of chemicals.

Just after the Second World War the village was still quite small, with a population of about 200. The houses were mostly old farmhouses of the 17th and 18th century, with some cottages and a few council houses. The parish church of St Mark was built in 1879 and there is also a Congregational church. At that time there were only six or seven cars in the village, no mains drainage and no tarmac roads. One small school with 14 pupils served the village well. Now there are five new housing estates, a school of nearly 100 pupils and a population of about 700.

The only public house is called The Lime Burners Arms. Lime-burning was the major industry of the village. Old lime kilns are still to be seen, but once there were 40 of them. Now the local industry is crushing the lime for modern road building instead of burning it.

The village has a thriving social life and 40 to 50 years ago the social life was, it seems, just as enterprising. There were then three football teams – one of them all ladies and to judge from an old photograph, a very pretty team they were too. There was once also a brass band in the village, disbanded it seems during the First World War. Old minutes of the meetings in the reading room tell of many whist drives and billiard matches held to raise money to send parcels to village men serving in the armed forces.

In limestone country there are caves, and Nether Kellet has its own, known as Dunold Mill. In 1760 it was described by a visitor –

'A large stream, which after turning a cornmill at the mouth of the cave, runs in by several beautiful cascades, and continues underground for two miles, appearing again near Carnford (Carnforth). The entrance to this underground channel has something pleasingly horrible about it.'

Great echoes and majestic horror accompanied their underground exploration for two miles. Exploration is no longer possible – just as well! There was, however, a hermit who lived in the cave until he was 100 years old. He must have had a bit of company, as some of his descendants are still living in the village.

In 1860 the village was notorious for cock-fighting, drinking and ruffianism, so perhaps that is why a Sunday school was established shortly after that date. The lady preacher was Elizabeth Bateson, a local farmer's daughter, who now has a memorial house named after her.

154

Newburgh 🦢

Newburgh lies on the Leeds–Liverpool Canal, between Ormskirk and Wigan. The population has more than doubled since three housing estates were built in the 1960s in what was previously a small farming hamlet. Many of the villagers today are professional business people who travel to neighbouring towns, but in the early part of the century most of the villagers were farmers. Coal miners, working in Skelmersdale, also lived here and several bargee families lived in Cinnamon Nook and down Culvert Lane. The bargemen went away for weeks on end and often took their families with them.

The majority of the farms in Newburgh were arable, although nearly all of them kept cows and horses for their own use. Only one cow was sold at the last of the Newburgh Fairs, about 70 years ago. Most households kept a pig which was fed and fattened for their own table. Pigs were reared and slaughtered at Hunter's (now the post office) where Mrs Hunter, senior, turned them into home-cured hams, black puddings, sausages, savoury ducks and pork pies. The bacon was sold as far away as Wiltshire and all her cakes, plus loaves and barm cakes, were baked in an oven fuelled by wood. Most houses had their own home-cured hams hanging in the larder or cooking over the fires.

Shopping was mainly done in the village. Hunter's supplied a host of edibles, the most famous of which was the 'Newburgh Cake', made from a pure butter mix of pastry and currants and moulded into oblongs about 6 ins by 4 ins. Hundreds were made and people came from miles away to sample them. A thriving tailoring business was also carried on here at Hunter's and the tailors could be seen sitting cross-legged in the upstairs window sewing jackets, trousers and even all the gamekeeper's suits for Lord Latham's estate.

A weekly shopping excursion could be enjoyed if you were lucky enough to get a seat upon the waggonette which left Parbold bound for Ormskirk market every Thursday morning. If it was full, people then set off to walk there through Lathom Park. One lady even walked to Preston to buy her butter!

Trips to Wigan Market were a real occasion. The farmers started out at 2 am loaded up with vegetables, and an extra horse was taken along to the top of Parbold Hill to take over at the summit. The tired horse was then taken back home and the farmer carried on to Wigan.

Potatoes were dug by hand, by Irishmen brought over by Ainscough's

Newburgh post office

and billeted in what was known as the Paddie House at Giant's Hall Farm. Strawberries were just as popular during the early 1940s as they are now and the plants were sold all over the country.

In those days, all the village was owned by Lord Derby and rent was paid on a special rent day at the Red Lion.

Newburgh Fair originally began in 1304 and, for the first 600 years, it was held annually on the three days before, during and after St Barnabas' Day – the 10th to the 12th June. Livestock was bought and sold and then stalls and amusements gradually appeared along with village sports and merry-go-rounds. The stalls sold, amongst a wide variety of produce, 'Fairing Cakes' and cheeses. In 1977 the fair was revived for the first time since the First World War, to celebrate Queen Elizabeth's Silver Jubilee. It is held every year now on the first Saturday in June and begins with a procession of floats, all designed and decorated by the villagers. Everyone joins in to make the fair one of the highlights of the year.

Before electricity came to Newburgh in the early 1930s the village streets were lit by oil lamps – one outside the post office, one on the end of the green and one half-way down Ash Brow. Each evening, Mr Greener would walk around the village lighting the lamps.

Life today in Newburgh is far more hectic with the constant stream of traffic pouring along these narrow roads but, apart from the arrival of electricity, gas and machines, the people have remained the same and there is a wonderful community spirit.

Newchurch in Pendle 🎋

Newchurch is a Pennine hill village which squats on a terrace partially man-made. The name originated on 4th October 1544 when John Bird, Bishop of Chester, consecrated the new church of St Mary in Goldshaw Booth. Prior to that a chapel had stood in the village, possibly as far back as 1216. Many villagers worked at farming and weaving. In the year 1826 a survey was carried out in the village which showed it had 769 inhabitants with 387 hand looms. These skilled weavers lived to see their skills taken over by machinery. The one mill remaining in Newchurch is now a carpet mill.

Before the First World War there were two shops in the village, with hawkers visiting regularly. The village had two travelling greengrocers who carried their goods by horse and cart and a butcher whose slaughter-house was behind one of the two pubs in the village. Houses were lit by oil lamp and candle, coal was brought into the village, but many outlying farms used peat and the very poor cooked on open fires.

Newchurch was a thriving, busy village in the early 19th century, with two pubs, two shops, a football team and brass band. The Pendle Forest Cycling Club, which is still going strong, was formed by the workers at Spenbrook Mill. Nowadays, however, times have changed with only one souvenir shop and one pub remaining.

Some traditions are still followed, such as the Annual Rushbearing when dry rushes are strewn on the floor of the church and in the pews to keep the congregation warm. With the advent of central heating this is no longer necessary, but the villagers still process through the village carrying rushes and singing hymns accompanied by a brass band. The Rushbearing Queen is also crowned, and after a short service in the church, tea is served in the school.

One of the characters of Newchurch in the 18th century was a lady called Nanny Maud. She lived in a house at the top of the road out of the village, to this day still called 'Nanny Maud', and at one time she collected a toll from every cart that passed her door, until the carters found another route. Nanny Maud was a 'wise woman', skilled in the use of herbs and the ways of nature. In earlier times she would have been called a witch.

The area around Newchurch and Pendle Hill is well known as being the home of the Lancashire Witches. In the churchyard is the famous so-called witch's grave, reputed to be the burial place of the witch Alice Nutter.

A significant feature of the 16th century church is the Eye of God in the west side of the church tower. This is believed to give extra protection to the parishioners from evil.

With the advent of the newly built motorway, and with many people working in nearby towns, the village is left almost empty during the day. The village school, which had over 100 pupils in the early 1800s now only has 35 pupils, with worries that this number could diminish each year.

Newton with Scales 🖎

Along with Salwick and Clifton, Newton is in the parish of Lund, bordered by the Preston–Lancaster canal, Savick Brook, Dow river (now only a stream) and the river Ribble. All the villages are mentioned in the Domesday Book. Originally the land was very marshy and it can still be seen where the Ribble rose at high tide, as a banking has formed from the marsh to Clifton and Newton. The villages are all on the Roman road running from the settlement outside Kirkham to Ribchester, which explains the historic interest of the parish.

Newton with Scales was originally two hamlets. There was Newton Hall and Scales Hall, the latter being demolished in the 1960s. Newton Hall, originally Highgate Hall, was used as a Quaker meeting house in the early 1800s. During its years it has had numerous alterations and names, and is now one of the two local hostelries, The Bell and Bottle, the other being the Highgate Hotel. The name 'Highgate' still appears on many buildings.

Quite a few 200 year old buildings are in evidence in Newton, but they are not recognisable as the old farms/cottages which they once were. Many of the cottages have been altered over the years. Some started life as one-roomed houses with attached shippons, and others were the dairy, laundry etc belonging to Highgate Hall.

Up until the late 1940s the village was a farming community with many smallholdings, expanding first with a council development and then with private housing. In the 1950s there were 17 worked farms and many garden nurseries, now there are eight worked farms and three nurseries.

Until the 1970s the village shop was part of Moons Cottage in School Lane. When a purpose-built store and hairdresser's were erected in Bryning Lane the village shop closed. Mr Joe Eastham was the local barber for many years, cutting the village people's hair in his barn. There is a DIY and garden centre in what was once a dairy.

The first petrol pumps in the parish were at 'Mayfield Jucntion', erected in the 1920s. The pumps were still in use in 1953, but removed a few years later. The business then transferred to Highgate Garage, which is still a petrol station today. The front of the garage is new, but the buildings at the rear of the petrol station were in evidence before 1845. There were two transport cafes on the A583, one is now a private dwelling and the other an Indian restaurant.

In 1987/8 over 100 houses were erected. With the growth of the village the main work is now out of the area. Quite a number work at British Nuclear Fuels at Salwick and at British Aerospace at Warton, but many commute to Preston and Blackpool, or even further.

Newton Blue Coat school was founded in 1709 by John Hornbie, of Scales Farm, 'to educate boys and girls to 14 years of age'. The main subject was farming for the boys and livestock was kept by the school. The girls were taught academic and household subjects. Until after the Second World War poultry was kept at the school. The old school was demolished in 1969 and a new school built in its grounds. Records are still available relating to the school's beginnings.

Many of the old names have been retained, eg Bryning Lane, originally Brynings Lane, named after the Bryning family of Highgate Hall, and Scales Hall Lane, after Scales Hall. A field off Parrox Lane is still known as the 'pissing hole' from the old word 'pis' or 'pea' – it was where peas were planted. Parrox Lane is the only lane in Newton without buildings.

Newton Clifton & Salwick Field Day is held every year on the 2nd Saturday in July. It began in 1948 and has altered very little over the years. The decorated floats now set off from Clifton, and the Rose Queen is crowned at the school. Before there was such a heavy volume of traffic on the A583, the procession ended in a field by the Highgate Hotel. This is the only occasion the local pubs stay open all day.

Before Lund church was created a parish, funerals took place in Kirkham, and a 'resting stone' can still be seen in New Heys Lane, where the pallbearers stopped for a rest.

Over Kellet 🍂

Over Kellet lies on the old high road between Lancaster and Kendal. Legend has it that a Christian temple existed here in the 10th century, and that a century before that the sacred body of St Cuthbert rested in the village during the seven years of wanderings that followed the destruction of the Abbey of Lindisfarne, before his bones were finally laid to rest in Durham Cathedral. The village is mentioned in the Domesday Book as Chellet, but by 1206 it had become Kellet. The name Over Kellet means 'higher hill spring'.

The parish church of St Cuthbert has an old embattled 14th century tower which was renovated in 1863. Until recently, after the morning service on Good Friday, the village children would climb out on to the top of the tower and sing *There is a Green Hill Far Away*. An old font was found in the gardens of Hall Garth (the Georgian manor house on the green) and was restored to the church, so that it now has two fonts.

Close to the church are two dated farmhouses, Birkland Barrow and Kirk House. Birkland Barrow is said to have been a monastery long ago and there is still a bell hanging at the side of the house which may have been used to call the monks to prayer. In the garden was a malt kiln where the monks were said to have distilled whisky. The house was once owned by the Lee Booker family of Swarthdale House. Earlier members of this family were engaged in the slave trade, and two iron figures of negroes, said to have been figureheads from slave ships, are still in the garden at Birkland Barrow. Rumour has it that an underground passageway existed between Birkland Barrow and Kirk House.

The pedestal of the cross on the village green is very old. Two sets of hinged staples, now sunk out of sight, on the bottom steps held the original stocks in place. The upper part of the cross has been restored. The schoolchildren have planted many daffodil bulbs on the green and these are a very attractive sight in springtime. A large Christmas tree, complete with lights, is erected each year and enjoyed by everyone. Various groups in the village have sung carols around the tree.

At the top of the hill is the tiny Methodist chapel. Until 1880 this was a barn before being converted to its present use.

A house on the village green was a dame school. This old house later became the village post office and is now a private residence.

Over Kellet has had a school for over 300 years. The present school, founded in 1677, was an endowed grammar school built by Thomas

Wilson. Now it is a Church of England primary school. The old school had no playground, so games were played out on the road. There were few cars and hardly any lorries in those days. In 1973 the school moved to new premises and the old building has been converted into two houses.

Limestone quarrying has provided employment in the area for many years. There are still remains of several old lime kilns where farmers would collect lime for their fields, and housewives to whitewash their outside buildings.

The Withers Charity, founded in 1715, benefits children living in the village, giving grants towards education and careers. Originally the charity assisted boys in apprenticeships and girls in service with gifts of tools and clothing. Much of the capital was derived by a toll of one farthing per ton of material quarried locally and which passed over the Trust land.

Old crafts in the village included a clogger. He was kept busy as all the children went to school in clogs – which were well cleaned the evening before. Even the village postmistress walked around the village delivering the mail wearing clogs. There was also a shoemaker, a basketmaker, a butcher, a dressmaker and a joiner who was also the undertaker. All these, together with the farmers, made the village virtually self-sufficient. There was also a well known sweet pea grower who would take his flowers by horse and cart to Carnforth railway station for the midnight train to catch the early morning market in the cities. More recently there was a taxidermist, one of only five in the country.

The village children could buy a halfpenny worth of sweets in a paper poke in the village shop, which was once run by an old lady called Mary Stephenson. The villagers would bring jam jars to her to be filled with treacle and syrup. Mary's cat used to sit on the counter keeping her company, which was not very hygienic but everyone seemed to survive.

Over Kellet has indeed a special charm. It nestles on the hillside with its many old stone cottages dating back to the 17th century outshining the newer developments. There is no finer sight at the end of the day than to stand at the top of the hill and watch the sun set over Morecambe Bay and disappear behind the hills of Lakeland.

Overton

Overton has antiquity, for there are traces of an Iron Age settlement and it was mentioned in the Domesday Book.

Up to 30 years ago when bungalows were built, little had changed over the centuries. Nestling on the estuary of the Lune, with its salmon, it has been a fishing and farming community, self-sufficient by its very setting, often cut off by high tides.

Its lifeline has been the river, one of the sources of which, near Newbiggin-on-Lune and 50 miles from Overton is St Helen's well; here, overlooking the estuary is St Helen's church. It has stood for a thousand years, the bell in the Saxon tower ready to warn in times of danger and its great oak door strong enough to keep out invaders from the sea.

Years ago there was a precarious way across the marsh to Lancaster, but it was safer and quicker by boat. Goods and mail were ferried across from Glasson and in times of need a midwife made her journey to Glasson by post-boat.

Salmon has been fished by haaf-net and from boats, the latter built in the village. When a new boat was ready to be launched the local schoolchildren were given a holiday to attend the ceremony.

It would then be a village of activity and noise, with the sounds of boat-builders, stone masons, quarry workers, a blacksmith, the shoe maker, farm horses and the clatter of clogs on the cobbled street.

Change came in the 18th century when the narrow promontory, with its village of Sunderland Point, became a busy port. Ships were built for Lancaster owners for trade with the West Indies, America and Africa. Some goods were unloaded at Sunderland and taken by road to Lancaster, passing through Overton.

Some handloom weaving was done in the village, for raw cotton was coming into the country. By the riverside lane to Lancaster stands an attractive inn, the Golden Ball, but always referred to locally as 'Snatchems'. Here, the Press Gang was known to operate.

Access becoming easier, the early 19th century brought people in great numbers to enjoy sea-bathing which was beginning to be fashionable. Visitors arrived, the affluent in their own carriages, others by landau from Morecambe, or by pony and trap and horse-drawn carts. Overton became a busy holiday place, with tea gardens, outdoor stalls by cottage front doors, swings and boating.

Visitors nowadays should make for the river after viewing the church.

Take the road past the post box leading into Bazil Lane. This becomes a private road so it is wise to leave the car well before this. There are steps down to the rocky shore. If it is a time of low tide you can walk safely along the track, passing a high bank of wild flowers and seeing haaf-nets stacked. When you see a stile, climb it and you are on an embankment which will keep you above what is often a muddy path. Follow the route by ladder-stiles which will take you to the top of a low hill, Hall Greaves. On a clear day you can see Pilling church and Blackpool Tower. Further away look for Black Combe, many of the mountains of the Lakes, the How Gill fells, and ever majestic Ingleborough. Turning slightly you will see the graceful curve of the Lune as it goes to join the sea. Climb the last stile into the lane, pass the post office to Main street, interesting in itself with old cottages, two inns, two farms and a garden centre.

Sunderland Point, which is part of the parish of Overton, is in another world. The tidal road is about one and a quarter miles long, with restricted speed for cars. It is now a small community of about 30 houses and the only vehicle approach is by the tidal road. At one time it was a fishing and farming community, with some holiday trade. The decline of old industries and the advent of the motor car have altered the way of life. Most of the inhabitants now commute into town for their various jobs, leaving a mere handful of fishermen and only one farming family. What a change from the days when ships arrived with their merchandise, tobacco, sugar and kapok from the West Indies! Some of the vessels carried gunpowder and cannon to protect them from privateers, mooring at the Point where they tied up to posts, one of which remains and is called the Powder Stump.

The cargo was discharged and stored in warehouses, three storey buildings. One is now converted into homes for villagers. The cargo stayed there until it could be carted by horse or ox to Lancaster, taking the windy route across the marshes and picking the way by shifting channels.

Sunderland Point is now peaceful, in that it can't be altered by nature of its position. The residents like it this way; they do not feel isolated, for many visitors come to look around, perhaps searching for the 'Cotton Tree' and the grave of Sambo, a coloured servant, about which much has been written.

You will want to visit this hamlet again and will come to realise, even after an interval of years, that it hardly changes and remains just as magical.

Parbold

Parbold today is a pleasant compact residential village, with three largish estates and several smaller ones filling in the gaps between the old road network, the river, the canal and the railway. It is well supplied with shops, banks and building society agencies along the road past the station. However, all this has developed over the past 100 years.

The old township of Parbold extended up the slopes of Parbold Hill from the river Douglas, where it comes out of the valley from Wigan and turns across the West Lancashire Plain to the Ribble estuary. There used to be four little settlements. The first was around the water mill, by the bridge on the Ormskirk road. Only the Wayfarer Restaurant and a couple of newer cottages are to be found in that corner now. The second was along the river, where the old Douglas chapel stood. Only one farm remains of what was once a busy riverside (and later canalside) community. However, a network of footpaths radiating from the spot were used for centuries by churchgoers, before today's Sunday afternoon strollers.

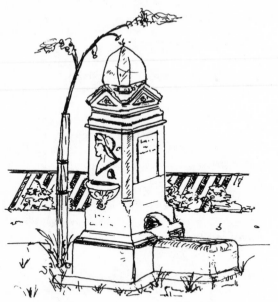

The Queen Victoria Jubilee horse trough, Parbold

Further east is the Gillibrand estate, no doubt a peaceful agricultural settlement until 1742 when the Douglas was made navigable through to Wigan. Then it developed into quite an industrial estate, with extensive quarrying and a substantial coal mine. This area is now an attractive wooded corner of the district. Finally on the top of Parbold Hill stood Parbold Hall, restored quite recently from a ruinous condition but with the nearby cottages now lost altogether. A few scattered farms made up the rest of the picture – only 69 houses in all as recently as 1801.

The Victorian village, centred on the railway station and the canal bridge, boasted a lime kiln, a corn mill, a boatyard and a brickworks – all now gone. However, as well as having an industrial past Parbold developed this century into quite a tourist centre. The Parbold Hill Cafe (now the Wiggin Tree Restaurant) catered for those who wanted refreshment after admiring the breathtaking view from the hill top. Nearer the village centre, the Delph Tea Gardens provided everything a Sunday school outing from Wigan could wish for. Three pubs catered for the cyclists coming out for a country ride from Manchester or Liverpool, and for a time there was even a golf course.

The present church replaced the Douglas chapel when the district became a parish in 1875 – it lies half way up the hill. It served both Parbold and Appley Bridge, the next village towards Wigan, in the days when people expected to walk a mile or two to get to church. The vicar has now moved from the big vicarage below Christ Church into the village, and the school above the church is abandoned in favour of a new one nearer the modern village. There is also a Catholic church, with its school, but no nonconformist place of worship. However, in 1662 John Schofield, minister of Douglas chapel, was one of the first nonconformists. He refused to use the new Prayer Book and was ejected. He founded England's first Presbyterian church at Tunley, in nearby Wrightington.

Parbold is a good place to live in now, with a number of active societies. The Chamber Choir make their own music, while the Music Society promotes professional concerts. The Drama Group, the Historical and Garden Societies are well established, and numerous other groups use the community centre (converted from a surplus government store) and the homelier WI hall. A new addition is a library, on a site reserved for longer than most people can remember. That has provided a plot for the Queen Victoria Jubilee horse trough, the future of which occupied the Parish Council for many happy hours after it was dismantled to make way for the telephone exchange. Maybe all this community spirit dates back to the 17th century, when the local worthies raised a rate for the support of a man disabled in a marl pit accident.

Parkbridge ✌️

Parkbridge lies at the foot of the Pennines with Hartshead Pike as its landmark (thought to be one of the beacons lit along the Pennine chain to tell of the coming of the Armada). It started off as an industrial village with an iron-works at its hub; the ironmaster, strangely for those days, was a woman, Mrs Hannah Lees. Most of the villagers were employed in the various departments of H. Lees & Sons, and lived around the works – rows of small cottages for the workers in the forge, and larger ones with bay windows for the office workers. A ten minute horse and trap ride away was a lovely old manor house at Westerhill for the Lees family, surrounded by large trees and with cottages for the house staff, dog kennels and stables.

This was a happy village in the 1930s, with 300–400 inhabitants, a church, a chapel and an institute built by the Lees family for the men of the village, where they could play billiards, cards and dominoes. There was also a bowling green where the village team entertained others from the league.

A great day was the Sunday school annual trip to the seaside. Almost all the villagers boarded the train with their sandwiches, bottles of pop and cold tea, clean faces, shoes, and best clothes, to return at the end of the day tired, dirty and happy, with traces of lollipop and candyfloss round their mouths.

Whit Friday was when both church and chapel 'walked', each with their beautifully embroidered banners carried on poles by two of the strongest young men. Hymns were sung at every farm and hamlet, and the walks finished at Westerhill House where both groups met and were admitted through the gates up to the front door. Mr and Mrs Lees would come out and sing with them and after handing a donation to each church leader, they would thank everyone for coming to sing for them.

The village had 'characters' too numerous to mention. One was an old man with a donkey and cart who used to collect rags. He wasn't always kind to the donkey, and a strict church lady, Mrs Sharratt, would chastise him whenever she saw him beating it. He was heard, on one occasion, saying to the donkey, 'Wait till I get thee past Mrs Sharratt's'. Always after, as he approached her house, all the children would shout

166

'Wait till I get thee past Mrs Sharratt's'. He was so ashamed that his treatment to the donkey improved considerably.

The ironworks closed after the Second World War and the Lees moved south. The cottages are now mostly occupied by workers from the neighbouring towns of Oldham and Ashton-under-Lyne.

Pendleton

Pendleton lies in a hollow below the 'nick' of Pendle Hill. A street village, the brook wends its way between the houses and farms. Like many English villages which were not consciously planned, therein lies its charm. It is a good working village with the sounds of lambs and livestock mingling with the rumbling of tractors. There used to be seven farms in the village, now with modernisation only four remain. Each has a dairy herd, which must go through the village and along the lanes to their various fields.

Pendleton was mentioned in the Domesday Book, but its history lies much further back than this for in 1969 a Bronze Age urn was excavated. This is now in the Clitheroe Museum.

There has always been an association between the adjacent hamlet of Mearley and Pendleton. Two of the farms are Great Mearley Hall and Pendleton Hall, the latter was the home of the de Hoghton family for nine generations.

High on the windswept slopes of Pendle is Wymondhouses which has a plaque recording that the first Congregational church in North East Lancashire was founded here by Thomas Jollie in 1667. Still higher on the Wiswell/Pendleton boundary is Jeppe Knave's grave. A pauper, he was murdered and no-one would pay for his funeral.

Clitheroe bypass was opened in 1971, separating part of the parish from the village, which was designated a conservation area in 1968. Some of the properties were listed as being of historical interest. Only seven houses have been built in the last 100 years.

A member of the Aspinall family, Mrs Blegborough, had the school built in 1837 and nine years later built the church of All Saints. She also built the vicarage in 1875. The buildings along with Dickinsons Farm circle the green at the top of the village. Unfortunately, the school closed in 1980. Later the vicarage had to be sold and Pendleton amalgamated with Sabden church.

Following the winding street, we come to Old Post Office Row. Here in the 1800s lived 'Little Ellen', the schoolmaster's daughter who kept the post office there. Very tiny, she had never seen a train and on bank holidays her treat was to visit the farm 80 yards away and stay for tea. She retired through ill health in 1912, and died at the age of 89. At the end of this row lay the well, which has now disappeared, where the villagers formerly drew their water, later piped from a spring at Pendleton Hall. The present post office is situated across from the new layby and small green and is still run by a member of the Nutter family who took over from Little Ellen.

There used to be a ford here, spanned by a stone in the shape of a fiddle – and always referred to as Fiddle Bridge. This now lies forgotten and overgrown behind Standen Hall. The road to Wiswell branches off here. During the war there was a searchlight battery known locally as 'Sunset Boulevard'.

In the 1940s there were two shops and a police station; none now remain. Then the Swan with Two Necks was just an inn, but now it provides food as well. In those days, the Miss Lunds of Brook House made afternoon teas. At East View, nearby, lived Mr Cawthorne, an artist whose pictures are now in great demand.

The majority of land and farms are now in the ownership of Huntroyde estate and Standen estate. Old traditions die hard in Pendleton and this to a great extent is the reason that it remains unspoilt and largely unchanged, still keeping its old traditions. In the past there were large families, all working on the land. Later many worked in the mills two miles away. Without transport, the entertainment was at home, concerts, dances, village sports and church activities were the order of the day. Now many visitors find their way here to admire the cottage gardens, bright with flowers, and to picnic by the brook.

Penwortham 🪶

Penwortham has historic roots, its existence being first recorded in the Domesday Book. Christian worship dates back to at least the 12th century with the establishment of Penwortham Priory as an off-shoot of Evesham Abbey. The present lovely church of St Mary dates from the 14th century, although only parts of the original building remain following extensive renovations in the middle of the 19th century.

Penwortham was an ancient crossing place of the river Ribble on the main route from Liverpool to York, and a bridge was built in 1755 – remaining still, with its cobblestones, but used now only by pedestrians. Towards the end of the 18th century a tram-track for horse-drawn trucks, spanning the river, was laid to convey coal from the south Lancashire mines to Preston, for use in its expanding industries, and for shipment, via the canal, to Lancaster and Kendal. This track is still clearly visible today.

At the turn of the century a bridge to carry the Preston to Southport railway line over the Ribble was built, immediately adjacent to the 18th century road bridge. Further upstream the river had been crossed 50 years earlier by a large railway bridge, within the parish, for the main line from London to Glasgow.

In modern times the village has developed in two separate parts, Lower Penwortham, by the 18th century bridge, and Higher Penwortham, round the parish church of St Mary and the priory. A community developed in the former area, and a workhouse was sited there but, later, was converted into a row of dwelling houses. This area was known as 'Bunnock' as the result of a treacle wagon travelling down Pear Tree Brow, on an icy road, coming to grief. Housewives rushed out to scoop up this unexpected bounty of treacle which flowed from the broken barrels. Oatmeal was cheap and large quantites of parkin or bunnock were baked to utilise it.

A large textile mill was built in the late 1800s which became a major employer. Lower Penwortham expanded in the last two decades of the 19th century and up to the outbreak of the First World War in 1914. Many steets of terraced houses were built to accommodate the employees of Vernon's factory. The company's name is now Vernon-Carus and the business has found a niche in the highly competitive textile industry by specialising in surgical dressings.

Large houses were built in the surrounding rural areas; the most notable being Penwortham Priory rebuilt in 1832, and Penwortham Hall owned by John Horrockes, the cotton magnate. The Priory was demolished in the early 1920s to make way for the building of, what we now call, 'executive residences'. This type of development has gathered pace over the last 20 years, infilling the green fields and leafy lanes which hitherto separated the two parts of the village. Contact with the past has been maintained by the retention of old names like Priory Lane, Abbots Way and Monks Walk.

1915 saw the opening of a new wide road bridge, and due to the ever increasing road traffic, and the loss of the Cop Lane railway station, a bypass with bridges over the Liverpool Road and the Ribble was opened in 1985.

The population has increased from 5,000 to 21,000 in the past 60 years, and there are now eight primary schools and three secondary schools in the area. None of these changes has robbed Penwortham of its village atmosphere which is maintained by its schools, churches, clubs, associations and two libraries. There are now two Anglican churches, St Mary's and St Leonard's; the Roman Catholic churches of St Mary Magdelene and St Teresa; Penwortham and Kingsfold Methodist churches and the United Reformed church.

There is an 18 hole golf course and a leisure centre which, at present, is expanding to include a swimming pool. There are several good shopping areas. An annual gala is held each June and many groups participate to make this a highlight in the calendar.

Penwortham boasts its own coat of arms, in the centre of which are three water bougets, representing the three principal wells which served the villagers before the building of the water tower. Although now unused, this is still a well known landmark at the junction of Cop Lane and Liverpool Road.

Except for employment at Vernon's factory, and those employed in the schools, shops and in the provision of local services most residents work in nearby Preston and district. A local charity still exists which will help apprentices to buy the tools of their trades.

A unique attraction to Penwortham is the presence of the Lancashire mounted police training school, and fine horses are seen regularly exercising around the lanes and roads. It is a marvellous spectacle to see a troop making their way to attend major public events.

Following local government reorganisation in 1974 it was decided that the parish council should change its designation to a town council, and the first mayor was Mrs J. S. Tye. This could be said to be entirely appropriate as the first suffragette in Preston lived in Penwortham. In 1913 she set fire to Lord Leverhulme's bungalow at Rivington Pyke. Sufficient to say she was secretary of Hutton and Howick WI and served on the Executive Committee of the Lancashire Federation!

Pilling 🌿

There is no better way to introduce Pilling than to quote from *The History of Pilling* by the late Mr F. J. Sobee, former headmaster of Pilling Church of England school.

170

'Pilling is a small township, with a population of approximately 1,500 and an area of 6,003 statute acres, tucked away in a southern corner of Morecambe Bay. It is a tiny remnant of old Britain; an independent entity cut off from the rest of England for more than 2,000 years by the sea and the bog; until recently rich in dialect and folklore; a bird sanctuary and a happy hunting ground for the botanist and the lover of nature; with wild untouched expanses of moss, marsh and shore, each anxious to tell its story to help build up the whole.' The name 'Pilling' is derived from the Celtic meaning 'a small creek'.

As well as its legends, Pilling's real history includes stories of shipwrecks, smugglers and the quicksands, which have claimed many lives and possessions over the years. Quite recently, a new sea wall has been built to keep back the high tides that caused serious floods in the past.

Pilling has five churches and the site of an earlier one. Two of them and the site are dedicated to St John the Baptist, the others being the Roman Catholic church dedicated to St William Fitzherbert of York, the Methodist chapel and the church of St Mark at Eagland Hill. The foundation stone of the latter was laid by the founder and 'father' of Eagland Hill, Mr James Jenkinson; the church's altar stands on the hearth of his former home.

Pilling has had two famous vicars. One, Rev James Potter (here 1802–1825) was a fighter and the other, Rev George Holden (here 1758–1767), wrote the 'Holden Tide Tables' used to this day. A sun dial, placed over the door of the old Georgian church, bears his name. This church, recently restored, is now the property of the Redundant Churches Fund.

Over the years many archaeological finds have been made dating back to the Neolithic Age, including the skull of a Bronze Age girl. The present house at Bone Hill was, in the past, reputed to have been an infamous baby farm.

Pilling also had its own railway and engine affectionately called the 'Pilling Pig', because of its whistle sounding like a pig with its throat being cut! The track ran from Garstang to Knott End via Pilling. Opened in 1870, sadly the last passengers were carried in 1930 and the last goods in 1950.

There has been a water mill at Pilling since 1242. The present windmill, dating back to 1808 and built by Mr Ralph Slater on a raft of brushwood, is now a private residence. The church tower was also built on a raft, but of cotton bales.

Pilling has had a brass band since 1786. The present Pilling Silver Jubilee Band, formed in 1935, gives regular concerts and takes part in many village events, one of which is the Coffee Feast. This is a unique event believed to have its origins in celebrations held by the monks of Cockersand Abbey to mark the festival of the beheading of St John the Baptist and is documented from 1754. The Feast is held annually at the end of July.

The village of Pilling, still a peaceful haven in this hectic, modern world, is a farming and market garden area famous for its potatoes and tomatoes, which are supplied throughout Lancashire. The vast bog and moss, which formerly occupied so much of the township of Pilling, was systematically and successfully drained from the early 19th century, creating the highly fertile fields to be seen today. Most of the peat, or turf, which the monks of Cockersand named 'The Black Lake', was cut for domestic fuel, and gave rise to the saying 'Pilling moss, like God's grace, is boundless'.

Quernmore

The parish of Quernmore lies at the head of the Conder valley, about three miles east of Lancaster. In Norman times the area was Royal Forest, reserved for the King's hunting. Some land was cleared and enclosed in a few places to make farms, and a deer park was enclosed at Halton, until then a small village which had been mentioned in the Domesday Book.

Much of the valley remained open common land until the beginning of the 19th century, when it was all enclosed. Before then, there had been considerable industrial activity, including several coal mines, stone quarries and a hat factory. The quern stones, or grinding stones, produced from the quarries provided the origin of the name Quernmore. Several quarries were on the slopes of Clougha Pike, which was the site of the beacon for Lancaster in Tudor times. Today the area is predominantly agricultural, providing grazing for sheep and cattle. Most of the farms in the valley are owner-farmed, passing down through the generations.

The central point of Quernmore is the post office at the foot of Quernmore Brow, alongside a cluster of houses. It was established in 1883 next door to the Dog and Partridge inn, which first opened its doors in 1826, but the licence was surrendered at the turn of the century so that the youth of the village would not be corrupted! It was renamed the Temperance Hotel, and became a cafe combined with the post office and general store. It served the community well until the mid 1980s, when the

172

'Temp' as it was known locally was sold. It is now a private home, but the post office continues to flourish.

In the 1970s houses were built either side of the Methodist church, which has stood since 1877. The Methodist schoolroom was added in 1954, next to the church, a result of a large Gift Auction of livestock and provisions. It is also used as a community centre for village activities.

St Peter's church lies a mile north of the post office. First built in 1834, it was rebuilt in 1860 in 14th century style, the stone quarried locally on Clougha. An interesting feature is the east window, which was salvaged from the wreck of the *Fairy Vision* at the mouth of the river Rhone.

Quernmore primary school stands alongside the church, with a master's residence. An old school house a couple of miles away was originally for the master, but this was sold, and the money placed in trust for future needs of Quernmore scholars.

The children carry on a long tradition with the annual Egg Service at St Peter's just before Easter. This service goes back to the war years, the children taking gifts of fresh eggs in beautifully decorated baskets, which are then distributed amongst children and old people's homes in Lancaster.

The highlight of village events takes place in May with Quernmore Field Day. These sports, known as 'L'ile Grasmere', have produced some well-known Cumberland and Westmorland wrestlers. A Fell Race scaling Clougha Pike started some years ago proves very popular, with over 100 entrants in 1989.

For generations collies have been used for the gathering and shepherding of sheep on the fells and lowlands of the Quernmore valley. The working sheepdog is essential for the success of efficient shepherding and nowhere more so than with the local Longton family who have won both national and international recognition.

So Quernmore life has changed little over the years. Mushroom growing is now part of the valley life, with a snail farm being the latest venture. Tourists drive through on their way to the Trough of Bowland, and there are now craft centres to visit. A male voice choir is kept busy, and a youth club caters for the teenagers. Church and chapel are well supported with a growing Sunday school.

Rainford 🏵

Rainford is a semi-rural/residential village with a pleasant mixture of old and new which blend together to make a desirable area for both Rainfordians and 'newcomers'. It covers 5,877 acres and consists mainly of agricultural land with two light industrial estates at each end of the village. It was first mentioned in documents in 1198.

Mossborough Hall, which was formerly moated, is the oldest building having been built in 1300 and renovated in 1703 and today is the home of a tenant farmer. The Lathom family and then, through marriage, the Stanley and Molyneux families were residents until 1786 when it was sold to the present owner, the Earl of Derby. Scythestone Delph Farm was built in 1682 of local sandstone and the inside walls are wattle and daub, and other cottages throughout the village also date from the 17th century. A conservation order covers the older buildings but six housing estates have been built over the years to meet the demand of the growing population, from 70 to 80 people in 1641, 3,745 in 1881 to 9,500 in 1989.

Rainford's coal, sand and clay, combined with rich arable land, influenced the lives and occupations of generations of Rainford families in past decades. Mining, clay pipe manufacturing, potteries and farming were some of the best in the country. As these rich sources dried up land was reclaimed to give way to housing, attracting town and city dwellers into the area. Slowly small industrial estates are growing consisting of units giving services to industry and the community. Rolling fields of agricultural land can still be seen amidst this growth, but modern machinery has taken over from man. No longer are pea, bean, carrot and potato pickers needed. Grown-ups and children can no longer enjoy the fun and companionship whilst picking, not to mention the extra money at the end of the day.

A highlight of the summer is the 'Walking Day', which was officially the 'Day and Sunday School Treat' and goes back over a hundred years. Today all the churches take part in the Walking Day and the whole village is united in a common witness.

Before and during the Jubilee Year of 1887 the elderly people of the village were entertained to an annual tea and concert by Mr Pennington of Muncaster Hall. After his death, the Hall changed hands several times and was eventually demolished. The village people formed an 'Old Folks Committee' to raise money to continue to give the elderly an annual outing by coach to Blackpool with dinner included – some 330 people enjoyed this outing in 1989.

Other annual events are the 'Arts Week', when the artistic efforts of the schoolchildren and adults of the village are displayed in the village hall. The Rainford Horticultural Show is held at the same venue, when residents and visitors from surrounding areas compete in the many classes of horticulture, handicrafts, flower arranging, baking, preserving and photography.

In the days of Elizabeth I drunkards were placed in the stocks for all to see. The renovated stocks are to be seen on the original site – no deterrent to present day living!

Rainhill 🦋

Rainhill village is situated on the main Liverpool to Warrington road, crossed at Kendrick's Cross by the Cronton to Eccleston road and close to the river Mersey which used to divide Lancashire and Cheshire. Although it has grown considerably over the last few decades, it is still a pleasant leafy place in which to live.

The earliest known record of the village was in 1190, and the name is believed to derive from Regna, a man who once lived on or owned the hill which rises from the Mersey plain. It must have been a small sleepy little place, mainly a scattering of farms, until the 19th century arrived heralding the Industrial Revolution. Luckily, Rainhill didn't suffer too badly during the Industrial Revolution, although a lot of the villagers abandoned their rural jobs and became out-workers for the watchmaking industry, worked in the iron foundry doing railway repairs, or in the brass foundry making brass fittings for the Liverpool ships. A glassworks also sprang up at Kendrick's Cross, as did a tar distillery, but these were short-lived, and all are no longer in existence.

Following the turnpiking of the Liverpool to Warrington road in 1753, a toll gate was set up at Kendrick's Cross, and the resulting improvement in the road surface allowed a coach service to be operated between Liverpool and Manchester, and Liverpool and London. The journey to London took three whole days and must have been extremely uncomfortable. A daily event was the sight of the London Mail coach flying through, fairly promptly at 9 pm. Bartholomew Bretherton ran the coaches, and built a fine house in Rainhill in which to live, with stabling for 240 horses at the inn across the way. He eventually built St Bartholomew's church, which stands today as his memorial.

However, the railways were soon to put coaching firms out of business. In order to provide a passenger service, it was decided to hold a competition to find the best locomotive, with a prize of £500, quite a sum in those days. Of course, a line had to be provided, so in 1826 a 1¾ mile stretch of level line was built through Rainhill, which involved cutting through rock and the building of a skew bridge to carry the main road. George Stephenson was the engineer, and he had the bridge constructed by George Findlay, from local sandstone blocks, and set at an angle of 34° across the line. It was the first example of its kind, and was completed in June 1829. It is still carrying the heavy traffic of this century, and is an amazing engineering feat.

The Trials were set to begin on 6th October 1829 and there was great excitement in the village. Five locomotives were entered, *Sans Pareil*, *Rocket*, *Novelty*, *Perseverance* and *Cycloped*, and the first day attracted a huge crowd of over 10,000 spectators. Rainhill had never seen so many people! The competitors' machines were to run 40 times along the line to simulate the distance from Liverpool to Manchester and back, at not less than ten miles per hour. The Trials took four days, there were many mishaps and breakdowns to entertain the crowd, but only George and

Rainhill Station

Robert Stephenson's *Rocket* fulfilled all the expectations of the organisers, and was declared the winner.

Rainhill celebrated the 150th anniversary of this event in 1979/80, when *another* 10,000 visitors descended upon the village. Many railway enthusiasts still come to see the station and visit the Trials Exhibition housed in an old railway carriage behind the library.

Another 150th anniversary has been celebrated, that of the consecration of St Ann's church on 21st June 1839. It was built of the lovely local red sandstone (which was also used in Liverpool Cathedral) and paid for largely by the wealthy Liverpool wine merchants and chemical manufacturers from St Helens who built grand houses on the hill during the 19th century.

The large houses are too expensive to keep up these days, and mostly have other uses such as schools, nursing homes and homes for the elderly.

Although Rainhill has grown considerably and its population has more than doubled only in recent years, there is still a strong community spirit. The village hall had to be extended, and although five rooms, apart from the main hall, are available for use, it still doesn't seem enough to cater for the 32 organisations which thrive here!

Read 🐚

The villages of Simonstone and Read, although they adjoin one another and share quite a lot of ancient history, are very different in character. Read's two mills influenced the village's development, and when the first one, Victoria Mill, was built in 1870 it was run by David Kemp and his son Joseph. Many terraced houses were built for the mill workers who worked there as winders and weavers, working from 6 am to 5.30 pm, five and a half days for 25 to 30 shillings a week. Another mill was built at the other end of the village called Friendship Mill, and both mills wove good quality cotton. Unhappily, trade worsened and the Kemps went bankrupt, putting many villagers out of work. Friendship Mill still stands and is divided into several small units, but the Victoria Mill was demolished in 1989 for redevelopment.

In the late 1890s a three storey Co-op was built, having one large room on the top floor, used for dancing. This building has now been converted into three flats. An amazing number of shops and tradesmen served the villagers at that time. There were two butchers, a joiner, a wheelwright (doubling as the undertaker), a black-pudding maker, a blacksmith, a greengrocer, a tailor, a dressmaker, a plumber, a café, a draper, a newsagent, three bakers, a barber, two coal merchants and a shoe shop where they also made clogs for the mill workers. Now there are nine shops and a well used launderette.

There has been a post office for many years, usually in someone's front room, and in the early days the sub-postmaster would walk down to Simonstone station to collect the mail and would also walk to deliver telegrams, often to outlying farms.

Unusually, for a village, Read hasn't a 'pub', but early in the 1870s a Literary Institute was opened where people could read newspapers, and much later the institute was granted a licence. In 1890, the Read and Simonstone Constitutional club was built where the men could play snooker, but this didn't have a licence until 1948 and no lady members until 1968! It is still a well used centre today.

During the 1920s a Silver Band was formed for which Joseph Kemp bought all the instruments and paid for the conductor. The band room was a large wooden building in the Victoria Mill yard.

For many years the local farmers supplied milk to the village by horse-drawn floats or hand carts but during hot weather children went with jugs to Speak's farm and got the milk straight from the cow. No worries about 'green top' unpasteurized milk then!

Christmas was tea party time, and early in the century there were three; one in Read Congregational school, one in Read Church of England school and one in Simonstone school, each on a separate day. Sit-down teas were provided by the ladies of the schools, and the villagers enjoyed roast beef, jelly and cake. The evenings were rounded off with concerts by local artists.

Until 1965 Walking Day was held on the first Saturday in June when the procession, led by a band and the banner, walked around the village, finishing at Read Hall for sports, coffee and buns. Read Hall was once the home of Roger Nowell, before whom the Lancashire Witches were tried in 1612.

St John's church was built in 1886, followed in 1888 by the school, which replaced the old one. Also in 1888, the Congregational church-cum-school was built.

Read Cricket Club was formed in 1877 and joined the Ribblesdale League in 1892, being the only club having an unbroken membership, and in 1949, 1973 and 1975 won the League Championship. These days, many, if different, activities flourish in the village.

Ribbleton 🌿

Ribbleton is now a suburb of Preston, but not so long ago it was still a village. The battle of Preston, so savagely fought in the Civil War, took place here, remembered in the street name Cromwell Road. Dating back even earlier is Watling Street originally built by the Romans and still running through Ribbleton.

In the memory of older people the old village sites live on: Primrose Dell, the bridge with the cat's face in it, 40 steps which led past the sandpits for the brickworks at Thorn Street. The road led on, past the farm to Uncle Tom's Cabin and Watling Street Road. Children were taken for picnics to the little Hills and Hollows.

There were Addison's Farm, Home Slack House, Forrest's Farm and Butler's Farm. There were at least six more farms and today three are still working farms. There was a farm behind the cemetery where the farmer would fill boys' caps with apples for 2d.

Close to Halfpenny Bridge there was a tall old house with beautiful gardens. Across the bridge was a hut where sweets were sold and another hut selling chips on a Sunday evening. Today the large hotel called The Tickled Trout occupies the site.

Behind Red Scar House were Brockholes Wood, Squire Anderton's wood and the Dingle, where bluebells grew in profusion. There was also Sandy Bottoms, where children could paddle and make sandcastles.

The village church of St Mary Magdalene celebrated its centenary in 1989. When it was first built it was a small church with underfloor heating provided by a coke boiler underneath the grating with pipes running down the centre aisle. It has since been altered and a church hall added. What was once the 'new cemetery' with a few graves now spans a large area.

Blackpool Road is still called the 'New Road'. Ribbleton today is a continuation of the Ribbleton of past years. Churches, schools, houses have come and gone, but something of the essential character remains.

Ribchester 🌿

The village of Ribchester is beautifully situated, well clothed with woods and hedgerows and surrounded by farmland. Ribchester is the only village which actually lies on the banks of the river Ribble. It dates back to Roman times and was originally called Bremetennacum Veteranorum. The Ribchester museum is a source of a great deal of information about the village's past.

Some of the houses in the village housed hand looms in their back rooms, the weaving being performed by members of the family. These have been altered and are now ordinary dwelling houses. The village also boasts a splendid parish church, St Wilfrid's, built in the 13th century on the site of a pre-Norman church.

Walking down Church Street into Water Street one comes to the 18th century White Bull public house. The four columns supporting the entrance porch are thought to be of Roman origin, and the mounting steps are still in place outside.

Whereas Ribchester once had 13 shops and two weaving mills, the introduction of the motor car meant people were able to travel into towns and cities to work and also to go shopping, and so led to the closure of many small village shops and one weaving mill. The remaining weaving mill is owned by Banister Bros & Co and is still thriving, with a mill shop where excellent cloth is sold. The engineering works across the road are to be demolished and the site used for the building of modern housing.

The riverbank is the perfect place to spend a leisurely afternoon and the Riverside Tea Gardens are popular. There is also an excellent recreation playing field with picnic tables and two tennis courts.

In Water Street there is an excellent fish and chip shop and cafe, and across the way is a craft shop. The Museum of Childhood is also housed in Ribchester.

The Ribchester Arms has an entrance area ablaze with tubs of glorious flowering shrubs and colourful flowers throughout the year.

Up School Lane is St Peter and St Paul's Roman Catholic church which is a barn-type church, built in 1789. Around the corner one finds the 'ding-dong-bell' well and pillared facade of the almshouses which John Shireburn of Bailey endowed in his will of 1726 to be used by five poor widows or spinsters 'to live separately therein'. A little further along the dirt road is Stydd chapel, once part of the religious house of the Knights Hospitallers of St John of Jerusalem. Only the chapel now remains but it is still occasionally used by St Wilfrid's at harvest time and for Christmas carols.

The field day staged in June brings out all the villagers. St Wilfrid's holds a garden party in July and the village market is held each year on Spring Bank Holiday Monday, with stalls run by the many charities in the village.

Rimington 🌿

Rimington means 'farmstead on the boundary' and, as Rimington has been on the boundary between Lancashire and Yorkshire at various times, this seems appropriate. Over the centuries, Rimington has been transferred from Lancashire to Yorkshire and back again. The last transfer was made in 1974 when those people Yorkshire born and bred became Lancastrians overnight, albeit very reluctantly.

Francis Duckworth, the composer of many well-known hymn tunes, the most famous of which is probably the one he called *Rimington*, was born in the village. His parents kept the post office and shop next door to the Methodist chapel and a plaque on the chapel, now a house, commemorates him.

The lead mines, once the source of local employment, are disused, but the legend of the fraudulent minting of counterfeit 'shillings' by Pudsey of Bolton Hall lives on. Crime is nothing new, it seems. With the exception of the station house, the old station buildings have been demolished, and the railway workers are gone. Gone, too, are the garage and the haulage business, and many farms are now private dwellings, the land having been sold to enlarge other farms or for building. Many barns have been converted and so too has the old sawmill. Farming no longer dominates the economy, and a high proportion of residents are either retired or work elsewhere in managerial capacities.

Now that the grass is cut much sooner than it used to be the meadows are not so full of flowers, but the hedgerows are fairly prolific and the village in the main is prettier.

Several old cottages and farms are listed buildings, and there are still three wells from which villagers used to obtain water, and, indeed can still do so. The village hall is the war memorial. The villagers also raised money for a sports field and pavilion.

Rimington is in the parish of Gisburn, where the ancient parish church is situated. The only place of worship in the village is the Congregationalist chapel, with a sundial on the front of the building, situated at Martin Top.

From past centuries the three-storey cottages of the handloom weavers remind us of life long ago and the wisdom of 1819 speaks to us from the words carved on the wall at Field House: 'Repeat no grievance and mind your own business'. But the village is very much alive today. It won the Best Kept Village Competition in 1987 in the First Time Entry class, and in 1988 the Small Village class. Newcomers remark on the friendliness of the villagers, something of which Rimington is very proud.

Rivington ❧

'When Rivington puts on her hood
She fears a rainy day
But when she doffs it you will find
The rain is o'er, and still the wind
And Phoebus shines away.'

This old weather rhyme refers to Rivington Pike, which at 1,192 ft dominates the skyline above the village and is a prominent landmark for miles around. The present tower at the summit was built as a hunting lodge from the stones of an old beacon, one of a chain which could be lit to spread news of national emergencies. It is recorded to have been lit when the Spanish Armada was sighted in 1588.

Traditionally, a ghostly horseman haunts this site on St Bartholomew's Eve, and ancient burial mounds are found on the moor. It was customary to worship here at sunrise on the first Sunday in May, but nowadays the pilgrimage takes place on Good Friday when hundreds of visitors climb to the summit, where there is also a fair and refreshment stalls.

The Pike Race takes place on Easter Saturday when around 300 fell runners are attracted from all over the country.

The picturesque village is situated in a miniature 'Lake District' of scenic beauty. It is unspoiled by new properties, mainly due to the construction of the reservoirs during the middle of the last century, and is a delight for visitors from the nearby industrial towns of South Lancashire.

Although not mentioned in the Domesday Book, historians record that the area existed as a manor before 1066. Ruhwinton, Rovington and Roynton are names from which Rivington was derived, indicating a settlement by a rough hill. The village green with its water trough and stocks is overlooked by the Unitarian chapel and a cluster of houses which include the post office. Other buildings are the 16th century church and church hall, the primary school, and the village club on the site of the former Black-a-moor's Head inn.

Rivington Hall was occupied by the lord of the manor and the Pilkington family who held it from 1202 to 1616 had great influence on the village. In 1541 Richard Pilkington built the church and in 1566 his son James, the first Protestant Bishop of Durham, founded Rivington grammar school. Rebuilt in 1714, it is now the village primary school with 40 pupils on roll. In 1875 a new grammar school was built along Rivington Lane nearer to Horwich and amalgamated with Blackrod grammar school. The charter granted by Queen Elizabeth I is in the school library.

The parish of Rivington has a scattered population of only 135. More than a century ago it was double the present number. A few dwellings were submerged by the reservoirs and many have been demolished in order to prevent pollution of the water supply to the city of Liverpool.

Farming, quarrying, blacksmiths and the cottage industries of hand-loom weaving and bleaching of cloth were the chief occupations. Many farms and cottages retain the names of bygone days and occupants – Moses Cocker, Bradley's, Hamer's, The Crosses, Pall Mall and Mill Hill to name a few.

The area known as Lever Park was purchased in 1900 from the squire of Rivington Hall by William Hesketh Lever, later Viscount Leverhulme. It includes the Hall, the two barns, several houses and farmland. The two barns are of Saxon origin but have been altered several times, though keeping the cruck trusses which support the roof. Lord Leverhulme opened the barns for shelter and refreshment and provided an open-air zoo, the first of its kind, long before Whipsnade. He also built, as a folly, a replica of the ruined Liverpool Castle on the shore of the Lower Rivington reservoir. Beautiful terraced gardens were constructed and opened annually to the public. He donated this area as a country park for the benefit of the people of his native Bolton and surrounding towns. It was controlled by the Liverpool Water Corporation, now the North West Water Authority.

Lever Park is now part of the West Pennine Moors Area. As more visitors are attracted to the area the increased volume of traffic has become a problem in the village, though new car parks have been provided. An information centre has been set up in Great House Barn and there is also a craft shop and a Park Ranger's office.

New proposals for further development are of great concern to the residents and the many friends of Rivington who wish to preserve the informal atmosphere and character of this lovely village.

Roughlee 🎵

Roughlee is in an area of outstanding natural beauty. It spreads out along the valley of Pendle Water overlooked by hillside farms and two pleasant caravan sites.

Focal points of village life in recent times have been the school and the Bay Horse Inn. The Methodist chapel was demolished in 1976. The nearest places of worship now are St Mary's at Newchurch in Pendle and Barley Methodist chapel.

The village school was built in 1852. Opposite the school is a shallow stream where children spend many happy hours catching tiddlers. Further downstream is the waterfall, even more attractive when it is in flood or frozen. There have been at least two floods when the usually benign stream became a raging torrent. In July 1881, there was a storm which resulted in severe flooding in Roughlee. A local paper reported that when the cellar at the Bay Horse Inn flooded, the strong smell of rum which permeated the vicinity indicated a great loss of spirits. The most recent flooding occurred in August 1967, when part of the main road through the village was washed away.

A magnet for tourists is Roughlee Hall, now divided into cottages, once the home of Alice Nutter, one of the Lancashire Witches. One recent resident was the late Jimmy Crewdson, one of the oldest Scouts in the world.

Recent building developments have included a few individual bungalows and three small clusters of detached houses.

Most villagers commute to work as there is little employment in the village. In the 19th century there were two cotton mills, Roughlee Mill and Thorneyholme Mill. They spun cotton yarn for the handloom weavers. By 1909 Roughlee Mill had become a laundry. Soon after this a boating lake and pleasure gardens were developed there. Until quite recently, this was popular with local people. The lake is now used for fishing.

Only one shop remains. Twenty years ago there were several. Many residents tell of the time when jugs of tea could be bought in many cottage gardens.

Rufford

Rufford, a village of 1,500 inhabitants, lies on the busy main road which runs from Preston to Liverpool.

The population has doubled since the end of the 19th century, and recently many new houses have been erected to accommodate the commuter population which has replaced the old farming community.

There are still many reminders to be seen of the past when Rufford was an estate village, and the Heskeths were, for over 600 years, paternal landlords.

On the northern approach to the village lies the half-timbered Old Hall, now owned by the National Trust, but begun by Sir Thomas Hesketh in the early 15th century, and added to by his descendants in 1662 and 1821. A very rare movable screen of great antiquity is to be seen in the great Tudor Hall where the early Heskeths once held court, and a small museum illustrates aspects of village life.

Across the road, and set in the large park, is Rufford New Hall, built as a more elegant and convenient seat for the family in 1760. Since the departure of the Heskeths it has served as a hospital.

Just beyond the red brick Victorian church of St Mary, which stands on an ancient foundation, is the new Fermor Arms; this replaces an imposing building which had to be demolished when it started to subside on its foundations of cotton bales. The sloping floors and bar were famous in local circles, and with day trippers.

On the main road the Hesketh, recently modernised, was formerly registered as an inn, and had stabling for twelve horses. Home produced ham and pork were the specialities of the house.

In 1339 Sir William Hesketh obtained the King's charter for a weekly market and annual fair to be held at Rufford. The market vanished long ago, but the fair has continued in various forms over the centuries. For over a hundred years from 1846 a major agricultural show was held in the park, and now the medieval fair held in May attracts people from far and wide.

Sabden

Sabden probably derives its name from 'Sappe Dene', the valley of the spruces. A lovely name for a lovely valley, situated between the Ribble and Calder rivers with Pendle Hill on the north side and Padiham

Heights (Black Hill and White Hill) on the south side. There is no through road up the valley, but motorists travelling to Sabden from the Whalley direction must, on reaching the village centre, turn either left or right, over the nick of Pendle to Clitheroe, or over Black Hill or White Hill to Padiham service area. Should, however, the visitor care to walk up the valley, a footpath will lead him via Sabden Brook from its source near Spen Brook down the valley to join the river Calder at Cock Bridge. Perhaps the music of the brook stirred the hearts of Sabdeners in days gone by when church and chapel choirs were renowned for their singing and the village brass band was in its tuneful glory.

Those were the days of the churches' annual Walking Days, when their congregations turned out in procession around the villages, pausing to sing rousing hymns of praise. The custom still survives but on a much smaller scale. Other customs have gone, such as the arrival of the fair and the erection of swings and roundabouts and coconut shies on Holme playing field. There were maypoles on May Day and quaint local games. Bonfires marked Guy Fawkes night and at Christmas time carol singers went from door to door.

The practice of medicine was rather different from that of today. Tonsils were removed on the kitchen table and the vapour from the local lime kiln was a sure cure for whooping cough! A visit to the dentist meant a walk of three or four miles, plus the same distance back.

Eventually a bus service was started, at first on Saturdays, which meant that a visit to the 'pictures' was made much easier. Then came electricity, street lamps and a daily bus service.

Now the new houses sometimes jar on the older residents who see their old village being altered out of all recognition. Light industry has replaced the textile mills, but agriculture still flourishes and some do not think the new and the old clash. And for the incomers Sabden offers a picturesque retirement haven with much going on and involvement if it is desired. Whatever the nostalgic reservations of some 'natives', new arrivals quickly feel accepted.

Saddleworth

Fourteen villages, all within walking distance of each other, lie within the parish of Saddleworth: Springhead, Grotton, Lydgate, Grasscroft, Friezland, Greenfield, Uppermill, Dobcross, Diggle, Austerlands, Scouthead, Delph and Denshaw. Mossley, a village built below Lydgate on the steep

186

bank of the river Tame is divided by altitude: Bottom Mossley and Top Mossley. Part of the latter, Roughtown, was so called because navvies had their quarters there during the building of the canal and railway. Originally it was part of Lydgate parish and so can claim to have been the 14th village in Saddleworth.

Saddleworth has been part of the Metropolitan Borough of Oldham only since 1974. Always closer to Oldham than any Yorkshire town, its large boundaries extend well into Yorkshire but over uninhabited moorland. Its villages have always been in the valley bottoms on the western side of the Pennines. Formerly in the West Riding, the white rose embellishes road signs as you enter the area.

Nearly all the villages are geographically, culturally and socially united in one entity called Saddleworth, the only part of Lancashire whose sons may play cricket for Yorkshire! Uppermill, being large, central and the nearest village to the now isolated Saddleworth parish church of St Chad, may be said to be the 'capital'.

Saddleworth's moors are probably best known for their grisly connection with the 'Moors Murderers' Brady and Hindley. Their victims' bodies were brought down from the A635 road to the small mortuary at Uppermill. Locals remember another murder connected with the same road. At the now demolished Bill's o' Jack's Inn a landlord and his son were brutally murdered by persons unknown in 1832. St Chad's churchyard has a huge tombstone with the full tale carved upon it.

The many streams which flow from the moors fill and feed several reservoirs, the river Tame and the Huddersfield Narrow Canal (begun in 1794). Unused for many years the canal has been dredged and fitted with new locks. Tourists may take a short pleasure trip on a narrow boat from Wade Lock basin. Here the 70 ft long and 9 ft wide boats are able to turn round.

The canal crosses the river Tame on an aqueduct which contains a lock and a skew arch and then passes under Saddleworth viaduct. Just beyond Diggle, having passed through nine locks from Uppermill, it enters Britain's longest canal tunnel (now closed), 3 miles 133 yards long and 645 ft above sea level. As it is just over 9 ft wide, boats had to be 'legged' through the tunnel on their journey from Ashton to Huddersfield.

On the banks of the canal at Uppermill stands Saddleworth Museum. Founded by our own Knight of the Garter, Lord Rhodes, it is manned and has been extended by volunteers, notably Mr Roger Tanner and members of Saddleworth Historical Society.

On the moors near Denshaw, flint arrow heads and other findings indicate Neolithic, Mesolithic and Bronze Age habitation of the area, when the Pennines were covered with trees. Stumps of birch, alder and hazel are still to be found in the peat bogs. In AD 80 a Roman road led through Saddleworth from Manchester to York. There was a Roman camp at Castleshaw near Delph (now a study centre for schools) and the remains of Buckton Castle, a Romano-British earthwork, are to be found just beyond Greenfield. Saddleworth is written as Saedela's Weorth on some old maps. The last lord of the manor was James Farrer who died in 1791. The Farrer's Arms at Grasscroft is named after him.

Quarries in the Castleshaw area were worked from the Middle Ages to the beginning of the 20th century to provide bakestones and roof tiles from the local mudstones, which have some of the properties of slate. There are many gritstone quarries which provided a particularly coarse stone suitable for the foundations of the great steam engines which powered the mills during the Industrial Revolution.

The hill farms which stand on the spring line and surround the parish have seen many changes in the valleys below. To the area of pack horse tracks, tiny farm cottages and larger loom houses, where handloom weaving was carried out, came Huguenot weavers driven from their native France. They gave the place name 'Frenches' to part of Greenfield and brought the surname Mallalieu.

Things changed with the advent of technology in the form of water power. Diggle had a water wheel second in size to the Isle of Man's Laxey Wheel. Later steam power led to cotton spinning and the rapid growth of Uppermill and Greenfield in the 1850s, as roads, canals and railways were developed.

In 1849 the Huddersfield and Manchester Railway was opened. Engineering feats involved another three mile long tunnel at Standedge and Saddleworth viaduct, which crosses the river Tame and is built on an arc. A later branch line from Oldham to Greenfield involved another tunnel at Lydgate, 1334 yards long. Five years earlier a single line to Delph had been worked by a horse and was known as the 'Delph Donkey', it closed in 1955. Of the eleven stations and halts within the parish, only Greenfield survives as a working station, sadly minus its buildings.

Saddleworth industry is very much alive and well despite the loss of the railways. The old mills still stand and house modern units involving such diverse things as electronics, plastics and quality piano felts (Royal George Mill). The mill in Chew Valley (Robert Fletcher's) is the largest producer of thin fine papers in the UK, famous for '40 row', a terrace of 40 back to back houses built to house its workers half way up the hillside. Large firms like Clear Span and Compoflex are also located in Saddleworth. The Alexandra Mill at Uppermill is currently a craft centre where hand-made goods are sold direct to the public, who flock here at weekends.

In the days when textiles reigned supreme, it was Dobcross which was the commercial centre of Saddleworth. Its picturesque houses clustered around the crossing of the two pack horse trails and amongst the loom houses and weavers' cottages are to be found the larger dwellings of prosperous merchants and the former headquarters of Saddleworth Bank (a forerunner of the present National Westminster).

Whit Friday is Saddleworth's great day, when after the Procession of Witness (eleven churches took part in 1989) and the children's sports, the evening heralds the Saddleworth Brass Band contests, held at most villages, attracting the best of Britain's brass bands. Some local bands still manage to win prizes.

Prompted by a love of music and an appreciation of artistry, locals organise the Saddleworth Festival of the Arts, lasting one week and taking place every four years. It is a celebration run by volunteers and attracting internationally famous artists and VIP's (including Royals). The Festival was founded by Lord Rhodes of Saddleworth.

Cricket is a religion in Saddleworth. Many a test cricketer has played on local grounds. Sonny Ramadhin played then stayed, as landlord of a Delph pub! Near Denshaw 'Cricketer's Row' was built by a local mill owner to house his team. Naturally it includes a house for the 12th man.

The great Rush Cart Procession tours the parish for two days in August, attracting Morris Dance teams from all over England. A gurning contest and many other entertainments culminate in a service at St Chad's, where the sweet scented rushes (sadly no longer gathered locally but imported from East Anglia) strew the church and the gentle tinkling bells of the Morris Dancers' clogs accompany the service.

There are over 70 listed buildings in the parish. The workhouse at Runninghill near St Chad's still stands but the area enjoys better prosperity now than in the bitter days of the cotton famine and the strikes of the 1890s. Co-operative Societies were formed all over the parish to eke out low wages, and the old Co-op shops survive in most villages.

Local Yorkists say they have been 'Lancastrated' but Saddleworth folk are friendly folk and no 'comer in' who moves into the new houses being built on these green valleys feels a stranger for long. The villages are busy and sometimes noisy, but there is peace and quiet to be found a hundred feet up on the 'tops'.

St Michael's-on-Wyre

St Michael's-on-Wyre is in the heart of the lovely Fylde countryside almost equidistant from the towns of Preston, Blackpool and Lancaster. The ancient parish church, situated close to a safe crossing point on the south bank of the river Wyre, was dedicated to St Michael the Archangel around AD 627–640. It was one of only three churches mentioned as being in existence in the Hundred of Amounderness when the Domesday survey of 1086 was carried out. Most of the present church structure dates from the 16th century with parts dating back to the 12th century.

The date of the first settlement is not known but Stone Age implements have been found nearby. Since the 12th century, the village has taken its name from the church and the river but its former name of Upper Rawcliffe with Tarnacre is still used in local government circles.

St Michael's-on-Wyre, circa 1920

190

During the last century, many thatched whitewashed cottages bordered the tree-lined roads. Cottagers were provided with allotments where fresh vegetables and flowers were grown, whilst some kept a cow and became members of the United Cottagers Cow Club – a form of insurance in case a cow should die. Insured cows, after a six month probationary period, were branded on the horns with the letters CC. Some cottagers had the right to cut turf from a moss dale and turf stacks were a common sight outside each cottage.

St Michael's is one of only a few parishes where the parish registers have been transcribed and indexed and they reveal a number of interesting occurrences. In June 1738, a most unusual event took place in the village. Ralph Dickinson and his wife Jane were blessed with quadruplets, or, as the parish register puts it, 'twin sons and twin daughters at one birth'. Sadly, the eldest only lived until he was six years of age. The parish registers also reveal times of great tragedy. The burial registers for the winter of 1728/9 record burials taking place at the rate of one a day. The most recent tragedy to occur to the inhabitants of the village took place on 23rd May, 1984 when 16 people were killed and many more were badly injured in a dreadful explosion in a Water Authority outfall station at Abbeystead, when a party from St Michael's were being shown round. A memorial plaque to the memory of those killed can be seen inside the parish church.

Through the ages, a number of wooden bridges have been built across the river. The first stone bridge was built c1696 and was replaced by the present stone bridge in 1803. Large volumes of traffic now pass over the bridge and the present inhabitants are pressing the County Council for a bypass which will restore the village to its previously peaceful condition.

The river Wyre provides an idyllic setting on long hot summer days, with the lovely mature beech trees overhanging the weir. However, this tranquil scene can quickly change, for the river has a much darker side to its character. In periods of heavy rain, it can quickly become a raging torrent, for just upstream from St Michael's, the river Brock joins the river Wyre and large volumes of water have often burst through the banks and flooded out the inhabitants. The last major inundation occurred in October 1980 since which time the Water Authority have completed a multi-million pound scheme which it is hoped will eliminate this risk.

Village institutions such as the bowling club, fishing and tennis clubs, provide healthy outdoor summer enjoyment (the bowling club remained unbeaten at home for 75 years) whilst the reading room and badminton

191

club provide endless winter pleasure for the indoor sports enthusiasts. In the last century, St Michael's was famous for its annual hare coursing event which attracted entries from far and wide. Both the hare coursing and the frequent otter hunts along the banks of the river have long since been abandoned. The annual children's gala, held early in June, now incorporates a raft race on the river and this has become one of the highlights of the village year. A garden party is also held each year at the home of the Hornby family, whose forebears were vicars of St Michael's for over 140 years.

St Michael's has become the base for a microlight aircraft school and enthusiasts can be seen over the village at regular intervals. A number of local people have 'defied the elements' and have been for a trip in one of these strange craft. Three fishing lakes have recently been opened where large trout and carp can be caught, which are proving to be a very popular venue for many fishermen.

Despite the risk of flooding, St Michael's is a delightful place in which to live and has often been described as the 'Jewel in the Fylde'.

Salwick ✺

Salwick – the farmstead in the willows – was a small farming hamlet, the only buildings besides farms being the railway cottages. Salwick station opened in 1840, was the only station serving the three villages of Salwick, Newton with Scales and Clifton, being on the main route from London to the Fylde coast.

The Clifton Arms (locally known as the Hand and Dagger) was named after the Clifton family. It was built at the side of the Preston/Lancaster canal in the late 18th century, to serve the needs of the canal people. The other hostelry is the Smith's Arms, although this could now be classed as being in Lea Town.

Salwick Hall, now owned by the Duchy of Lancaster, was an impressive building, and was the home of the Clifton family. Although the date of building is uncertain, records show Cuthbert Clifton as the owner in the late 1500s. Until 1798 there was a Roman Catholic chapel at the Hall.

When British Nuclear Fuels built the Springfield works at Salwick in 1945 it transformed the landscape but the farms surrounding the works continue to be worked. Otherwise, the village has not been developed.

Samlesbury 🦢

Motorists speeding along the M6 know Junction 31 as the Samlesbury (pronounced Samzbury) Exit – signposted Blackburn and Clitheroe. Those travelling southwards can glimpse the tower of Samlesbury church amidst trees on the southern bank of the river Ribble. Many delights lie in wait for those wise enough to leave the motorway and explore this part of the Ribble valley.

There has been a church on the site of St Leonard's the Less since at least 1196 and the gable end of the present church contains the outline of the 14th century chapel. Rebuilding took place in 1558 and a further restoration at the end of the last century. Fortunately the parishioners managed to save the amazing box pews which are carved with the initials of their 17th and early 18th century occupants. Some also bear early Victorian brass plates, engraved with the names of the farms – 'College', 'Hoolster', 'Intack', whose inhabitants occupied them. Preserved too, was the two deck pulpit (cut down from three) and the beautiful and simple 17th century communion rail.

Adjoining the churchyard is the still thriving parish primary school. In this churchyard, only a stone's throw from the motorway, there is the grave of a reputed witch.

Witches were nothing new here. Three Samlesbury women, Jennet and Ellen Brierley and Jane Southworth, were committed for trial at Lancaster in the notorious Lancashire Witch Trials of 1612, accused of witchcraft and sorcery. The main prosecution witness was Grace Sowerbutts, the 14 year old granddaughter of Jennet. She later retracted her evidence and the women were freed. Even at the beginning of this century certain elderly women in Samlesbury were regarded as having the 'evil eye' and a cottage in Nab Lane had a large bat pinned over the door to ward off evil spirits.

Near the church are a group of whitewashed cottages. Their spacious cellars were probably used as handloom weavers' workshops. You can continue past them along Potter Lane but you will find no village or centre of population. Samlesbury's inhabitants dwell in scattered farms or small communities along the long winding lanes which thread their way through undulating, fertile, often wooded farmland.

Just up the hill from St Leonard's, standing hidden from the main road by trees, is Southbank, a sturdy late Georgian-style house with what appears to be a barn attached. This is no barn but the Catholic chapel built in 1818 to resemble one when laws against Catholic worship were still on the statute book and Catholics had no desire to draw attention to themselves. It is a plain simple building little changed inside or out.

At Samlesbury aerodrome in the Second World War, the Handley Page Hampton and Halifax aircraft were assembled. Nowadays it is owned by British Aerospace and the very latest types of plane take off into Samlesbury's skies.

In the early 19th century Samlesbury, whose inhabitants had always combined handloom weaving and farming, acquired two cotton spinning mills, both standing in the valley of Samlesbury's other river, the Darwen. One, at Roach Bridge, is now a paper mill, the other in Samlesbury Bottoms houses several industrial units.

Samlesbury Bottoms is a romantic place with a slightly melancholy air, lying in what is almost a ravine. Not so long ago stone cottages clustered along the river bank, now a handful of modern houses have replaced them. In earlier times Samlesbury folk brought their grain to be ground at the water mill here.

To reach the Bottoms from the 'New Road' you use Nab Lane, passing through Sowerbutts Green. Along this lane are dwellings representing every century from the 16th to present day. The Nabs Head is a substantial four square Victorian pub. Facing it is the former Methodist chapel, now a private house. Nearby is Samlesbury's only remaining shop, a general store cum post office in Further Lane.

Situated on the main road almost opposite the entry to Nab Lane is Samlesbury's gem – the beautiful black and white half-timbered Samlesbury Hall, commenced in the 15th century. In later centuries the Hall fell on bad times. The 'New Road' of 1824 was built so close to the house that it cut across the moat. Only in the 1920s was its future made safe by the setting up of a trust. Today Samlesbury Hall is a centre for the sale of antiques and collectables.

Stanley Grange, in a lovely position near the Hoghton boundary, is another large house given a new lease of life. This red brick Victorian mansion is now a 'Care Village' and the ornamental gardens house bungalows in which the mentally handicapped live in family units. The former kitchen gardens produce shrubs and plants to sell to the public.

Sawley 🌿

Sawley is situated by the middle reaches of the river Ribble, at the northern end of the Ribble valley. It lies just a quarter of a mile from the busy A59 York to Liverpool trunk road. This once ran directly through the village via the notorious Sawley Brow.

To the south of the village lies Pendle Hill, infamous for its connections with devil worship and witchcraft. To the north and north-west are the Bowland Fells and to the east the rolling scenery of the Craven lowlands.

Sawley is now firmly part of Lancashire, although for most of its history it was in the West Riding of Yorkshire. The evolution of the village began in the 12th century, when in 1146 Sawley Abbey was founded by William de Percy. Salley or Sallei means 'land of the willows' and the site was chosen because of the presence of water and an abundant supply of fish.

The abbey, although smaller and poorer than the abbeys in Whalley and Yorkshire, flourished as a Cistercian community until its dissolution during the reign of Henry VIII. The monks returned to the abbey during the 'Pilgrimage of Grace', which called for the restoration of the old religion, and remained in possession until the collapse of the insurrection in 1537, when the last abbot was executed.

Little of the abbey now remains, much of the stone being incorporated into the village building and walls. The site is however, well maintained and is a peaceful haven of tranquillity, very popular with visitors to the village.

For the next 250 years the village was a quiet rural hamlet of scattered farms and smallholdings, 16 of the houses being built before 1785. A major development occurred around this time, when a calico printworks was opened in the village by the Peel family of north-east Lancashire. The printworks became a major employer and imported into the area many families, increasing the population to 580 people. In 1818, the printworks closed and the Peel family moved to Staffordshire. With the closure, the village population fell to around 250.

The village was always a self sufficient community and in 1840 a Wesleyan chapel was set up in the old printworks building. In 1876, Countess Cowper, then lady of the manor and local benefactor, founded the village school. This was to serve the community for 100 years.

The village originally had two public houses, the Spread Eagle and the Sawley Brig, which was situated by the bridge over the river Ribble.

Although the Spread Eagle remains, the Sawley Brig was pulled down around 1880. The village retained its rural, self contained identity well into the 20th century, with its own shop, joiner's shop and post office. The post office closed in 1972, the school in 1976 and the joiner's shop in 1978.

Currently the residents of the village, numbering around 200, are a mixture of farmers, retired people and business people who commute daily to the industrial towns of Lancashire. Employment within Sawley is restricted to the Spread Eagle Hotel, the local farms or the Riverside Rest Home for Retired Gentlefolk. The Spread Eagle Hotel is a well respected eating establishment, offering first class hotel accommodation.

There has been an upsurge in house building with 15 new properties being built including the conversion, into three storey cottages, of the old calico printworks. There is a thriving men's club and the school has taken on a new function as the village community centre. Indeed the village community spirit continues to thrive.

Scorton 🐚

A couple of miles north of Garstang to the east of the A6 lies Scorton. Words that spring to mind to describe the village are words like 'charming', 'picturesque', 'unspoilt', even, heaven forbid, 'sleepy'. They all smack of tourist brochures and as with most clichés have an element of the truth.

For most people the essentials of a village include a church, a shop, a school and a pub. Scorton has all of these, except the last. It is one of the few villages that for years has not had a recognisable 'local'. But with the new licensing laws and a licensed restaurant that does a brisk trade, perhaps the 'village with no pub' label can no longer be justified.

There is not just one place of worship, but three; St Mary and St James Roman Catholic church, consecrated in 1861, the Anglican church of St Peter, founded in 1879, and the Wesleyan Methodist chapel which is older than either and dates from 1842.

Oddly enough, the building known as 'The Priory' has now no religious connection. It is used as a gift shop and restaurant, but was at one time the home of the local Catholic priest.

On the opposite side of the road is the sub post office and Priory stores. This is a typical village shop which stocks an amazing variety of goods. As a bonus you can hear all the local news when you pop in for a packet of biscuits or a postage stamp.

In the centre of the village is Scorton school, over a hundred years old and still going strong. Several years ago it was threatened with closure along with a number of other small rural schools. A vigorous campaign to Save Scorton School earned it a reprieve and now there are more than 50 pupils in the school.

As well as these amenities, Scorton has a public hall, a playing field, a bowling green and a lawn tennis court. There are the usual village societies, a Mothers' Union, a WI, a Bowling Club and an Over-60s club.

Sefton 🖋

The river Alt bounds Sefton parish and in the olden days the village folk were ferried by boat to the parish church of St Helen, and the harvest carried on rafts. Little wonder then that the name Sefton means 'village of the reeds'. Nearby is the ancestral home of the Molyneux family, followers of the Conqueror and earlycomers to these parts. They rose to become Earls of Sefton, their great house at Croxteth a palace within a vast park.

Both the Molyneux family and the Blundells of Little Crosby lie beneath the floor of the 14th century Sefton church, where each claimed right of burial during the generations when both families were firm Papists. On the north side of the church lie two effigies of knights; one is thought to be Sir William Molyneux who was a Crusader and knighted in 1286, and the other probably dates to the early 14th century. An outstanding feature of the church is its 16th century carved woodwork. The pulpit with its canopy and the reredos dating from 1728 would be fine enough to grace a Wren church in London.

In days gone by, Manor Courts were held at the Punch Bowl, the old inn. Gatherings were also held there of the Ancient and Loyal Corporation of Sefton, which drew in prosperous Liverpool traders and merchants to choose mayor, bailiffs, recorder, etc. The Mayor's Sunday meant morning service at the 'Cathedral', as they called Sefton church, dinner at the Mansion House (the old Church Inn), church again, and the rest of the day spent in 'conviviality and harmony'.

Local girls threw pins into St Helen's wishing well, which was said to have healing properties. Stray cattle were impounded in Brickwell Lane pinfold, and there were stocks and a ducking stool, but these were rarely used.

Over two centuries ago, Sefton had fine meadows reaching almost to the sea, supplying Liverpool with hay. These were watered by the river Alt, a small trout stream, but were under water the whole season after the first winter floods. After 1777 an Act was passed, and a tax levied on all owners or occupiers of improved land. The Alt was cleared and cleansed, and a new channel cut, as part of the Great South West Lancashire Reclamation Scheme. Until the 1950s ice skating was a popular winter pastime when the water froze.

Sefton manor house was demolished in 1720 and nothing now remains. In fact few of the old village dwellings are left. Two hundred years ago, Sefton church looked just as isolated as today, and the corn mill erected in the 1590s is no longer in use. Trees are few in number, and ditches take the place of hedges.

In recent years a certain amount of renovation of old barns and buildings has provided housing for people wishing to live away from suburbia. Some fine new houses have been erected, including the rectory, and the population now numbers in the region of 900 together with neighbouring Lunt.

Shevington 🥀

Shevington is a thriving village four and a half miles north-west of Wigan. Although surrounded by beautiful countryside the village is cocooned between the M6 motorway to the west and the Manchester/Liverpool railway line to the south, making it ideal commuting territory. This has resulted in the large growth in population in recent years from approximately 900 in 1900 to 12,000 today.

In earlier times inhabitants earned their living by weaving, agriculture, basket making and mining. Coal mining has taken place here from as early as 1350 and soon became the predominant industry with almost every household having its own small mine in the garden. At its peak in the 18th and 19th centuries there were seven collieries within the village boundaries. When the M6 motorway was being constructed on the outskirts of the village no fewer than 53 mineshafts were discovered. None of these collieries are working today and very little evidence is left of their existence.

The Leeds/Liverpool canal runs along the village's southern boundary and this was very important to Shevington's mining industry. However, today, thanks to the Waterways Board, the canal and towpath have been restored and have become a leisure area used by walkers, fishermen and pleasurecraft.

Past inhabitants seem to have been an industrious lot. Not content with toiling all day in the mines or mills, they found time to raise the money to build two schools and two churches. The earliest school was built by public subscription in 1814 and is still in use today as one of the three primary schools within the village. The first headmaster, Mr William Blight, was appointed in 1892.

Shevington has also had its share of disasters. The earliest ones recorded are earthquakes that occurred in 1570 and 1580. On 1st November 1861 there was an explosion at Tillywers Colliery in which 13 men died. That colliery closed in 1877. In the southern part of the village is an ICI Roburite factory which manufactures mining explosives. In May 1916 an explosion occurred there killing nine men. The manager of the works, Mr Cooksey, received a medal for gallantry in saving lives at the time.

Most of the older village buildings have now gone, but some still remain. The 17th century Victoria Bowling Green Inn is now the Conservative Club, Club House Farm built in 1660 is still occupied by an old Shevington family, the Hiltons, and Coach House Farm, in which Cromwell once slept, is still in use as a private residence.

Shevington is a healthy mix of old and new, the old fashioned community spirit intermingled with the vitality of a contemporary society. A truly modern village.

Simonstone ✒

Simonstone today has numerous new estates housing new 'in-comers' to the area but the village's roots are buried deep in history. One of the earliest visitors was John of Gaunt, who came because of the plentiful supply of game. He built himself a hunting lodge in the place where Huntroyde Hall now stands.

There are some very ancient properties in Simonstone, some of these being the West Cottages, built in about 1600 to house workers on the Huntroyde demesne. At one time the public footpath passed near to these and to the Hall itself, but a hundred years ago the then incumbent of the Hall had the path re-routed to give himself more privacy. When this new path crosses the lane it leads to a field close to woodland where the pack of hounds attached to the local hunt was kennelled at one time.

Beyond Higher Trapp, going towards Sabden, the road crosses a road called an 'ancient road', or 'Roman road' on maps. This at one time was the only road connecting Simonstone with Whalley and there is at least one exciting occurrence associated with it. During the Civil War, the Starkies of Huntroyde and the Shuttleworths of Gawthorpe supported Cromwell. One day, the Royalists left Preston and headed in the direction of Simonstone, and when the Nowells of Read Hall heard about this they asked that the soldiers should make as little noise as possible behind the Hall as a family member was seriously ill. The Cromwellian forces on the 'ancient road' met the Royalist forces at Old Read Bridge, and, although they were outnumbered by five to one by the King's forces, they put them to flight. This has been regarded by many historians as a turning point in the Civil War. Perhaps, one day, some historian will discover what happened to the sick person!

Two other old buildings are the Eveson's Tenements, again built around 1600, now used as dwellings, not as farmhouse and cottage.

Present day members of this fairly affluent village, would be surprised to learn that Simonstone once had a workhouse. The Poor Law Act required every Parish to have an Overseer of the Poor, who collected a rate, to relieve the sick and aged, bind poor children as apprentices, set the able bodied to work and punish 'sturdy beggars' and others, who would not work, to a whipping.

The village has never been known for industry, but within living memory there has been a paper-making mill, a slaughterhouse and a fire-lighter factory. Neither has it, in recent years, produced anyone of very great renown, but some time ago a Cyril Hanson trained high stepping horses, his most famous being *Simonstone Sunspot*. An enterprising man, he exported his horses to America. Another, with a claim to fame, was Tom Noble whose greyhound *Church Street* won the Waterloo Cup.

Every family these days can find something of interest. The WI produced a 'What's On in Simonstone and Read' leaflet for newcomers and it lists 26 organisations in the two villages. The village has an interesting past and looks foward to a developing future.

Singleton ✵

Singleton was first mentioned in the Domesday Book. Today it consists of Singleton Hall, a church, a church hall, a school, a bowling green, a pub, a garage, farms and about 90-odd houses and a post office.

The village, according to Ekwall, gets its name from the type of roofing that was used on the houses – 'shingles', thin pieces of wood used as house tiles.

Singleton once had a witch named Meg Shelton. She lived alone and never wanted for anything by reason of her powers. Many tales surrounded her and she was supposed to have been seen riding a broomstick into the night sky. She is buried in Woodplumpton churchyard. The grave is topped by a huge boulder-stone, because when she was first buried she scratched her way out!

Robert Gillow, who lived in Singleton during the first half of the 18th century, left to be an apprentice joiner at Lancaster. He later started the cabinet making business which became Waring & Gillow of Lancaster.

Alderman Thomas Miller, cotton manufacturer of Preston, bought Singleton for £70,000 in 1853 and pulled the old village down. He then began rebuilding it. He built the church, the school and most of the houses. His son, Thomas Horrocks Miller completed it. Singleton Hall was built in 1855.

Hewitson, a journalist from Preston, said of Singleton in 1872 'the houses are ranged in couples, they have pretty garden plots, you meet first two whitewashed houses and then a couple of red brick houses, the

Singleton fire station

population is altogether agricultural and in regular employ on the estate'. It also had a tanner, a joiner, sawyer, blacksmith, shoemaker, miller and wheelwright. In the latter half of the 19th century there was also a grocer, bricklayer, gamekeepers, gardeners and grooms. The produce from the farms was taken by train for sale in Preston and Blackpool.

The fire station (which still stands) was built in 1882 by T. H. Miller. The fire brigade was made up of volunteers from the estate workers, consisting of a captain and 14 men. They had one manually-operated fire engine pulled by a horse, but first they had to catch the horse!

T. H. Miller was a keen shire horse breeder. *Honest Tom*, one of his stallions, won first prize at the Royal Show six years running, and was one of the most famous sires in the record of shire breeding. His body is buried and marked with a gravestone in the grounds of the Hall. When the Hall was sold his head, which was stuffed and hung in the Hall, was moved to Preston Auction Market.

The appearance of the village has altered little since the years of the Millers. The garage replaces the blacksmith's and there is now a post office and a bowling green. The houses are still two whitewashed and two red brick. The Hall is now used as a boarding school for handicapped children. On Singleton Gala day a village child is queen for a day, and the children dance around the maypole as in olden days.

Slaidburn 🍃

The village of Slaidburn, lying eight miles north of Clitheroe, has seen very little change over the years and attracts visitors from all over the world.

St Andrew's church is one of the main attractions, a handsome building made of redfell stone in the Gothic style, with a tower. The church was rebuilt in about the time of Henry VII and is now in a good state of repair. The tower contains a fine peal of six bells and inside the church itself is a list of rectors dating back to 1245. It has a fine Jacobean three-decker pulpit. The verger sits in the lowest deck, the rector conducts the service from the second deck and preaches from the top deck. There are a number of family box pews, four of which are placed in the chancel behind a superbly carved oak screen.

There is also a sanctuary bar – a huge wooden pole which can be slotted into the church door, therefore giving a fugitive sanctuary for some little time. In a case in the vestry are a pair of dog whips, which were used to drive fighting dogs out of the church.

Adjoining the churchyard is the village school. Brennand's Endowed School is a grammar school founded in 1717 by John Brennand, who bequeathed £200 towards its building. An estate was left in trust out of which £50 per annum had to be paid to a master and £30 per annum to an usher for teaching the Classics and English grammar to the children of the parish. It has now been taken over by the Education Authority as the local Church of England primary school. The old stone building, now used as an assembly hall, originally had a top storey which was a dormitory for the boys.

Another fine building situated in the centre of the village is the Hark To Bounty inn, dating back to the 13th century. Until 1875 it was known as 'The Dog', when the squire of the village, who was also the parson, had a pack of hounds. One day whilst out hunting, he and his party called at the inn for refreshments. Their drinking was disturbed by loud and prolonged baying from the pack outside, and high above the noise could be heard the squire's favourite hound, which prompted him to call 'Hark to *Bounty*'.

The inn contains a remarkable courtroom which was still in use as a court as recently as 1937. From the 14th century onwards it was visited by the travelling justices, being the only courtroom then between York and Lancaster.

Beneath the reservoir to the north of Slaidburn lie the remains of Stocks-in-Bolland (or Dalehead). This village, part of Slaidburn parish until 1871, consisted of about 20 cottages, a shop and a post office. On the shores of the present reservoir stood a church with a graveyard and a vicarage, together with a school and school house.

In 1925 when the Fylde Water Board received permission to establish the reservoir, these latter buildings were demolished though the foundations of some are still visible. The remains of deceased persons had to be removed away from the gathering waters and the present graveyard was formed with a church built of stone from the old one. This little church is much visited and stands out in the forest along the Clapham road with no house in sight.

In very dry summers, the island, a breeding ground for black-headed gulls and Canada geese, becomes accessible from the shore and the remains of the old Chapel bridge can be seen spanning the original Hodder river, along with the foundations of house and field walls.

Slyne with Hest 🥀

For nearly 900 years the villages of Slyne and Hest, now formalised as Slyne with Hest, have given rest and refreshment to travellers on their way to and from Lancaster. The village story is one of a community obliged to grow, by influences outside its control, to its present position as a dormitory for the nearby conurbations.

There is a date stone on the manor house that locates the Greene family in 1681 and the stocks are where they always were, close by Hanging Green meadow. The tithe barn however was demolished as recently as 1960 to make way for a Wimpey housing estate. There is a stationmaster's house but no station and the warehouses by the canal are now cottages.

The village is still a landmark on the A6 northwards out of Lancaster and it is the first point at which the visitor can pause on the greensward to take a leisurely look at the hills of the Lake District, reflected, if he's lucky, in the still waters of Morecambe Bay. On the old Green Lane above Slyne, which was a thoroughfare long before turnpikes and motorways, there is a fuller view that reaches from the Pennine peaks of Ingleborough in the east to Walney Island at the tip of the Furness peninsula in the west.

The first recorded travellers passing Hest Bank were the monks from Furness Abbey on the other side of the bay, on their way to collect salmon from their traps at Halton, possibly using a route established by the Romans on their way west to subdue the tribe of the Brigantes in what is now Cumbria. In 1322 the Scottish armies of Robert Bruce passed through on their way to sack Lancaster and over 300 years later the area suffered violently at the hands of both the Parliamentarians and the King's men. In 1745 Bonnie Prince Charlie came down the Green Lane from the border and took refreshment at the manor house on his way south to the debacle in Derbyshire.

By the 16th century the procession of travellers had grown enough to justify the licensing of the Hest Bank Hotel – in 1554 identified simply as The Sands Inn – and by 1760 the same inn was sustaining the daily coach service, across the sands of Morecambe Bay to the Furness peninsula.

As the desire to travel boomed, the area blossomed and in 1805 the inn boasted a lantern room to guide travellers across the bay and accommodation for 16 horses, six ostlers, four drivers and a rescue team, not to mention the footwarmers and ironing and starching services. The coach service lasted through until 1856 when competition from the Furness railway finally left Hest Bank to its coastline and birdlife again. Today the coaches occasionally cross the bay by the same route, but seldom serviced by the ostlers of the Hest Bank Hotel! The guiding still relies on branches of broom known locally as 'brogs' to locate the safest route through the quicksands of the bay and across the channels of the rivers Keer and Kent.

Between the periods of the coaches and the railway the canal made its impact on Slyne with Hest. In 1820 the first pier in Morecambe Bay was opened to provide a transhipment point for goods bound via the canal for Kendal, and briefly sustained a tourist trade to the well-known watering point of Hest Bank.

The 20th century came slowly to Hest Bank and Slyne. The church was not built until 1900 but the population, at that time under 500, could also support the Congregational church that was opened in 1903. The school, opened in 1877, was attracting an average attendance of about 30 at the turn of the century. A nine-hole golf course was opened in 1905 in Hatlex Lane, and subsequently closed, and the station on the main line to the north that thrived between the wars was closed in 1967. The so-called Coast Road was opened in 1933 to serve the modern tourist and the building developer, and to make sure there were to be no green fields between the sea and the A6.

Staining 🌿

The village is approached along narrow, winding lanes and has a church, an inn, a school, a caravan site, a windmill and several farms. Its size has increased in recent years with the appearance of several small housing developments.

The church, dedicated to St Luke, began over a century ago as a school, used on Sundays as a mission church. There is a new school now, and the church serves the community during the week as a meeting place.

The windmill stands proudly at the junction of Smithy Lane and Mill Lane, alongside the path of a Roman track from Freckleton Naze on the river Ribble to Skippool on the river Wyre. Weavers used to walk that track as they came to work in a building which is now part of Baines' Farm. The windmill stands four storeys high, with a revolving wooden dome. The position of the sails is set by a long rope. They are canvas sails which can be taken down like a ship's sails. Other mills in the Fylde have wooden slats like venetian blinds. After the mill was gutted by fire the village was fortunate enough to have a family come along who have renovated it so well that the sails have actually begun to turn again.

The old brewery has seen its neighbouring ice cream factory go up in smoke. There is a story associated with the nearby natural spring: 'A handsome stranger appeared before a woman at the spring and gave her some fairy ointment to put on her child's eyes. The woman decided to try it on herself first and put some on her left eye. A few days later she went to Preston market and was surprised to see the same gentleman stealing corn while no one else seemed to notice. He was amazed that she could see him for he should have been invisible. Realising she had been using the ointment herself, he dealt her a blow that destroyed her left eye.'

The village pub of 110 years stood on one of the blind corners and was renowned for its pianist. However, there is now a new Plough Inn with a large grassy frontage where its predecessor stood. It was built from bricks reclaimed from demolition work in Preston and its roof slates have an attractive pattern created with green slates among the grey. It would be interesting to hear what the workers involved in building Blackpool Tower thought of the new pub – they used to call at the old one for refreshment as they walked home each evening.

Stalmine with Staynall

The village of Stalmine is unique among its neighbours as it lies almost entirely on the salt beds. Thousands of gallons of brine are pumped daily from beneath the rich agricultural land to give support to the ICI factories at Thornton in their manufacturing processes. The three miles of riverside and saltmarshes give a varied landscape, with minor population centres at Staynall, Coldrow and Wardleys. The river Wyre flows to the sea at Fleetwood.

The village encompasses 2,312 acres of most interesting countryside. On a gently rising hill 75 ft above sea level, it clusters around the ancient church, very much the same in layout as it was hundreds of years ago, the newer properties blending with the old. At Staynall the cottages and farmsteads are exactly as they were in 1710 before either Blackpool or Fleetwood were established.

At Wardleys, formerly a flourishing port and now a modern yachting centre there is a horseshoe harbour, which once held three-masted ships. At Coldrow there was once a busy smithy. At the Heads (taking its name

206

from the Saxon 'haywood', meaning an enclosed space) Russian ships loaded up with rock salt as they returned down river from Wardleys where they had discharged cargoes of tallow and flax.

A curious wooden track of split oak trees laid on birchwood scrub, known as Kate's Pad, crosses the moss. Pollen tests have established that it pre-dates Roman times. Farmers have dug up trees of 50 ft in length.

The parish church of St James was once dedicated to St Oswald and the registers are complete from 1583. They contain many interesting and poignant entries including references to many deaths during the plague year of 1623–24. There was an ancient cross at the Four Lane Ends at Staynall, known as the Combelaw Cross, and at Stalmine, the Lawrence Cross. There are also the remains of an ancient preaching cross in the churchyard, restructured into a sundial in 1690.

After a Customs House had opened at Poulton le Fylde in 1708, Wardleys and Staynall became notorious for smuggling. At Wardleys smugglers gathered at No 4 on a little road near the quayside, later known as Velvet Street as the rolls of French cloth were said to be hidden there. Kegs of rum were thrown out on the banks of the river and hidden at High Gate in an old barn.

The first mention of 'Stalming Scoole' was in 1674, although there were others at Coldrow and Moss Side. What is now Stalmine post office where the old bar is now the serving counter, was once an inn with a cock pit. 'Mains' (cock fights) were held at all seasons and the schoolmaster attended with his pupils!

The rise of Fleetwood in the 1830s led to the decline of Wardleys as a port. But waggonettes brought visitors from Blackpool and Wardleys toffee became very popular.

After the Second World War the population doubled. The village school has been renovated and extended and a fine secondary school, St Aidan's, has been established in Preesall. The Seven Stars and the Wardleys Hotel meet the new social scene while retaining their antiquity. There are two village shops and a restaurant.

Gradual subsidence to the west of the village will limit the future extension of Stalmine, although building is planned for 80 acres around the school. The once-pure Wyre, where the Prince Regent walked with Mrs Fitzherbert, is now polluted by effluent from five urban districts and by the discharges of the ICI. The flukes and samphire are inedible.

Such is the price of progress that the Stalmine people have paid in their pleasant village, 'far from the madding crowd'.

Tarleton ✤

Tarleton, a busy village in West Lancashire, seems to have been known from as early as the 13th century, though in those days it was known as Tharilton. Several houses dating from the 17th century are in the village, one in Plox Brow having a date of 1635.

Early houses would have been built near the river Douglas, the river being very busy with shipping by the 16th century. By the 1800s trade had increased tremendously, with schooners sailing from Tarleton with cargoes of slate, iron ore, gunpowder for quarrying and coal. The river Douglas and the canal run side by side. Local people can remember coal being brought along the canal in barges and stored in boat yards at Bank Bridge and Plox Brow. Local coalmen weighed and bagged the coal and delivered it to houses on horse-drawn carts.

After a complex historical and religious background, the church of the Blessed Virgin Mary was consecrated on 24th July 1719 by the Bishop of Chester. It was built on the site of the ancient church of St Helen. Now the old church is only used once a year on the first Sunday in August. This day has become a reunion for people who have loved ones buried in the grounds and for people who have moved away from Tarleton through marriage or work. A larger church was required and on 7th June 1888 Holy Trinity church was consecrated by the Bishop of Manchester.

Methodism was first recorded in the village in the early 1800s, with the building of a chapel in 1851. Behind the chapel a row of cottages was built. When the old chapel was demolished the cottages remained. The new chapel built at the side was consecrated in 1896.

The Ram's Head, dated 1640, was an old coaching inn, situated on the road from Ormskirk to Preston. Years ago there was a toll gate across the road at Windgate Corner. Coaches would pass through there from Liverpool to Preston. The Cock and Bottle in the village was reputed to be a venue for cock fights. One landlord tried to change the name to 'Tarleton Hotel' but local people preferred the original name.

Tarleton has always had farming as its main occupation. Life was hard for farmers years ago on the Moss. The land was peaty and had to be drained, the peat being used for fuel. Today, in every direction, there are greenhouses. The first greenhouses were built at the end of the 19th century. Tomatoes and lettuces are grown under glass in great quantity, creating employment for many in the area. Many vegetables are grown on the land today.

Many craft occupations thrived in the early part of the century in the village. Mr Hugh Cookson had a basket-making shop near Gorse Lane End. In a large wooden building, the locally grown willow twigs were boiled and thrown on a bench for workers to peel. The story goes that the experienced workers picked out the thicker twigs, throwing the thin ones for others to peel. The workers were paid by weight of twigs peeled so they knew how to earn the most money.

J. Webster & Sons Ltd is a large shop in the village which has celebrated its centenary. Beginning with a small shop and a travelling van, it has progressed to a large shop selling furniture, china, clothing etc. Travelling shops were the vogue for years, even into the 1920s. Mr Baybutt went round the village selling material by the yard, towels and red spotted handkerchiefs. He also carried paraffin and candles in his horse-drawn van.

In 1924 about six Tarleton women got together to make money to buy a large car that was for sale. They bought it and had it converted into a temporary ambulance. In 1928, Tarleton had its own two District Nurses, who lived in the village.

Many of the older inhabitants regret the passing of the 'good neighbours' – the way one could leave a door unlocked or leave the insurance money on the table for the man to collect and for it not to be stolen. None the less they welcome the modern amenities of the Health Centre, Mark Square shops, bus services, better roads and local authority services.

Tatham Fells

This scattered community covers eleven square miles including Tatham Fells and Botton, and contains almost 100 dwellings. But only 14 are in the village of Lowgill, with three completely new houses, two barn conversions and a recently restored derelict cottage. In spite of a slump in population 50 years ago there are ten more families than there were in 1881 when most of them were employed in agriculture.

But the countryside hasn't changed much. This is still the most beautiful place on earth. In summer hedges are scented with blossom, elder flowers, roses and honeysuckle and an abundance of wild flowers and native trees on the steep valley sides in full leaf. These hedges and stone walls divide pastures and meadows, some dark green, others almost white when grass has been recently harvested. Looking south the fells are shading to brown. In autumn they sport purple patches of heather when grouse fly for their lives from sportsmen's guns.

Legend has it that a Celtic road traverses the western side of the valley while traces of the Roman road from Ribchester to Burrow can still be clearly seen on the eastern side.

On the Roman road stands Robert Hall (named after Robert Cantsfield), part of which was a Catholic chapel. This house hides a priest's hole, as does Cragg Hall.

The present road from Slaidburn, no longer gated, has the stone base of the Cross of Greet at the watershed. This pack horse trail was served by three inns, Higher Craggs long ago, the Moorcock up to 1889 and the Rose and Crown until 1961.

The great stone of Fourstones is a landmark, said to have been dropped by the Devil when his apronstring broke. The other three were broken up to fill holes in the road over Burnmoor. Nearby is Ringstones farm, possibly the site of a stone circle, not far from the Good Shepherd church, rebuilt in 1888.

The Wesleyan chapel was built in 1866. There is said to have been a Quaker meeting house at Lanshaw and schools at Noggs near High Thrushgill, Croasdale Grains and Tunstall House, as well as the Old School which was rebuilt in 1863 and closed in 1961 when the new school was built in the village.

Thornley-with-Wheatley 🌿

There is little resemblance to the traditional village yet Thornley-with-Wheatley boasts a church, public house and school. Thornley, meaning 'pasture amid the thorns', and Wheatley, 'lee where wheat grows', is recorded as 'Watelie with one carucate of cultivated land' in the Domesday Book. Evidence of the wheat beds is still visible when long shadows highlight the fellside. From Jeffrey Hill, the Bowland and Bleasdale Fells and the coast are clearly visible. The present population, 279, is the lowest since figures were recorded, the highest being 516 in 1831.

The village was once a much more lively place, even within living memory. The water mill, its leets and dams now dry, houses an agricultural machinery repair shop, the lime kilns and pits at Arbour Farm have become a fossil-rich Site of Special Scientific Interest with quietly browsing sheep, and the quarries are empty of carts and men. Cottages no longer echo to the thump of the handloom, and the carpenter's shop is empty. The great cheese presses are museum pieces, and a garage has replaced the role of the smithy.

The one constant occupation is farming, the lifeblood of the community. Modern concrete and iron buildings mark the new age of agriculture, dairying and sheep rearing, and chemical fertilizers have replaced the 'marl' once brought from still-existing pits. Yoghurt is commercially produced, and the leisure industry catered for by a golf club, an hotel and an inn. In 1989 many barns were converted to dwellings, but in 1712: 'Thomas Seed of Thornley' was allowed 'to turn the house . . . of Thomas Eccles into a stable'.

Important in local history is Thornley Hall and its connections with the lords of the manor: a priest hole and secret room are worthy of particular note. The site of the manorial mill is nearby, where the 'kuck-stool' may have been positioned, and the stock stones still are. Before Thornley school was opened in 1880, children had to attend school at Chipping. Now they are transported to various venues, the village school having closed in 1977. The bulding is now used as a community centre.

St William's Roman Catholic church, founded 1735, and arguably the most turbulent of places in the past, is once more under threat of closure, as its mission school at Lee House Farm was many years ago. Watering Trough Garage and the Derby Arms still serve the wayfarer, but the latter no longer hosts the Trinity Tuesday Court Leet. Happily the building called 'Bedlam' is not needed as a corrective asylum for the present parishioners.

Through the centuries certain notable inhabitants have lived and worked in the village. Miss Ann Cutler, well known as 'Praying Nanny', was born in Thornley in 1759, converted at an early age, and 'her joyful patience through all adversity' in turn converted countless persons before she died at the early age of 35 years.

Memories of the oldest inhabitants tie the past to the present, with stories and traditions. Some tell of the days when boys were paid 1d for scaring crows, or of the 'big snow' which cut Thornley off from the rest of the world for two weeks, with hedge-high drifts. The 'head in the wall' at Wheatley has a tale attached of a grieving mother placing it there as a memorial to a son killed in the Wars of the Roses. A more historical tradition relates how a certain Father Trappe moved a stone cross base from Wheatley to Lee House cemetery, against all local advice and superstition. It took twelve horses and eight men to transport it and dire consequences were foretold. The late incumbent of the church honoured it with a new cross in 1988. In 1879 an epidemic of diphtheria decimated the children of the area, the population dropped by 100! The story is told of the miracle cure from America, of painting the throat with 'sulphur and glycerine', which was small comfort for those who had already lost five children.

Though occupation and population may vary, the wild life of the area is ever present: the deer, hare, grouse, partridge and pheasant, a reminder of the old hunts and the new 'shoots'. The trout swim in the Loud, where once freshwater oysters were found, the heron glides overhead, the kestrel hovers and 'tuwits' and plovers wheel and call across a landscape with a magical beauty all its own.

Thornton-le-Fylde 🌿

The sun rises on Thornton over its eastern boundary, the river Wyre, and sets over the sea at the holiday resort of Cleveleys, into which the west of Thornton merges. The main road through Thornton is wide and straight, connecting Poulton-le-Fylde from its southern boundary to Fleetwood's northern peninsula. Gravel from the beach was used to form this road, the first over Thornton Marsh, in 1805. The Highway Rate for Little Thornton in 1827 is recorded as sixpence in the pound!

Victoria Road is now an attractive avenue of bungalows and semi-detached houses with well kept gardens, decoratively lined with tall, old horse chestnut trees. The public gardens around the cenotaph, library and bank at Four Lane Ends and at all the major road junctions are attractive and colourful, reflecting the pride and caring nature of its inhabitants to visitors, passers by and newcomers.

Of the four local day schools, the oldest dates back to 1717, when the woollen merchant James Baines provided an opportunity for the local children to receive a free general education. The foundation stone can be seen on an existing wall of Baines Endowed School, which was rebuilt in 1908. Money he invested in farmland and property paid for the school's upkeep and on Candlemas Day, when the farmers paid their annual rent, the schoolmaster was given his salary and the scholars enjoyed a day's holiday. The trustees were provided with 'a sumptuous meal' at the Bay Horse Inn, across the road.

There are no less than six places of Christian worship – two Church of England, two Roman Catholic and two Methodist. The first Methodist church on the Fylde was built in Thornton in 1812, on a site alongside the present Wignall Memorial Methodist church, where the church hall

212

and Sunday school buildings now stand. It is said that the Wesley preachers would come by boat during the night to Wardleys Creek, fearful of the Anglicans who would fight to keep them out. The parish church of Thornton, Christ Church, and the parsonage on Meadows Avenue, were built in the 1830s at the expense of the lord of the manor – Peter Hesketh Fleetwood. St John's is the newest church in the area, built in 1961 to create a new parish in Little Thornton, due to the increase in population during the 1950s.

The Preston and Wyre railway line opened in 1840 with a station in Thornton called Ramper. Alas, its life was short as it was closed within three years. A nearby station called Cleveleys was more successful and in 1905 had its name changed to 'Thornton for Cleveleys'. It was replaced by a new station north of the level crossing in the 1920s and was finally renamed 'Thornton Cleveleys' in 1953. It closed in 1970. The line provided transport for the busy docks and salt works at Fleetwood but also attracted holidaymakers to the Fylde coast. During the holiday season, crowds standing five deep were said to have lined the length of the platform.

The salt works, which became part of the United Alkali Company, began production of salt at Burn Naze, on the boundaries of Fleetwood with Thornton, in 1890, using local girls as salt packers. By 1926 it was under the control of ICI, extending along the banks of the Wyre, and to this day provides the major source of industrial employment in the area.

The river Wyre has provided further important industry and employment for several centuries. Cotton and flax were regularly delivered at Wardleys Creek and Skippool Creek, where Russian and other foreign cargo ships called. Today, Skippool boasts a marina, busy with leisure boats and as a mooring for Skippool Yacht Club. The river banks form part of the newly developed Stanah Country Park with designated picnic areas. Further up the river, situated near the cockle beds, was a small white cottage called Cockle Hall, belonging to Peter Hesketh. Near to the Hall and salt marshes, samphire (sea-fennel) was gathered and sold for pickling.

Another feature is Thornton Marsh Mill, which was built in 1794. Standing at 70 ft, with its sails towering above the houses, it is the tallest windmill in the Fylde. From its platform, on a clear day, views of Lancaster and the Lake District can be seen. It was the only windmill in the Fylde containing all the necessary machinery for grinding corn and it remained a working mill until 1922. Restoration work was carried out in 1935, following a frightening and damaging gale.

Standing alongside the old millyard were two cottages, a joiner's shop and a blacksmith's. A new project is now in hand to restore the mill to working order and incorporate it into a Craft Village.

In close proximity to the mill, but with its entrance on the main Victoria Road, are the very popular Ashdell bowling greens and a new leisure centre with facilities for all the popular indoor sports. Community amenities include a health centre, with its forward-looking well-woman clinic, a local dentist, chemist, post office, library, several banks and all the shops for daily needs.

Thurnham 🦡

Thurnham is a small scattered village community situated about five miles south of Lancaster, made up mainly of farming families. The manor of Thurnham used to belong to the Dalton family who lived at Thurnham Hall. They were descendants of St Thomas More and at one time owned many acres of land in Lancashire. Death duties took their toll and the last of the family, Miss Alzira Eloise Dalton, who died in 1983, sold the Hall and lived in the cottage just inside the gates which bear the Dalton family crest. Thurnham Hall has been restored and is undergoing alterations to become a time-share development.

The ruins of the Abbey of St Mary of the Marsh at Cockersand are buried under the fields of Abbey Farm; only the chapter house remains standing. This appears to be a rare example of octagonal form in a Premonstratensian house and is thought to date from the 13th century, although there was a hermitage founded here about 1180 by Hugh Garth which later became a hospital belonging to Leicester Abbey. The ceiling of the chapter house is beautifully vaulted in red sandstone. Much of the stonework of the abbey is now incorporated in local farmhouses, including Crook Farm opposite Sunderland Point which has windows and doorways from the abbey in the house and shippon. The field adjacent to the farm is named Chapel Hill leading one to suppose that there was once a chapel of ease there.

Salmon fishing using heave, drift and whammel nets is still carried on though the number of fishermen declines each year.

The estuary and salt marshes are also home to vast numbers of wading birds, oyster catchers, cormorants and sheld ducks and is one of the few remaining pieces of unspoilt, undeveloped coastline in Lancashire. The sea walls hold a wealth of wild flowers but unfortunately Spartina Grass is growing on the marshes, destroying the mud flats where the wading birds feed.

Farming is mainly traditional although silage has replaced hay due in part to the changeable weather. Dairy farming and sheep are the dominant forms of farming. Hawthorn hedges surround the fields and many bear testimony to the gales, being almost horizontal in some cases.

The gales coupled with high tides result in the whole of Thurnham being flooded on occasions, the last being on 11th November 1977 when water covered the land as far inland as Briggs Brow, the site of the former school which has been converted into a house.

St Thomas and St Elizabeth Roman Catholic church is beyond Thurnham Hall and is surrounded by woodland which is rich in flora and fauna. It is a beautiful church with a rood screen and is well worth a visit. In the wood there is also an ice house, which used to belong to Thurnham Hall and where meat would be stored before the days of refrigerators.

Trawden ✣

The name Trawden was probably first given to the trough-shaped valley which contains the village of the present day. Trawden is now in the borough of Pendle and lies near the foot of Boulsworth Hill. There is no main road through Trawden so villagers grew up and married within a compact community, producing many families with the same surname. This led to people being better known by their nicknames than by their proper names. It was said by outsiders that all 'Trawdeners' owned their own house and the one next door – meaning that they were very thrifty and did not easily part with their hard-earned wages!

Rennie o'Cobs, whose name was actually Wilkinson, lived at No 4 Slack Booth. This building was once a dandy shop where people could buy wool which they took to their own cottages to be woven into woollen cloth on a hand loom. When power looms at the local mills took the place of handloom weaving, the price of hand-woven cloth fell and many villagers were forced to seek work in the mills in Trawden and the nearby town of Colne. Today there are still two mills operating in Trawden – Forest Shed and Hollin Hall Mill. Although other small industrial businesses flourish in Trawden the majority of villagers now work outside the village.

Children up to the age of eleven attend the village school, which was built in 1910 and nicknamed 'Trawden High School' because it is at the top of a very steep street.

Trawden also encompasses the villages of Winewall and Wycoller, the latter having a famous house known as Wycoller Hall (allegedly being the Hall described in the novel *Jane Eyre* as Ferndean Manor). In about 1865 the porch of Wycoller Hall was bought by David Bannister and brought to Trawden where it was rebuilt on to Scar Top Mill to enlarge the living accommodation for his family of eleven children. The youngest of these was named Ralph and he was the father of Dr Roger Bannister, who was the first athlete ever to run a mile in under four minutes.

A favourite beauty spot is 'Lumb Spout'. Situated higher up the valley in a pleasant wooded clough, a small stream falls in a single spout clear of the rock face down to a deep pool at the base of the rocks. On the way to Lumb Spout is Midge Hole between Seg-Hole Farm and Greenbank Cottages. This was the headquarters of the Midge Hole Club. Each Saturday at noon, when work finished at the local mills, many of the men made their way to Midge Hole where they gambled away their wages. They did not return to their homes until Sunday evening and some even stayed until it was time for work on Monday morning. Many wives and children suffered great deprivation because of their husbands' gambling.

There are still two clubs in Trawden today. White Lea Head Club, more commonly known as the 'Cock Hill Club', is situated near Slack Booth whilst the Grand Club is on Colne Road. Both are still 'men only'.

Being on the slopes of the Pennines, Trawden gets its fair share of rain and the North West Water Authority land on Boulsworth Hill is a gathering ground for water. A reservoir supplying Trawden with water was situated at Alderhurst Head Farm and this has now been supplemented by the further construction of another reservoir near to Dyke Farm. This water is of a high purity and softness. However, in times of drought the moors become tinder-dry and in 1942 Boulsworth Hill was on fire for many weeks, the fire covering approximately 18 square miles.

Floods occur from time to time in both Trawden and Wycoller and the most recent one, on 19th May 1989, was described by the Meteorological Office as a 'once in a thousand years' thunderstorm. Nearly nine inches of rain fell in just two hours. Wycoller was particularly badly hit with a flash flood 4 ft high sweeping through the village. Cars were swept away, houses flooded, and the historic 1,000 year old Clam Bridge in Wycoller Dene was broken into several pieces and swept downstream.

One of the oldest houses in Trawden is Dent House situated at 'T'top o' Trawden'. The house is roofed with stone slates and on the middle chimney is the date 1604. Further along Colne Road, Trawden Hall, which was built around 1900, replaced an older house once belonging to the Foulds family. Miss Mary Foulds, who died in 1817, gave money for the building of Trawden church in 1845. The church is dedicated to St Mary and it was built of local stone taken from Rock Lane quarry. The vicar of Trawden from 1908 to 1949 was Canon Hugh Paul Dempsey, well known by all his parishioners who often met him on his visits around the parish wearing his familiar garb of cassock and clogs. It was a rare occasion to see him wearing shoes.

Treales, Roseacre & Wharles

This parish consists of some 4,100 acres of typical Fylde countryside. Total population of the three villages is approximately only 379. It was a much higher figure 100 to 150 years ago when local industries employed many locals and agriculture was more man-intensive.

At Tile Farm in Treales, a tile works, made all the drainage tiles required on the estate and a local brickworks in Wharles turned out the lovely red bricks (hand thrown in the early days) which can be seen on local buildings today. Unfortunately the clay pits of the brickworks were filled in some years ago.

The parish is bisected by the M55 but it is otherwise untouched by any main roads, and comprises quiet country lanes, small woods and farm-steads. Treales, pronounced 'Trails', is the main centre of population with its church, school, village inn called the Derby Arms, and groups of cottages.

The parish church, Christ Church, was erected in 1853 and endowed five years later by the Dean and Chapter of Christ Church, Oxford. Treales school was acquired in 1876 and is a listed building of architectu-ral importance. There is an old inn called the Eagle and Child at Wharles, very pleasing visually with a recently thatched roof. A thatched cottage called Pointer House is reputed to have been a coaching inn.

The parish is, for the most part, flat and well-suited to arable and dairy farming. Much of the land formerly belonged to the Earl of Derby and later the Church Commissioners' estates until 1971, when it was trans-ferred to the Pension Fund Property Unit Trust. In 1987 the estate was acquired by Mountleigh, an investment company.

There are several listed buildings. Rhododendron Cottage and Ivy Dene Farm have been beautifully restored and both have gained conser-vation awards.

An old windmill in the village of Treales has recently acquired a new cap roof in the style traditionally used on this type of windmill. The sails no longer turn to grind corn and the windmill is now a beautiful home.

Rural pursuits, clay pigeon shooting, retriever dog trials, riding and shooting are part of the history of the parish and many people still enjoy these sports today. The local shooting club do much to enhance the area with the ducks, pheasants and partridge reared each year. Over the last decade foxes have returned to this area, and a family of deer live in the surrounding woodlands.

Tunstall

The parish of Tunstall lies at the northern edge of Lancashire, sharing a border with North Yorkshire and Cumbria.

Each of the settlements of Tunstall, Cantsfield and Burrow has a separate entity, but all are in a highly-organised agricultural setting, based predominantly on dairy cows, fattening cattle and sheep. The lush green pastures cultivated for animal fodder are an integral part of the landscape.

Tunstall has several facilities common to the parish. It has a fine, mainly 15th century church of St John the Baptist, well kept and admired. This is said to be the 'Brocklebridge church' of Charlotte Bronte's *Jane Eyre*. The footpath the young Brontës trod from Cowan Bridge Clergy Daughters' School, and the room above the church porch in which their food was eaten after morning service, witness this link with the past. The post office and shop is situated in a row of white-washed cottages opposite the Lunesdale Arms on the main road.

Moated Thurland Castle, in a majestic setting of parkland, is glimpsed from Church Lane. Now privately owned and being carefully restored, it has all but lost its links with the area. Only the chime of its clock reminds us that it is still there.

The generosity of a former vicar of Tunstall, Rev Lees, provided the site for a parish hall over 60 years ago. The days of village dances and whist drives are sadly past. The tennis court next door, recently refurbished, provides a welcome sports facility for all ages.

Going towards Kirkby Lonsdale, from Tunstall on the A683, Burrow is glimpsed as a hamlet of stone-built houses, bright with flowers in the summer. Behind the Highwayman Inn a redundant barn has been converted to three dwellings. A rural workshop has also been built and

Church of St John the Baptist, Tunstall

created from former farm units. Burrow Hall was built on the site of a Roman fort. Privately owned, the site is not accessible.

Travelling from Tunstall in the other direction and turning towards Ingleton at the Greta Bridge, beautifully constructed but bearing far too many heavy lorries, the river Greta flows towards the river Lune. Follow the A687 and you come to Cantsfield, yet again a large agricultural area but one may think of it as that small cluster of stone-built dwellings on the road to Burton-in-Lonsdale. Cantsfield Hall Farm is a fine example of a 17th century building, and had considerable influence in the area during that era.

Events in the farming calendar provide a quality of life for residents – young lambs in the spring, the whirr of machinery in high summer, cows slowing down traffic on the A683 as they return for milking. There is the call of the curlew, herons idly flying over to the becks, and ducks, geese and swans flying in formation at dusk to find the Lune, a river which provides one of the choicest salmon fishing stretches in the country.

Nearby Kirkby Lonsdale with its busy streets appears to be an overflow from the Lake District. Yet here in Tunstall, four miles away, the pace of life, despite the buzz of traffic at busy times, could be described as a 'rural idyll' which many envy.

Ulnes Walton ❧

There is much of interest in this small township, a part of Chorley Rural District, situated between Croston and Leyland, with the ecclesiastical parishes of Croston and St James, Leyland, within its boundaries.

In the 13th century the manor of Walton (also spelt Waleton) was in the possession of Ulf of Walton, and was part of the barony of Penwortham. Legend has it that the original Ulf was a Danish pirate who sailed up the river Douglas, into the river Lostock and settled at Littlewood. Ulf's manor house was on the site of Littlewood Hall, about two miles from Ulnes Walton school.

A short distance north of Lostock Bridge, on the eastern side of the road to Leyland, there was until recently a small three-cornered piece of ground enclosed by hedges. This was the pinfold where straying animals were kept in charge of a pinner or pinder, who released them to the owners on payment of one shilling to the overseers of the township. The pinfold is now levelled, the trees bounding it cut down and no trace of it remains.

The bases of two crosses, one behind Lostock Bridge and the Roecroft cross at the junction of Ulnes Walton Lane and Southport Road, are all that remain of praying crosses where coffins were rested on their way to Croston or Eccleston church. There was no church at Moss Side, the west end of Leyland, until 1855.

The story goes that when the Roecroft cross base was moved during road widening it was brought back overnight to its original place. Several times the stone crossed and re-crossed the road until some local lads dressed as ghosts moved it to its present site, and it was not moved again.

Did deer once roam on Barber's Moor and Roe Moor? There is also Roecroft Farm and Roe Cottage along Ulnes Walton Lane. Over 50 years ago a house which had been roofed by corrugated iron was stripped to reveal the original thatch. Hidden in the thatch was a pair of deer's antlers. Deer poaching brought severe penalties, and this was evidence which could not be destroyed easily; hence the secure hiding place.

Within the boundaries of the township there has been a brickworks and a pottery. The pottery was known as 'The Lancashire Pottery Company, Ulnes Walton', and specialised in the making of glazed earthenware for domestic and garden use.

The oldest established business, which continues to flourish, is that of J. H. Mayor and Sons' saw mills. The firm was established by James Mayor, great-great-grandfather of Henry Mayor, now head of the firm. James Mayor made handloom shuttles and bobbins. His son made bungs for brewers' barrels and clog blocks. The family business progressed and expanded under the next generation, headed by John Henry Mayor with his sons, the eldest of whom, Robert, was the father of the present owner. The firm suplied timber for joiners and wagon builders, as well as smaller items, such as mangle rollers.

Tradition says that Mr J. H. Mayor was able to save a piece of history, for amongst the timber received at the yard was a manger made from a tree trunk, which had been used for feeding horses when Lathom House was besieged by the Parliamentarians in 1645.

There was an old windmill behind the saw mill, described even in 1808 as 'the ruins of a windmill'. It had been used as a malt kiln and had a good well of water, but later fell into disuse, except for storage, and was demolished when the structure became unsafe.

Toll Bar House, no longer standing, on Southport Road, was much used when cockle-gatherers passed on their way from Banks to Chorley Market.

Waddington 🌿

Much of Waddington's history can be traced from its buildings. The fine church, for example, though largely rebuilt at the beginning of this century, is in the Perpendicular style of an older church. The coat of arms on the tower is a reminder that Richard Tempest, lord of the manor, was concerned with its building in 1500.

Among the monuments are some to members of the Parker family of Browsholme Hall. Since 1630, as owners of the advowson, they have appointed the vicars. All the 19th century vicars were members of the Parker family. Some old church customs, such as rushbearing and 'beating the bounds' of the parish continued into the 19th century. The dog-whipper whose duty it was to control any dogs straying into church was, until 1840, paid six shillings for his services.

The stocks are still to be seen in their original position by the church. They were kept in repair and used until the late 18th century, as was the nearby pinfold where stray cattle were impounded. Also near the church is the former smithy, now a private house. Older villagers remember gathering there to watch the smith at work at his anvil and to hear the latest news. During the First World War the smith spent one day a week making horseshoes for the cavalry.

The Methodist Sunday school stands on the site of a second smithy. Originally, the Wesleyans worshipped in a cottage in Back Fold, but in 1824 they built a chapel which also served, until 1889, as a Sunday school. In the years when there was no day school in the village the only education was that given by their two 'ABC teachers' and others teaching writing and spelling on Sundays. Over 100 children were then attending the school.

Although today many of the residents of Waddington are retired people and commuters, the village was, until a hundred years ago, almost a self-supporting community made up of farmers, craftsmen and weavers. Up the clough there was a cotton spinning mill supplying yarn to the handloom weavers; behind the Sun Inn, bobbins and chairs were made in a small factory; there was a tannery at the back of the village. The back-to-back houses in the square may well have been the homes and workshops of weavers; later, one of them served as the lock-up. Around the Square, the centre of village life, were the wheelwright's shop, the post office, houses thatched with straw or ling and several shops. At the Higher Buck – then known as the Buck i'th Vine – in 1838 members of the Waddington Branch of the Order of Foresters were enrolled by 'Robin Hood' and 'Little John'. Until only a few years before this there had been bull-baiting in the Square.

At one of the three inns 40 yards of blue cloth were distributed to the poor on the feast of St Michael. A lady called Ellen Wilkinson had made provision for this in 1694 and for over 200 years the terms of her charity were observed.

It was in the attic of the Sun Inn that the parish chest was discovered and presented to the newly formed Parish Council in 1896. Its contents – accounts kept by the Poor Law overseers and constables – are now in the Preston Record Office; the chest itself seems to have disappeared.

A short distance from the Square is the hospital founded by Robert Parker 'to the Honour of God' and 'for the convenient reception of ten poor widows'. The original homes and a chapel where the Reader took services twice daily were built in a row behind the old pump dated 1700. Eventually provision was made for 30 widows and new cottages were built. The founder's birthday is still observed on 13th June each year.

Down the road from the Square stands the Old Hall with the words 'I will raise up his ruins and I will build it as in the days of old' inscribed over the gateway. John Waddington who bought the Hall – then a rather dilapidated farmhouse – in 1900, restored it to something of its former glory when it had been the manor house of the Tempests and a refuge for a king. During the Wars of the Roses, Henry VI, having been defeated at Hexham in 1464, stayed first at Bolton Hall and then at Waddington. One evening at dinner, warned of the approach of his Yorkist enemies, he escaped from the Hall and crossed the Ribble at Brungerley Hippings, but was captured in the nearby wood and taken to the Tower of London.

On the outskirts of the village near Brungerley Bridge is Waddow Hall, a much older building than its 18th century facade suggests. This too belonged to the lords of the manor but is now a Girl Guide training centre. Wade's Hill, allegedly the site of Wada's Saxon encampment, is behind the house. The bridge itself indicates the former boundary between the old rivals, Lancashire and Yorkshire. Today Waddington, proud of its Yorkshire past, is part of the Red Rose County.

Walmer Bridge

Walmer Bridge in Little Hoole is first recorded in 1251 in the chartulary of Cockersand Abbey as Waldemurebruge. Part of Longton, the hamlet is situated around Walmer Brook, a tributary of the river Douglas. The original bridge was demolished and the brook culverted in 1901 but after repeated flooding the culvert was rebuilt in 1970.

One of the oldest buildings, Walmer Hall, stands at the corner of Dob Lane in Little Hoole, still occupied and now divided into two houses.

The Wilkins brothers, owners of a local malting, brewing and bottling business, originally owned the Walmer Bridge Inn and the nearby Longton Arms. They also owned four other local inns and some hotels in Southport. They gave the site for the new Methodist chapel which was opened in 1894. Previously the Methodists had to meet in various houses.

They also built Rawcliffe Row, Sea View and School Street in 1855. Most of the occupants worked at the local mill opened in 1852 by Crewdson and Grierson, making velvet and furnishing fabrics.

The local school was supported generously by them after its opening in 1860 for it provided most of the workers for their factory later on. A red brick gabled building, it has been carefully preserved by the present occupiers and the original clog scraper can still be seen at the door. A new school was opened in Dob Lane in 1937.

The factory closed in 1931. After its demolition in 1979 the site was cleared. It is now a sheltered housing estate called 'Old Mill Court'. A local Co-op opened in 1909 has also closed, and is being converted into shops and flats.

The local industries include a ladies lingerie factory, mushroom, dairy and poultry farms, a cash register assembly and sales, two motor service stations, a dressed poultry factory, a cellophane and polypropylene packaging firm and a prestige car distributor. There is a local ambulance station and a post office.

Walton-le-Dale

The village of Walton-le-Dale, known in the Domesday Book as Waleton, lies at the confluence of the two rivers – the Ribble and the Darwen. There was a settlement in the area even before the Romans built a camp on their road from Wigan to Lancaster.

Much of the land in Walton-le-Dale is cultivated as market gardens. On the site of one, Mosney, was a mill where in 1780 the first roller printing machine was installed for the printing of calico.

In May 1840 the Cuerdale Hoard was discovered by men repairing the river bank in the area named Cuerdale on the south bank of the Ribble. The hoard was probably the war chest of a Danish king which was buried hurriedly as the Vikings retreated to the coast after a defeat in battle.

At the top of the hill aptly named Church Brow, stands St Leonard's church. There has been a church on this site since 1162. Some fascinating gravestones are to be found in and around the church. One in particular, set into the floor of the chancel, states 'Here lies the body of Samuel Brooke killed going to the Assizes, by William Buckley August 9th 1722'. Stories are told of the ceremony of 'Raising the Dead' in the churchyard in 1560, when a local alchemist is reputed to have raised a newly-buried man who prophesied correctly about local people. Strange goings-on indeed!

Next to the church is the Old School – built about 1832. This is now used for meetings, offices and a fitness club. The new school on the bank of the river Darwen was officially opened in 1974, access to it being along Walton Green, one of the oldest and most picturesque roads in the village.

John Wesley came to Walton-le-Dale in 1784 while on a visit to Preston. Methodism started in this area in the early 1760s, but it was only in 1868 that the first Methodist chapel was opened for services. The present chapel at the foot of Church Brow was opened in 1882 and cost £1,653. The other church in the village, built in 1880, is the Roman Catholic church of Our Lady and St Patrick. The church and school adjacent to it were built on land donated by Sir James de Hoghton.

There are very few industries now in the village – Dalgetty being the largest employer. Well known firms such as Atkinson's Vehicles, Haworth and Airey, J. A. Ley, Calvert's Cotton Mill and Hankin's Haulage have changed, closed down or left the area. Some of the old buildings are being used for new enterprises and the new complex of stores along the new London Way bypass has altered the area in the last few years.

Many landmarks in housing have disappeared, some of the larger historic houses having fallen into disrepair and then been demolished. One such was Walton Hall, which was demolished in 1880. It had been the home of some well known local families – the Bannisters, the

Langtons and the Hoghtons. Later another Walton Hall was built on the site, but that also was demolished in 1941.

The Unicorn Inn, a 17th century building (now known as Pinocchio's) was the posting station used by Parliamentary troops during the Civil War. It was said to be the headquarters of Oliver Cromwell during the battle of Preston. It was later the meeting place of the Jacobites in the area. A Walton man, Thomas Cowpe, who joined the Jacobites in 1715 was later hanged at Gallows Hill in Preston. His grave is in St Leonard's churchyard.

Cooper Hill, now demolished, was a large house overlooking the village. The owner was a great friend of the American scientist Benjamin Franklin who invented the lightning conductor, and who tested out his invention on the roof of Cooper Hill during a visit to his friend.

At one time there were many pubs or beer houses in Walton-le-Dale – The Unicorn, Queen's Arms, Black Horse, Sir Robert Peel, Black Bull, Grey Horse, Gardener's Arms, Yew Tree, Bridge Inn, White Bull, Ring O'Bells, the Beeftub (or Beefsteak) and the Red Lion, which is now a private house near St Leonard's church.

Villagers still talk of St Leonard's field day, when parishioners once walked through the streets to Walton Hall grounds where there were races, refreshments and two bands playing for dancing until evening, when everyone joined hands and danced back to the centre of the village.

Warton (near Carnforth)

From whichever direction one approaches the village of Warton its presence is dominated by Warton Crag. Travelling in from the direction of Carnforth one passes through low-lying pastureland with the river Keer leading out through marshland to the shores of Morecambe Bay to the west. This encompasses RSPB nature reserves and is part of the Area of Outstanding Natural Beauty. Beyond the farm and cottages at Town End lies the 'Weir' or 'Ware', an area of green commonland which was formerly a watering place for the locals to collect their water and take animals to drink.

Many years ago shire horses used to be brought to the Weir on the last day of March, decked out in their ribbons and finery for a Grand Parade. Now, each July, not horses but children gather here for the Children's Sports Parade and Crowning of the Queen. The Main Street of Warton

226

has many historical buildings and cottages including the Shovel Inn, St Oswald's church, the rectory ruins and, across from the post office, Washington House. The latter was the ancestral home of the forebears of the former American President, George Washington. On 4th July each year the American Stars and Stripes flag is flown from the church tower and it is believed that the design for this flag was derived from the old Washington coat of arms, which can be viewed inside the church tower.

Warton is a thriving, active community with many residents coming from old Wartonian stock and others from nearby villages and towns. In recent years new houses and bungalows have attracted people from further afield but the majority have blended into village life. Residents are well served with a post office, butcher's and baker's, two grocers and a fish shop. There are three public houses to quench one's thirst and a thriving village school. The church plays an active part in the community and the fortnightly lunches provided by the Methodist chapel are a popular venue for senior citizens and younger folk alike.

Amongst the simplest of pleasures within village life is the taking of a walk along the many lanes and footpaths throughout the area. A climb up the limestone crag reveals breathtaking views across Morecambe Bay, the Lakeland hills and the Pennines to Yorkshire beyond. Primitive man lived within the caves of the crag but today residents live their lives in harmony down in this beautiful old conservation area village where links with the past continue to thread their way into everyday life.

Warton (near Freckleton)

Warton is a small Fylde village of some 700 inhabitants. It is located on the north bank of the Ribble estuary, three miles up-river from Lytham St Annes – where the treacherous waters between Lytham and Southport join the Irish Sea. In winter, the climate is forbiddingly cold, windswept and rainy, but in spring, the whole scene is completely transformed in the sunshine and clear air, the lush pastures and meadows contrasting attractively with the newly whitewashed farm buildings and cottages.

In the 1920s dairy and poultry farming were the main industries, employing whole families and workers in the production of milk and cream, Lancashire cheese, poultry and eggs, for the quickly growing holiday trade of the Fylde coast between here and Blackpool.

In November 1927 came an unusually high tide and a very violent storm, causing the Fleetwood Flood Disaster, which claimed several lives and extended as far as Warton with the loss of livestock and poultry cabins.

As well as farming, the Lytham shipyard provided skilled work for many Warton men, who cycled the three miles to work as platers on the African river boats which were made there (the most famous of these being the derelict one used in the film, *The African Queen* starring Katherine Hepburn and Humphrey Bogart).

The cotton mill, one mile away in Freckleton, employed many young Warton women who either walked or cycled to weave 'Regina', a very strong cotton sateen used in the manufacture of velveteen – the looms making a deafening din and unfortunately causing much deafness. This mill, the 'Balderstone' as it was called, has been demolished to make way for a large housing estate.

The river Ribble, scarcely polluted at all in the 1920s, held many good-sized salmon and 'flukes' and provided a good harvest for the shrimpers, and regular work for river pilots, lamp lighters and fishermen. Shipping from foreign ports sailed through Warton to Preston docks. On clear evenings it used to be a popular pastime watching the 'Geest' banana boats, their tall masts bearing coloured lights. Cattle boats from Ireland unloaded their cargoes at Preston port, to be quickly sold at the cattle market to Fylde farmers.

Small plots of land were sold and new bungalows, with enough acreage to support several hundred head of poultry and perhaps a cow or two, were springing up like mushrooms about the village. The joinering of the cabins became a thriving industry and many people from East Lancashire mill towns came to try a more pleasant way of life here.

From 1930 onwards, tourists from Manchester and the East Lancashire cotton towns were beginning to enjoy themselves – motoring through Warton en route for the Fylde coast and Blackpool.

Farming families used to stand en masse in their fields, adjoining the main road, getting their entertainment from the constant stream of traffic passing through the village at weekends, dressed in their hessian 'Brats' (sacking aprons) and clogs. The 'grannies' wore beautifully made cotton sun bonnets, intricately tucked, generally heliotrope colour and most becoming!

Towards 1930, the 'Glasshouse Industry' developed in Warton and the whole Fylde – the climate and conditions being particularly suitable for the growing of 'Blackpool' tomatoes and lettuce. This flourished for many years, through the Second World War, in spite of enemy bomb damage and the vibration from the USAAF 'Liberator' bombers stationed here. Through the 1960s–70s, the ever-increasing price of glasshouse heating, foreign competition and freak gales and hailstorms brought this industry to a close and a way of life ended.

During the Second World War, all available land in Warton and Freckleton was commandeered by the Air Ministry and an enormous aerodrome was constructed with the biggest hangar (six acres!) and the longest runway in Europe. Thousands of USAAF personnel arrived and were here until the war ended.

Until the early 1920s, the old peg mill (windmill) still survived, but now only its millstone and the old anvil are preserved at the former smithy.

St Paul's Church school and the Church of the Holy Family school both flourish, as does the village hall. The hostelries – The Pickwick Tavern, formerly 'The Clifton Arms' and The Birley Arms, formerly 'The Red Heart', continue to flourish, as do the village public library and sub post office.

After the Second World War ended, the entire aerodrome was taken over by British Aerospace, which employs thousands of workers and is the biggest aircraft manufacturer in Europe.

In spite of this 'invasion', Warton still tries to survive as a village, now having a population of over 3,000 – instead of 700 as in 1926.

Weeton-with-Preese

As with many other places there are a number of theories as to how Weeton came by its name. One is that it could have been 'Willow Town' because of the willows that grew on the moss. In fact when the digging was done for the M55 motorway hundreds of bundles of osiers were found neer Weeton. Certainly its origins go back to pre-Roman times. Bronze Age and Roman axe heads and coins have been found, some quite recently, at Stanley House farm.

At the time of the Domesday Book there were 300 acres of arable land in Weeton. The history of Weeton with Preese has been closely linked with the small neighbouring villages of Esprick, Greenhalgh with Thistleton and Great and Little Plumpton, which today form one parish. The Butler (Botiler) family held Weeton from 1249 to 1673 when it passed to

The Eagle and Child inn at Weeton-with-Preese

the Earl of Derby through the marriage of Thomas Butler's daughter Elizabeth to the Earl's son. It remained part of the Derby estate for many years, the Earl granting land for the church of St Michael, which was built in 1842. The school adjacent to the church was built in 1886 and remains relatively unchanged and thriving today, unlike Esprick school which opened in 1857 but sadly closed owing to falling rolls in 1975.

In the centre of the village is the triangular green where for many years Weeton Fair took place on Trinity Monday, said to have been the largest cattle fair in the Fylde. The local housewives made and sold Weeton Fair Cakes, a kind of shortbread containing caraway seeds and beer. The recipe for these is now known only to Mrs Mary Smith whose grandfather kept the Eagle and Child inn. The fair ceased to take place many years ago, but until the early 1960s a farmer walked a cow from

Inglewhite on Fair Day and stood on the green to maintain the charter.

Candlemas day, 2nd February, was the start of the annual holiday for farmworkers and was also hiring day when servants were hired out for the following year. Rents to the Derby estate were paid annually. On Rent Day two halberds, still to be seen in the Eagle and Child, were set up, tied with blue ribbons, outside the inn door. A jury known as the Court Leet was also appointed on rent day, the members of which had to go out and inspect all dykes and watercourses during the first week in November. A dinner was provided for all tenants and members of the Court Leet.

The week before Easter was pace-egging time when young men and women dressed up as various characters, blackened their faces and visited the houses in the village singing the pace-egging song. They were given gifts of eggs, beer or money.

The Eagle and Child inn stands beside the village green; it dates back to Cromwellian times – in fact Cromwell was said to have stayed there. It was originally thatched, as were most of the dwellings in the village, but only one, Knowlesly Farm House, built in 1673 for Thomas Butler, retains its thatch today.

Weeton lies in the coastal strip of land called the Fylde in what used to be known as 'Windmill Land'. It had its own windmill, built in 1812 on the site of a 17th century peg mill. Flour was ground at the mill until 1916, but it was sadly demolished in 1960 and only the stone circle remains.

Weeton boasts its own saint. The Blessed William Harcourt was born in the village circa 1609. He joined the Society of Jesus, trained in Rome and worked in the London area. He was martyred at Tyburn in 1679 with other priests, a victim of the rumours of a 'Popish Plot' started by Titus Oates. There is a beautiful stained glass window commemorating his life in the local Roman Catholic church of St Anne at Westby Mill.

The village claims to have the oldest ghost in the Fylde, 'The Hairy Boggart of Weeton'. There are other stories of supernatural happenings. If you wander down Greenhalgh Lane at midnight at the time of the full moon you may see a coffin glide across the road to a pit in the corner of the field; and a ghost in the form of a cloaked figure has appeared in the middle bedroom of Manor Farm at Greenhalgh and has been seen by three members of the family on separate occasions.

Following its busy and interesting past Weeton maintains a lively community spirit, though the population is smaller than it was and many of the original buildings have disappeared. It has a recently renovated village hall and a croft used as a children's playground.

Perhaps the best known village character today is Mrs Mary Smith, who used to keep the village shop. Now in her 80s she has for many years written dialect verse and is still writing today.

Wennington & Wray

If you travel on the B6480 between Clapham and Lancaster you will enter the village of Wennington through a very narrow road between stone houses, which is typical of many villages in the area. The roads at those points were closed when fairs or cattle markets were held, to prevent the cattle escaping.

Wennington Hall was built originally in 1345. William Allen Francis Saunders, who was high Sheriff of Lancaster, rebuilt part of the Hall in

Cottages at Wray

B. Bellamy

1856, and later married Dorothea Morley, who was a descendant of the original Dr Morley who built the Hall. It is now a special school.

Crossing the bridge over the Wenning, on the right you can see a stone marking the boundary of Lonsdale, bearing the letters HL. The course of the river Wenning had to be altered when the Lancaster to Leeds railway was built and this can be seen in a painting of Hornby Castle, attributed to J. W. Turner.

As you follow the road you will see Tatham church of St James the Less. It was built in the 12th century and some rebuilding took place in the 15th century.

The road twists and turns and you enter Wray crossing Mealbank bridge, rebuilt in 1967, after the flood, on the line of a proposed bypass for the village. In 1967 the river Roeburn burst its banks and swept away a farm and an inn. A mark on the bus shelter erected in the Main Street, on a green sward beside the river, indicates the height the water reached.

Wray was once quite famous for its industry and crafts, quarrying, nail making, a silk mill, top hat making, clog making, tailoring, swill and basket making. Alas all industry has gone. The mill, standing beside the river Roeburn, has been converted into houses. The only remaining craft is swill making.

The village has its own school, which was endowed with £200 for ever by one of its residents, Captain R. Pooley, an officer in Cromwell's New Model Army, on condition the village built the school.

Parts of the Main Street are still cobbled. It is pleasant to walk along the Main Street, observing the date stones on some of the houses, over the bridge, along the lane towards the Silk Mill and over Kitten Bridge (so called because it is believed that people drowned their unwanted kittens there). Then back alongside the wood by the river, to see Ingleborough, with the chimneys of Wray still gently smoking, past the school and back on to the Main Street. There is still an atmosphere of bygone days.

West Bradford 🌿

The village of West Bradford was mentioned in the Domesday Book of 1086. Some men from the village paid the first poll tax levied by Richard II in 1379.

The present day village lies along the road between Grindleton and Waddington, the older part of the village being at the west end and the new estates in the east. A map of 1765 shows the village to have been a similar shape in those days with an open green between it and the Ribble to the south. In medieval times the green provided a place for the poor to tether their stock and a place to which all stock could be driven for protection. A market was also held there.

Access from the south was originally by way of a ford which entered the village where the road bends on the north bank of the river. A footbridge was in existence in 1822. It was a few yards below the present bridge and was privately owned. It was very narrow and consisted of three wooden beams set in four stone piers which carried the bridge about twelve feet above the water. The old foundations can still be seen when the water is low and clear. Before the footbridge was built, a ferry boat operated from the Boat Garth Field where West Bradford Brook enters the river. The road bridge was built in 1888 by public subscription.

The mill, situated in the centre of the village, was a corn mill and had a waterwheel until the Holgate family bought it in 1867 and it became a cotton mill. It remained in the family until 1960 when it was closed. Since then it has been used by various textile firms, and plans for residential development have been proposed.

Today most people work away from the village but formerly a wide variety of occupations were practised including joinery, chair-making, blacksmithing, stonemasonry, nail-making, farming, handloom weaving, lime-burning and hatting. At one time there was a clock shop at the corner of Westfield Drive. The firm Cottam and Buller made the Bowland Cycle and also had an eye-testing kit which villagers could use to have their eyes tested! There were also two grocers and two public houses. Nowadays only the post office and the Three Millstones survive.

The old chapel was built in 1797, just off Eaves Hall Lane, but only the graveyard remains as the building was demolished in 1906. The new chapel was built in 1904 on land given by Mr John Holgate. The West Bradford Mission Room was well attended in 1896. It used an upper room in the cottages opposite the Three Millstones, the entrance being by way of an outside staircase. When St Catherine's church was built in 1898, the mission room bell was housed in the church and can be heard every Sunday.

In the past the village had a cricket team which played in the Ribblesdale League and won the Garnett Cup in 1913. Twenty years later, the sons of the team won the cup again in 1933. Other village events included the Maypole and Sports Day. Today there is a football team and the Children's Sports Day and Fancy Dress Parade. The villagers are raising money for a permanent hall which, it is hoped, will keep the village a thriving community in the years to come.

Whalley 🌿

Whalley is one of the most famous villages in Lancashire, well known for its ruined Cistercian abbey, its parish church, its ancient grammar school and the field where the first 'Roses' cricket match was played.

It has an attractive situation at a crossing of the Calder, between the Nab and Pendle Hill, on a route between Yorkshire and the Lancashire coast. There has been a village here since at least Saxon times. Bronze Age tribes lived at Portfield and there is a Roman road marking the western boundary of the parish. At one time, Whalley parish extended from the Ribble to Cliviger beyond the village of Burnley.

The parish church of St Mary (Whalley's third) was begun in 1206 but in the churchyard are three 'Celtic' crosses of an earlier date. Inside are many treasures, above all the 15th century choir stalls which were brought from the abbey at the Dissolution of the Monasteries. They have beautifully carved misericords depicting various scenes such as a man shoeing a goose and St George and the dragon.

The church is older than the abbey, for the monks only came here in 1296. The western gateway (1318) with its Gothic arches still spans Church Lane and it is here that Whalley's first school began in 1350. The north east gate (1480) is still the entrance to the abbey grounds where the ruins of the cloisters, church and abbot's house can be visited. At its dissolution in 1537, Abbot Paslew was hanged and the monks dispersed. The buildings were sold in 1553 to the Assheton family, ancestors of the present Lord Clitheroe of Downham, and some of the stones were used to build a manor house. Today, this building is a conference centre for the Diocese of Blackburn.

The school over the west gate became a grammar school and was given its charter by Edward VI in 1547. The 'Old Grammar School' building was erected in 1725 and the school continued till the early 20th century. In 1954, Whalley WI raised the necessary funds to 'rescue' and restore the original part of the building which they leased from the Board of Governors. They were responsible for the letting of this hall until it was taken over by the County Education Committee. It is now a busy Adult Centre but still the WI meeting place.

235

In *The Lancashire Witches*, Harrison Ainsworth tells the story of Abbot Paslew and goes on to describe Whalley life in the reign of James I when witches were 'floated' above the weir on the Calder. The mill race and abbey corn mill are still there, though the water wheel stopped turning in 1961. There are still old cottages and Tudor houses to be seen, such as Poole End and the Toby Jug, which contains panelling supposedly taken from the abbey. There are Georgian houses in the main street, and three out of the four inns at the crossroads date from the 1700s.

Whalley never became a town, but increased in size after 1850 with the coming of the Blackburn to Hellifield railway line and the building of the viaduct. The next event was the building of Calderstones hospital for the mentally handicapped, just in time to serve as a military hospital in the First World War. The station was closed in 1961 and the future of Calderstones is uncertain.

The invention of the petrol engine has made village life attractive to townspeople. Like so many others, this is now a commuter village and, above all, a place to retire to. With four pubs and a night club, not to mention several cafes and restaurants, there are plenty of visitors in the evenings and at weekends. There is still one shop of each kind as well as antique, souvenir and arts and craft shops, and a modern library with art exhibitions and concerts.

The most dreadful local scandal of this century was in the 1960s when Whalley Co-op, including its cinema, furniture shop and shoe shop, went bankrupt. Many people lost all their savings and quite a few, their jobs. The former Co-op is now a high class fashion shop, attracting customers from far and wide.

The 1960s was also the period of traffic jams and queues along the main street, until the building of the bypass restored peace to the village.

Wheelton ✧

Wheelton became a thriving village with the advent of the cotton industry (originally handloom weaving) and the building of the mill by Peter Todd in 1856. It continued to grow as more houses were built to accommodate the workers and their families. The mill just off Victoria Street is no more, but the houses remain.

The Kenyon Brook, which is the boundary between Wheelton and Heapey, is culverted now and passes under the road in the centre of the village, flowing into the Leeds–Liverpool Canal. The war memorial stands next to a garage where the blacksmith's forge was previously sited. The old Blackburn road passed through Wheelton in those days, but with the opening of the bypass in 1966 this part of the village was isolated.

At the bottom of the hill is the Dressers Arms where the slate dressers used to slake their thirst after working in the slate delf. At the top of the hill just off Harbour Lane is a dirt road which leads to Munsill, a corruption of Monks Hill. It is said that the monks climbed 40 steps up this hill on their way to Whalley Abbey via Briars Brow, thought to have been 'Friars Brow' in those days.

At the highest point of Wheelton along Harbour Lane there is a beautiful view looking out over the Lancashire plain towards Southport, Blackpool, Morecambe and the sea beyond. The sunsets from this vantage point have to be seen to be believed.

White Coppice 🍃

White Coppice lies between Heapey and Wheelton, and is three and a half miles from Chorley, five minutes from the M61 going east and 15 minutes from the M6.

There are 20 cottages and houses and one farmhouse in the village. Living on the farm is the fourth generation of the same family. White Coppice was given the name because all the cottages were painted white; to this day there are still nine white cottages.

The small school is now a house. It was closed in 1963 as only ten children were attending the school. There are no shops and no public transport. The main attraction to the village is the cricket field which nestles within the hills all around. By popular belief it is the prettiest field and surroundings in Lancashire. The area is used by hikers and motorists all year round.

Many, many years ago the squire's wife who lived at Northwood fell out with the vicar and so started the Meeting Room. This was once the reading room belonging to the cotton mill which many years ago existed in White Coppice. It was the little church until it became unsafe and a new one was erected just down the road. Though non-denominational, this closed as a church in 1984 due to lack of attendance.

There are three small reservoirs joined by streams and a waterfall. At the top of the village water cascades down the moors into what is known as the Goit. In the early 1920s a quarry existed in White Coppice as well as the cotton mill. The chimney of the mill was demolished about 1950 along with three cottages nearby. When the Goit and the railway were built a number of Irishmen were brought in to do the work. At that time six beer houses were opened in the cottages. The railway closed in the late 1950s.

All the property in the village over the years has been either extended or improved and modernised. On the whole the looks have been improved while remaining in keeping with this tiny hamlet.

Winmarleigh

Don't blink as you travel through Winmarleigh or you may miss it. The church, school and village hall are the centre. The church steeple is different to our neighbours in that it is made of wood, similar to those seen in the Norfolk area. There may be some connection here with early settlers, as much of the village land is East Anglian-type flat black moss soil surrounded by water-filled ditches. Most of the land is owned by The Crown with eleven farmers being tenants of the Duchy of Lancaster, along with the village pub, the Patten Arms. In the mid 1700s John Wilson Patten (later Lord Winmarleigh) bought the township of Winmarleigh and built Winmarleigh Hall as his family residence. The family built the church and school in the 1870s.

In 1912 the estate was sold. It was bought by Frank Reddaway, who had to rebuild the Hall in the 1920s when it had been destroyed by fire. On his death in 1945 the estate was sold again, most of it being bought by the Duchy of Lancaster and the rest by private owners. Winmarleigh Hall and grounds with two farms was bought by Lancashire County Council and later became Lancashire College of Agriculture until the present college was built at Myerscough. Winmarleigh is still used for day release courses.

The Hall is a stately building with a magnificent staircase and fireplace in the hallway. It is set in lovely woodland so it is not easily visible from the road. Some residents can hear the chimes of the clock, depending on the direction of the wind and this gives an indication of the future weather.

On the west side of the village is an area of wild bog land which is an area of Special Scientific Interest going back to the Ice Age when the land flooded. On surrounding fields farmers still plough up large parts of trees that rise to the surface and have been preserved in the peat.

238

On the east of the village the Preston to Kendal canal provides our boundary, a lovely stretch of canal, busy with pleasure boats, winding its way past two very well kept caravan parks and the village garage, through peaceful countryside to the market town of Garstang a few miles away or north to the historic town of Lancaster. If you want a detour, take the branch off to Glasson Dock, a tiny port busy with pleasure and cargo boats.

Wiswell & Barrow 🦢

Wiswell village lies on the south-west slope of Pendle Hill and enjoys fine westward views towards the Trough of Bowland which leads to Lancaster. It is a village of considerable antiquity. From a charter dated 1193 (during the reign of Richard the Lionheart), lords of Clitheroe granted the de Arches family 'two ploughlands' which included Wiswell, also the 'free chase of Wiswell'. Huntsmen rode this land till the A59 bypass was constructed in 1972.

Wiswell was also part of Whalley Abbey estate and has always been used as pastureland. In bygone days farm women wove at home on their hand looms and some of the smaller farms were worked by the wives while their husbands toiled in the sandstone quarry above the village.

The tradition of beating the bounds has taken place since the 1300s, though infrequently in recent years. Families processed around the nine mile perimeter beating the ground with wands and at certain points, bumped the small boys on the ground to help them to remember the boundary lines so that they too could carry on the tradition.

Wiswell Shay Cross is one of the numerous wayside crosses dotting this area. It must have served as a prayer station for all kinds of travellers. The cross shaft is recent but the base is original and stands in a clump of woodland near the land leading up to Wiswell Hall Farm, built near the site of Wiswell Old Hall which dated back to before King Henry V.

The Old Hall was the home of the notable Paslew family in Tudor times and was the birthplace of Abbot John of the Cistercian abbey at Whalley. Legend has it that the abbot's ghost walks from Shay Cross to his home at the Old Hall.

Old Vicarage House holds a mysterious past. It is one of the old Lancashire houses which contains three secret rooms. Possibly, priests and others seeking refuge were glad to hide in those dark spaces. One bedroom has windows overlooking three aspects, with a clear view over to Stonyhurst College.

Cold Coates Farm lies at the edge of the village. One day a servant girl found a vagrant called Jack O'Napps in the dairy. She hit him and he subsequently died. As he had no money none of the surrounding villages would afford him a proper burial so poor Jack lies in a grave marked by stones on the side of Pendle Hill.

Nowadays this quiet little community is a residential area, apart from the farming families. The chapel and school have been refurbished as houses. There are two small housing developments, no shop, but the inhabitants can still take refreshment at the Freemasons' Arms.

Opposite Tythebarn, Wigga's Spring wells up. Another water source is noted for its medicinal sulphur content. Molly's well is now dry. When the bypass was excavated two forgotten artesian wells gushed many feet high. The water had to be piped away before the road could be constructed.

Barrow is Wiswell's industrial neighbour, lying one mile away like a ribbon along the A59. A water-powered spinning mill was built in 1785; by 1811 it had become a printing and dyeing works. The Calico Printers Association was later owned by Mr Bryce Smith from c1860.

'Barrer Printworks' closed in 1931 due in part to the general recession, but re-opened after the Second World War for engraving designs onto copper rollers for the cotton printing trade.

This firm provided good sports amenities for the village. Barrow's most famous son is the Lancashire and England cricketer Cyril Washbrook, who was appointed President of Lancashire County Cricket Club at Old Trafford in July 1989. He scored 996 runs in 17 tests against Australia from 1948 to 1956.

Sadly those sports amenities disappeared; the printworks were demolished in the 1970s. Washbrook Close and Trafford Gardens were built on their site. The Barrow works lodge is now kept stocked by a private angling club.

In 1662 Rev Thomas Jolly left the Established Church and built a chapel in Wymondhouses near Wiswell. People worshipped there or in Wiswell till 1886 when the congregation moved to Barrow into the Jolly Memorial chapel, built to commemorate their first pastor. It is still used today as the United Reformed church.

Barrow has two small pubs, a post office and two shops. Employment is found in surrounding towns. There are plans to develop housing and light industry.

Withnell 🦋

Withnell is a pleasant village situated on the edge of the West Pennine moors. It lies between Brinscall and Abbey Village and is surrounded by picturesque hills and open countryside. Its name is believed to derive from a white knoll of trees.

Originally a farming community, Withnell now has only half a dozen working farms and depends on the local woodyard, a small Forestry Commission depot, a factory producing ties and badges plus a few local shops for its industry. There is a post office, a modern health centre, and a well stocked chemist's shop. There was a small Methodist chapel, which sadly closed, but there are still two remaining churches. St Joseph's, Roman Catholic, stands off Withnell's main road, Bury Lane, and houses an infant and junior school of approximately 65 pupils below the church, an unusual feature in these modern times. There is a small statue of St Francis of Assisi which stands in the grounds of the church.

Across the road 50 yards further up, at the top of Bury lane, is St Paul's Anglican church. In the grounds stands a memorial dedicated to James Miller who was posthumously awarded the VC in the First World War. He bravely carried vital messages between front line troop commanders whilst under intense shelling.

Bury Lane is one of the oldest names in the district, descending from Adam de Withnell and Adam de Bury, knights of old in association with the barony of the de Hoghton family.

Withnell Fold 🦋

A 'withy knool' – or wooded hill – gives one a picture of the land in this part of Lancashire after the Norman Conquest when Henry de Withynalle became its chief landowner. For many centuries what is now the village of Withnell Fold consisted solely of two farmsteads and it was not until the Industrial Revolution that real changes took place.

In 1839–40 brothers Robert and John Parke from Longton near Preston purchased the whole of the parish of Withnell, which included the Fold, from William Talbot, then lord of the manor. Cotton mills were built in parts of the parish but it was not until 1843 that a son of Robert named Thomas Blinkhorn Parke built a paper mill near to Withnell Fold farm and by the bank of the Leeds and Liverpool canal. Workers experienced in paper manufacture were brought from Darwen and the first group of terraced houses built to accommodate them.

The village was laid out around a central square and consisted of 35 terraced cottages each with its own garden. They were built of stone from a local quarry and the excellent condition of the properties today testifies to the care taken in the original building. A property was made available to serve as a shop and a variety of social facilities introduced by the Parke family illustrate how well in advance of modern employee welfare schemes the firm was. A reading room was opened which was used for social gatherings, a recreation field made available for cricket, and a village school and chapel built.

As the firm grew so further properties were added and although in 1890 the business was taken over by Wiggans Teape and Company Ltd the village itself remained as a typical example of benevolent paternalism and Withnell Fold became known as a Model Garden Village. Of course to live in the village required that at least one member of the family had to work in the mill.

The village was a close knit community and regular concerts and dances were held for many years in the reading room. There was also a Silver Prize Band and cricket and bowling teams entered into spirited competition in local league matches. Two tennis courts were also very popular in the early days, particularly with the ladies of the village.

A Garden of Remembrance was later added and remains as a peaceful spot to rest and ponder upon the many changes which have taken place. A reminder of earlier days of rough justice takes the form of the village stocks now sited near the village centre.

Withnell Fold won the competition for the Best Kept Village in Lancashire in the under 500 population class in 1961, 1963 and 1964. Then came the first intimations of major change for many years – a development of eleven detached properties just above the existing village was completed in 1967. Later that year Wiggans Teape closed the paper mill and sold off the village properties. The old paper mill and the outbuildings were kept for several years but today only a much smaller part of the original works remains to house a car body firm, an air compressor service and other small businesses. The old mill chimney has been kept as an interesting feature but new detached properties have been built and the former reading room and works offices converted into dwelling houses. The village has become purely residential with residents, no longer tied to the local mill, often commuting many miles to their now more varied types of employment. A far cry from 'walking down to t'mill'.

Now there is a flourishing Conservation Society, which was formed in 1982 to look after and represent the interests of the village. The Society has instigated and waymarked a 'Village Trail' and produced a leaflet for walkers. A sports and social club provides tennis, bowling and cricketing facilities, a Women's Institute thrives and local anglers use the old mill lodges. The village school and chapel remain as does Withnell Fold Hall the former residence of the Parke family and now in use as a county old people's home.

Personalities of note connected with the village include *Kathleen Ferrier (1912–1953)* the famous contralto who married a local man.

Woodplumpton 🐚

Woodplumpton lies about five miles north-west of Preston in the Fylde district of Amounderness and was originally situated on the edge of a large forest which stretched from the Bowland Fells to the eastern limit of the Fylde.

Woodplumpton itself was recorded as Plunton in the Domesday Book. In the year 1256 it was Plumpton, and the prefix 'wode' was added in 1336 to distinguish it from the other Plumpton in the Fylde which became Field Plumpton. The name Plumpton simply means the plum tree farm or enclosure.

Woodplumpton church, dedicated to St Anne, was known to have existed before the year 1340, but there is evidence of a place of worship on or near the present site as early as the 11th century. Records show that the present church was rebuilt in 1639 and again in 1900, the vestry was added in 1850.

During restoration many sections of original stonework were found in the walls, portions of old shafts and notably an old capital dating back to the 12th century. Other ancient stones including part of a Norman tombstone have been found built into a recess in the vestry. The north doorway has early Christian symbols carved into the stonework and this, together with the nearby old window, is undoubtedly the oldest standing part of the present building.

The main entrance into the churchyard is through the lychgate which was erected in 1912, flanked on one side by the old stocks and a mounting stone used by patrons of the church who in earlier days arrived on horseback.

Woodplumpton church

A large boulder in the churchyard is said to cover the grave of old Meg Shelton, the Fylde witch. If cattle fell sick, crops failed or milk turned sour, this was said to be the work of Meg. She was reputed to be able to assumed the shape and form of animals, which enabled her to escape detection when about her nefarious deeds.

While her misdemeanours are wildly exaggerated, Meg really did exist. Her name was Margery Hilton, who was found dead in her cottage crushed between the wall and a barrel. She was buried by torchlight on the 2nd May 1705, but according to legend scratched her way out! She was buried a second time but again she found her way to the surface. The third burial was made to last. She was buried face downwards and a huge boulder, one of the largest natural stones ever to be found in the district, was placed on top of her grave. Meg never surfaced again and is now probably scratching herself in deeper and deeper!

Whether Meg ever had to suffer the indignity of being ducked by the cuckstool is not recorded, but many local harridans were subjected to this form of punishment. The cuckstool and pond are now gone but are remembered in the name of Cuckstool Farm which was adjacent to the pond.

Since the 1930s the village has doubled in size with homes extending as far as Whittle Hill and beyond. Many of the new inhabitants commute to various occupations but the main way of life in the surrounding area is still farming.

The church, school and Wheatsheaf pub are still the centre of village life, with an active Mother's Union, Over Sixties club and other youth activities taking place regularly.

The Woodplumpton & District Bowling Club is well supported with the associated tennis club regularly used. Whist and domino drives take place weekly at the club. The Women's Institute and Young Farmers' groups also meet here.

Wrea Green ✺

The village of Wray became known as Wrea Green because of postal confusion with the Wray near Hornby. The green is the largest in Lancashire and in the last century was even larger. In those days farms and cottages opened straight out onto the green, but in about 1900 people began to fence off front gardens for themselves.

A map of 1893 shows three ponds on the green. These were known locally as 'dubs' and it is supposed that they got this name from the word 'daub'. Early cottagers simply dug clay, or daub, from the green for their wattle and daub cottages. Later they took the clay for hand-made bricks.

There has been a school in the village for almost 300 years. In 1693 James Thistleton, a tailor, left £180 in his will for the building and maintaining of a free school, and then in 1716 a Nicholas Sharples, a London innkeeper who had spent his childhood in Wray, left £850 for the purchase of some freehold estate for the benefit of the school.

There have been many interesting village characters and perhaps Thomas Noblet, who at the age of 80 walked regularly to Preston and back, comes most readily to mind. John Porter in his *History of the Fylde* wrote of him in considerable detail.

Another extraordinary man was Evan Ainsworth. Everything about him was outsize and he had to have his boots made on a special last. He always wore a rather peculiar hat, a kind of half-tall shiner. Evan was a cattle dealer and his drovers brought cattle from Ireland. When they arrived in the village the cattle ran wild and if any cottage doors were open they would charge straight in!

Gypsies, pedlars and hawkers often came round the village and a familiar figure was 'Cockle Maggie'. She had a donkey and cart and used to travel to Lytham for shellfish and then hawk them round the villages.

A number of notable families have lived in the village and the Birleys had undoubtedly the most influence. Mr and Mrs P. L. Birley came to live at 'The Villa' in 1902. Mrs Birley was very autocratic. The girls were expected to curtsy and the boys to doff their caps and bow when they met her. She was well known in Guiding and became Chief Commissioner for England in 1930.

Another family of influence were the Duckworths of Ribby Hall. This Georgian mansion was built by the Hornby family in 1776. It was bought by Mr William Duckworth in 1903 and the family remained there until 1941.

After the First World War a lychgate was built as a memorial to the men of the village who were killed and, as far as possible, the material and labour used was all local. The oak was from Ribby Hall estate, the stone and the stone roof-slates were from a ruined and reputedly haunted cottage, the ironwork was forged in Mike Parker's smithy, while the woodwork was carried out in the Wareing Brothers local carpentry shop.

The oldest family are the Cooksons of Cooksons' Farm. They were yeomen farmers when most others were tenants and the deeds of the property go back to Elizabethan times. They were landowners in Warton, Freckleton and Lytham, where their property included the windmill on Lytham Green.

There are four good shops in the village and G. & V. A. Dobsons had the distinction of winning the National Award for Shopkeepers in 1979. The Dobson brothers were born in the village and their grandfather, Bill Eccles, was a real old village character. He used to love to tell tales of the days when he was young, 'when the old cottages were built all higgledy-piggledy, with some of them sticking out into the roadway and Wrea Green was a real quaint sort of place'.

The village remained quietly rural with agriculture as the main source of employment until the death of Mrs P. L. Birley in 1958. Soon after this her family left the district and 'The Villa' became a restaurant. The Birley farms were sold to sitting tenants, who sold land to developers, and Wrea Green doubled in size in a very short time. The population in 1951 was 697 but by 1981 it was 1,464.

Today only a small number of inhabitants depend on agriculture for their livelihood. The firm of J. Wareing & Son (Wrea Green) Ltd, agricultural and industrial building contractors, employs between 50 and 70 men.

Notwithstanding the increased residential development, Wrea Green remains a charming village. Wrea Green won the Community Council of Lancashire's Best Kept Village Competition for the first time in 1959. Since then the village has been in the Championship Class and has won the award several times. It has also won many other awards including Best Kept Church & Churchyard, Best Kept War Memorial and Best Kept Playing Field.

The old smithy, St Michael's-on-Wyre

248

Index

Abbeystead 9
Abbey Village 11
Ainsdale 11
Appley Bridge 12
Aspull 14
Astley 16
Austerlands (see Saddleworth)
  186

Bangors Green (see Halsall) 105
Banks 18
Barley 19
Barrow (see Wiswell) 239
Barton 20
Bashall Eaves 22
Becconsall (see Hesketh) 113
Belmont 23
Billinge 26
Bilsborrow 27
Blacko 29
Bolton-by-Bowland 30
Bolton-le-Sands 31
Borwick 33
Botton (see Tatham Fells) 209
Bradshaw 34
Brindle 36
Brinscall 37
Bromley Cross 38
Brookhouse (see Caton-with-
  Littledale) 48
Broughton (near Preston) 40
Burrow (see Tunstall) 218

Cabus 42
Calder Vale 44
Cantsfield (see Tunstall) 218
Carleton 45

Catforth 47
Caton-with-Littledale 48
Chapeltown (see Edgworth) 75
Cherry Tree 50
Chipping 51
Churchtown 53
Claughton on Brock 54
Clayton-le-Woods 55
Clifton 56
Cliviger 58
Cockerham 60
Coldrow (see Stalmine) 206
Copster Green 62
Cowan Bridge (see Leck) 137
Cragbank 63
Crank 64
Cronton 65
Croston 67

Delph (see Saddleworth) 186
Denshaw (see Saddleworth) 186
Diggle (see Saddleworth) 186
Dobcross (see Saddleworth) 186
Dolphinholme 69
Downham 70
Dunsop Bridge 72

Eccleston 73
Edgworth 75
Elswick 78
Esprick (see Weeton-with-Preese)
  229
Euxton 80

Farington 81
Farington Moss 81
Fence in Pendle 83
Feniscowles 85
Fernyhalgh 87
Forton 88

Freckleton 90
Friezland (see Saddleworth) 186

Galgate 91
Garstang 92
Glasson Dock 93
Goosnargh 94
Grasscroft (see Saddleworth) 186
Great Eccleston 95
Great Mitton 98
Great Plumpton (see Weeton-with-
    Preese) 229
Greenfield (see Saddleworth) 186
Greenhalgh (see Weeton-with-
    Preese) 229
Greenmount 98
Gregson Lane 99
Grimsargh 101
Grindleton 102
Grotton (see Saddleworth) 186

Haigh (see Aspull) 14
Halewood 104
Halsall 105
Halton 106
Hambleton 108
Hapton 109
Hawkshaw 110
Hesketh 113
Hest (see Slyne) 204
Higham 115
Higher Penwortham (see
    Penwortham) 168
Higher Walton 116
Hoghton 118
Hoole 120
Hornby 122
Hurst Green 125

Inglewhite 126

Ingol 127
Inskip 129

Kirkham 130

Langho 132
Larbreck (see Little Eccleston)
    139
Lathom 134
Lea 136
Leck 137
Lever Park (see Rivington) 182
Little Eccleston 139
Little Hoole (see Hoole) 120
Little Mitton (see Great Mitton)
    98
Little Plumpton (see Weeton-with-
    Preese) 229
Longridge 140
Longton 141
Loveclough 142
Lower Penwortham (see
    Penwortham) 168
Lowgill (see Tatham Fells) 209
Lowton 145
Lydgate (see Saddleworth) 186

Mawdesley 146
Mellor 148
Mellor Brook 150
Mere Brow 151
Mossley (see Saddleworth) 186
Moss Side 152
Much Hoole (see Hoole) 120

Nether Kellet 153
Newburgh 155
Newchurch in Pendle 157
Newton with Scales 158
Over Kellet 160

Overton   162

Parbold   164
Parkbridge   166
Pendleton   167
Penwortham   168
Pilling   170
Priest Hutton (see Borwick)   33
Primrose Hill (see Halsall)   105

Quernmore   172

Rainford   174
Rainhill   175
Read   177
Ribbleton   179
Ribchester   179
Rimington   181
Rivington   182
Roseacre (see Treales)   217
Roughlee   184
Roughtown (see Saddleworth)
   186
Rufford   185

Sabden   185
Saddleworth   186
St Michael's-on-Wyre   190
Salesbury (see Copster Green)   62
Salwick   192
Samlesbury   193
Sawley   195
Scorton   196
Scouthead (see Saddleworth)   186
Sefton   197
Shevington   198
Simonstone   199
Singleton   200
Slaidburn   202
Slyne   204

Sowerby (see Inskip)   129
Springhead (see Saddleworth)
   186
Staining   205
Stalmine   206
Staynall (see Stalmine)   206
Sunderland Point (see Overton)
   162

Tarleton   208
Tatham Fells   209
Thistleton (see Weeton-with-
   Preese)   229
Thornley-with-Wheatley   210
Thorton-le-Fylde   212
Thurnham   214
Trawden   215
Treales   217
Tunstall   218
Turton (see Edgeworth)   75

Ulnes Walton   220
Uppermill (see Saddleworth)   186

Waddington   222
Walmer Bridge   224
Walton le Dale   224
Wardleys (see Stalmine)   206
Warton (near Carnforth)   226
Warton (near Freckleton)   227
Weeton-with-Preese   229
Wennington   232
West Bradford   233
Whalley   235
Wharles (see Treales)   217
Wheatley (see Thornley-with-
   Wheatley)   210
Wheelton   236
Whitechapel (see Inglewhite)   126
White Coppice   237

Whittingham (see Goosnargh)   94
Winehall (see Trawden)   215
Winmarleigh   238
Wiswell   239
Withnell   241

Withnell Fold   241
Woodplumpton   243
Wray (see Wennington)   232
Wrea Green   245
Wycoller (see Trawden)   215